HIDDEN®

Oahu

"*Hidden Oahu* offers a glimpse at the Hawaiian island's one-of-a-kind lodging and dining opportunities, as well as innovative outdoor activities."
—*Denver Post*

"This guide focuses on the unique rather than the obvious."
—*San Antonio Express-News*

HIDDEN®

Oahu

Including Waikiki, Honolulu and Pearl Harbor

Ray Riegert

FOURTH EDITION

Ulysses Press®

BERKELEY, CALIFORNIA

Published by:
ULYSSES PRESS
P.O. Box 3440
Berkeley, CA 94703
www.ulyssespress.com

ISSN 1524-5934
ISBN 1-56975-378-4

Printed in Canada by Transcontinental Printing

10 9 8 7 6

UPDATE AUTHOR: Joan Conrow
EDITORIAL DIRECTOR: Leslie Henriques
MANAGING EDITOR: Claire Chun
COPY EDITOR: Lily Chou
EDITORIAL ASSOCIATES: Kate Allen, Laura Brancella
TYPESETTER: Steven Schwartz, Lisa Kester, James Meetze
CARTOGRAPHY: Ben Pease
COVER DESIGN: Sarah Levin
INDEXER: Sayre Van Young
COVER PHOTOGRAPHY: Douglas Peebles (Mokulua Islands, Lanikai)
ILLUSTRATOR: Jen-Ann Kirchmeier

Distributed in the United States by Publishers Group West and in Canada by Raincoast Books

For Claire,
my favorite kamaaina

Acknowledgments

A big *mahalo* to my wife Leslie Henriques, update author Joan Conrow, Claire Chun, Bryce Willett, Lily Chou, Kate Allen, Laura Brancella, Steven Schwartz, Lisa Kester, James Meetze, Sayre Van Young and everyone else who helped bring this book to press.

*

What's Hidden?

At different points throughout this book, you'll find special listings marked with a hidden symbol:

◄ HIDDEN

This means that you have come upon a place off the beaten tourist track, a spot that will carry you a step closer to the local people and natural environment of Oahu.

The goal of this guide is to lead you beyond the realm of everyday tourist facilities. While we include traditional sightseeing listings and popular attractions, we also offer alternative sights and adventure activities. Instead of filling this guide with reviews of standard hotels and chain restaurants, we concentrate on one-of-a-kind places and locally owned establishments.

Our authors seek out locales that are popular with residents but usually overlooked by visitors. Some are more hidden than others (and are marked accordingly), but all the listings in this book are intended to help you discover the true nature of Oahu and put you on the path of adventure.

Write to us!

If in your travels you discover a spot that captures the spirit of Oahu, or if you live in the region and have a favorite place to share, or if you just feel like expressing your views, write to us and we'll pass your note along to the author.

We can't guarantee that the author will add your personal find to the next edition, but if the writer does use the suggestion, we'll acknowledge you in the credits and send you a free copy of the new edition.

ULYSSES PRESS
P.O. Box 3440
Berkeley, CA 94703
E-mail: readermail@ulyssespress.com

Contents

1 THE GATHERING PLACE — I

Where to Go — 6
When to Go — 8
Seasons — 8
Calendar of Events — 9
Before You Go — 13
Visitors Centers — 13
Package Tours — 14
Packing — 14
Lodging — 16
Condos — 18
Dining — 18
Traveling with Children — 19
Women Traveling Alone — 22
Gay & Lesbian Travelers — 23
Senior Travelers — 23
Disabled Travelers — 24
Foreign Travelers — 24
Mail — 25
Transportation — 26

2 THE LAND AND OUTDOOR ADVENTURES — 32

Geology — 33
Flora — 33
Fauna — 36
Outdoor Adventures — 41

3 HISTORY AND CULTURE — 65

History — 65
Hawaiian Culture — 83
People — 85
Cuisine — 86
Language — 87
Music — 90
Hula — 93

4 WAIKIKI — 94

Sights — 96
Lodging — 103
Condos — 113
Dining — 114

Groceries   120
Shopping   121
Nightlife   123
Beaches & Parks   127

5 DOWNTOWN HONOLULU   128

Sights   129
Lodging   139
Dining   140
Groceries   146
Shopping   147
Nightlife   149
Beaches & Parks   150

6 GREATER HONOLULU   152

Sights   153
Lodging   163
Dining   165
Groceries   170
Shopping   170
Nightlife   171
Beaches & Parks   172

7 SOUTHEAST OAHU   174

Sights   174
Lodging   178
Dining   178
Groceries   180
Shopping   181
Beaches & Parks   181

8 WINDWARD COAST   184

Sights   185
Lodging   191
Dining   194
Groceries   196
Shopping   196
Nightlife   197
Beaches & Parks   197

9 NORTH SHORE   **202**
Sights   203
Lodging   208
Dining   209
Groceries   212
Shopping   212
Nightlife   215
Beaches & Parks   215

10 CENTRAL OAHU & LEEWARD COAST   **218**
Central Oahu Sights   219
Leeward Coast Sights   222
Leeward Coast Lodging   223
Leeward Coast Dining   224
Leeward Coast Groceries   224
Leeward Coast Nightlife   224
Leeward Coast Beaches & Parks   226

Index   229
Lodging Index   234
Dining Index   236
About the Author and Update Author   241

Maps

Oahu	3
Waikiki	97
Downtown Honolulu	131
Greater Honolulu	155
Southeast Oahu	177
Windward Coast	187
North Shore	205
Leeward Coast & Central Oahu	221

OUTDOOR ADVENTURE SYMBOLS

The following symbols accompany national, state and regional park listings, as well as beach descriptions throughout the text.

 Camping

 Hiking

Swimming

 Snorkeling or Scuba Diving

Surfing

Waterskiing

Windsurfing

Fishing

ONE

The Gathering Place

Oahu is the centerpiece of the Hawaiian archipelago that stretches more than 1500 miles across the North Pacific Ocean. In a sense, Oahu is a small continent. Volcanic mountains rise in the interior, while the coastline is fringed with coral reefs and white-sand beaches. In the parlance of the Pacific, it is a "high island," very different from the low-lying atolls that are found elsewhere in Polynesia.

The northeastern face of the island, buffeted by trade winds, is the wet side. The contrast between this side and the island's southwestern sector is sometimes startling. In the northeast, the landscape teems with exotic tropical plants, while across the island you're liable to see cactus growing in a barren landscape!

Dominated by the capital city of Honolulu, Oahu is the meeting place of East and West. Today, with its highrise cityscape and crowded commercial center, Honolulu is more the place where Hong Kong meets Los Angeles. It's the hub of Hawaii—a city that dominates the political, cultural and economic life of the islands.

And it's the focus of Oahu as well. Honolulu has given Oahu more than its nickname, The Capital Island. The city has drawn three-fourths of Hawaii's population to this third-largest island, making Oahu both a military stronghold and a popular tourist spot.

With military installations at Pearl Harbor and outposts seemingly everywhere, the armed forces control about one-quarter of the island. Most bases are off-limits to civilians; and tourists congregate in Honolulu's famed resort area—Waikiki. Both defense and tourism are big business on Oahu, and it's an ironic fact of island life that the staid, uniformly dressed military peacefully coexist here with crowds of sun-loving, scantily clad visitors.

The tourists are attracted by one of the world's most famous beaches, an endless white-sand ribbon that has drawn sun worshippers and water lovers since the days of Hawaiian royalty. In ancient times Waikiki was a swamp; now it's a spectacular region of world-class resorts.

Indeed, Waikiki is at the center of Pacific tourism, just as Honolulu is the capital of the Pacific. Nowhere else in the world will you find a population more varied or an ambience more vital. There are times when Waikiki's Parisian-size boulevards seem ready to explode from the sheer force of the crowds. People in bikinis and wild-colored aloha shirts stroll the streets, while others flash past on mopeds.

"Ua mau ke o ka aina i ka pono," the state motto, means "The life of the land is perpetuated in righteousness."

Since the 1980s this sun-splashed destination has also become a focal point for millions of wealthy tourists from Japan. As a result, Waikiki now has moneychanging shops, restaurants displaying menus in Japanese only, stores where the clerks speak no English and an entire mall filled with duty-free shops.

Today the development that created modern-day Waikiki continues, albeit at a slower pace and on a less intense scale, at the Koolina Resort, along the south central Oahu coast near residential Ewa Beach, with the JW Marriott Ihilani Resort & Spa providing a flagship hotel for the resort. Nearby, work continues on the development of Kapolei as a "second city" for Oahu, planned for as many as 200,000 people and designed to reduce the population concentration on urban Honolulu.

So hurry. Visitors can still discover that just beyond Honolulu's bustling thoroughfares stretches a beautiful island, featuring countless beaches and two incredible mountain ranges. Since most of the tourists (and a vast majority of the island's 876,100 population) congregate in the southern regions around Honolulu, the north is rural. You can experience the color and velocity of the city, then head for the slow and enchanting country.

As you begin to explore for yourself, you'll find Oahu also has something else to offer: history. *Oahu* means "gathering place" in Hawaiian, and for centuries it has been an important commercial area and cultural center. First populated by Marquesans around A.D. 500, the island was later settled by seafaring immigrants from Tahiti. Waikiki, with its white-sand beaches and luxurious coconut groves, became a favored spot among early monarchs.

Warring chiefs long battled for control of the island. Kamehameha I seized power in 1795 after landing troops along the coast just east of Waikiki, proceeding inland and sweeping an opposing army over the cliffs of Nuuanu Pali north of Honolulu. Several years earlier the British had "discovered" Honolulu Harbor, a natural anchorage destined to be one of the Pacific's key seaports. Over the years the harbor proved ideal first for whalers and sandalwood traders and eventually for freighters and ocean liners.

Text continued on page 6.

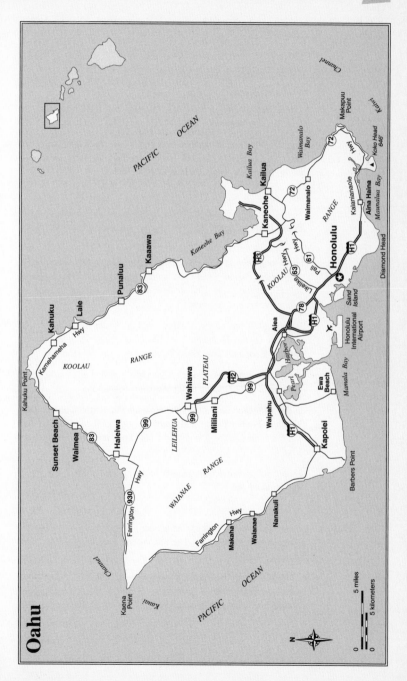

Oahu

Hawaiian Getaway

Oahu Three-day Itinerary

Day 1
- Check into a hotel or condo in Waikiki then make tour reservations for the next day for Iolani Palace and/or Pearl Harbor.

- Explore **Waikiki Beach**, take a stroll over to **Kapiolani Park** (page 100), or just kick back. In the evening, seek out a spot to listen to Hawaiian music. Dine in Waikiki.

Day 2
- Spend the morning sightseeing in Honolulu. If you are going to **Pearl Harbor** (page 157) try for an early-morning tour. (Allow 1.5 hours.)

- Head back downtown to visit the **Mission Houses Museum** (page 129) (allow .5 hour) and then continue along South King Street to **Iolani Palace** (page 130). (Allow 45 minutes for the tour of the palace, reservations needed.)

- If you opted not to go to Pearl Harbor earlier, drive up the Pali Highway to the **Nuuanu Pali Lookout** (page 157), stopping at **Queen Emma's Summer Palace** (page 157) on the way.

- Return to Downtown Honolulu and have lunch, then stroll through the nooks and crannies of **Chinatown** (page 135).

- In the afternoon either visit the **Hawaii Maritime Center** (page 135) and **Foster Botanical Garden** (page 137) or return to Waikiki for a canoe ride, a swim or a hike up **Diamond Head** (page 61).

- Hop on a bus and have dinner at an eatery in Ward Centre or Restaurant Row.

Day 3
- Drive around the island. Get up *early* in the morning (when the water is clear) and snorkel at **Hanauma Bay** (page 175). (Allow at least 1 hour.)

- Continue along the Kalanianaole Highway, Route 72, stopping at the **Halona Blowhole** (page 175) to see the ocean in its fury and **Makapuu** or **Sandy Beach** (page 182) to watch the body surfers.

- Continue on Route 72 to the bedroom community of **Kailua** (page 185), then take Route 83 (Kahekili Highway) to the **Byodo-In Temple** (page 188) for a short stroll through a peaceful oasis. (Allow .5 hour.)

- Continue along Route 83, stopping for a picnic lunch at **Kahana Bay** (page 189).

- Take a short hike through **Ahupuaa o Kahana State Park** (page 199), past small Hawaiian farms. (Allow 1.5 hours.)

- Continue along Route 83 to **Sunset Beach** (page 204) or **Waimea Bay** (page 206) for a dip in the ocean. (If it's winter and the surf's up, don't go swimming—just watch the surfers ride those magnificent waves.)

- Next, drive through **Haleiwa** (page 206), stopping at **Matsumoto's** (page 213) for a shave ice (with azuki beans) and a stroll around town.

- Take Route 99 to H2 to Honolulu, stopping in Chinatown for dinner.

By the 1840s, the city, originally a village called Kou, had grown into a shipping port and the commercial and political capital of the Hawaiian kingdom. Here in 1893 a band of white businessmen illegally overthrew the native monarchy. Almost a half-century later, in an ill-advised but brilliantly executed military maneuver, the Japanese drew the United States into World War II with a devastating air strike against the huge naval base at Pearl Harbor.

There are some fascinating historical monuments to tour throughout Honolulu, but I recommend you also venture outside the city to Oahu's less congested regions. Major highways lead from the capital along the east and west coasts of this 608-square-mile island, and several roads bisect the central plateau en route to the North Shore. Except for a five-mile strip in Oahu's northwest corner, you can drive completely around the island.

Closest to Honolulu is the east coast, where a spectacular seascape is paralleled by the Koolaus, a jagged and awesomely steep mountain range. This is Oahu's rainswept Windward Coast. Here, traveling up the coast past the bedroom communities of Kailua and Kaneohe, you'll discover beautiful and relatively untouched white-sand beaches. On the North Shore are some of the world's most famous surfing spots—Waimea Bay, Sunset, the Banzai Pipeline—where winter waves as high as 20 to 30 feet roll in with crushing force.

The Waianae Range, rising to 4040 feet, shadows Oahu's western coast. The sands are as white here, the beaches as uncrowded, but I've always felt slightly uncomfortable on the Leeward Coast. Theft can be a problem here. Wherever you go on Oahu never leave valuables unattended, but be particularly watchful around this coast.

Between the Koolau and Waianae ranges, remnants of the two volcanoes that created Oahu, spreads the Leilehua Plateau. This fertile region is occupied by sugar and pineapple plantations as well as several large military bases.

Geologically, Oahu is the second-oldest island in the chain; two million years ago it was two individual islands, which eventually were joined by the Leilehua Plateau. Among its geographic features is the *pali*, an awesome wall of sheer cliffs along the windward coastline, and three famous tuff-cone volcanoes—Diamond Head, Punchbowl and Koko Head.

Where to Go   Although many visitors bypass Oahu to vacation on the Neighbor Islands, it has much to offer. From the hustle and bustle of the largest city in the Pacific Islands to the quiet beaches of the Leeward Coast and the mountains of the interior, the island's diversity allows a variety of experiences unavailable elsewhere in Hawaii.

Waikiki is where the action is. People come from all over the world to stroll along its beaches, shop in its malls and be part of the scene. The competition among the vast number of hotels means there are good bargains in accommodations, which means most people stay here. Restaurants range from inexpensive fast food to elegant five-star hotel dining rooms highlighting Hawaiian regional cuisine to diverse ethnic fare. Shopping opportunities are endless.

The coastline of Oahu is 112 miles, offering approximately 130 different beaches to swim, surf, boogieboard, snorkel, dive or just plain relax.

The buildings of **Downtown Honolulu** trace the city's history from its early days as a mission outpost and royal capital to its current incarnation as a modern port and commercial center. This eclectic collection of architectural treasures includes old homes, commercial buildings, churches, the shops of Chinatown and the only royal palace ever to be built in the United States.

Greater Honolulu is the Honolulu of the locals. It is where they live and play in neighborhoods like Kalihi, a working class enclave to the west of downtown, inhabited by Hawaiians and Samoans, among others. Or in Kahala, the toney coastal district with its beachside homes and perfectly manicured lawns. Or Manoa, a neighborhood that stretches from the University of Hawaii campus to a valley verdant with tropical rainforest.

Beyond the hustle and bustle of Honolulu lies the rural tropical terrain of **Southeast Oahu**. This region of volcanic craters towering overhead, cliffs plunging into the sea and beaches strung out along the shoreline is waiting to be explored. Waimanalo, a rural town of fruit farmers and cowboys, sports another side of Oahu's many faceted personality.

Heading north along the **Windward Coast**, the spectacular scenery continues. The bedroom community of Kailua has become a low-key destination for windsurfers, kayakers and swimmers, with lots of bed and breakfasts and restaurants catering to the watersport crowd. Kamehameha Highway hugs the coast, passing a series of sandy beaches on one side and small farms on the other. The Mormons developed the town of Laie with its branch of Brigham Young University and the Polynesian Cultural Center, which brings to life the traditional customs of the Pacific islanders.

Perhaps nowhere is more legendary among surfers than Oahu's **North Shore**. Surfers from around the world come to try their skills at Waimea Bay and Sunset Beach. The area is also noted for its farms and ranches. Haleiwa, a mostly gentrified planta-tion town, serves as the commercial cen-ter of the North Shore and has scores of shops and restaurants that cater to the surfers, farmers and counterculturalists, all who call this beautiful coastal region home.

The temperature in Oahu ranges from lows of 65 degrees in January to highs of 88 in the summer months. The mean temperature ranges from 73 to 81 degrees. And there's usually a cooling breeze. Ahh.

Central Oahu and the **Leeward Coast**, which together comprise the western half of Oahu, are the only part of the island that have been relatively untouched by tourism. The last of Oahu's major plantations occupy the high central plateau that is nestled between two mountain ranges. The isolated Leeward Coast, with its rugged landscape, has some of the most beautiful beaches on Oahu. The area also serves as home to rugged, inde-pendent people, who are determined to preserve the customs and traditions of the past that have disappeared elsewhere.

When to Go

SEASONS

There are two types of seasons on Oahu, one keyed to tourists and the other to the climate. The peak tourist sea-sons run from mid-December until Easter, then again from mid-June through Labor Day. Particularly around the Christmas holidays and in August, the visitors centers are crowded. Prices increase, hotel rooms and rental cars become harder to reserve, and everything moves a bit more rapidly.

If you plan to explore Oahu during these seasons, make reser-vations several months in advance; actually, it's a good idea to make advance reservations whenever you visit. Without doubt, the off-season is the best time to hit the island. Not only are hotels more readily available, but campsites and hiking trails are also less crowded.

Climatologically, the ancient Hawaiians distinguished between two seasons—*kau*, or summer, and *hooilo*, or winter. Summer extends from May to October, when the sun is overhead and the temperatures are slightly higher. Winter brings more variable winds and cooler weather.

The important rule to remember about Oahu's beautiful weather is that it changes very little from season to season but varies dramatically from place to place. The average yearly tem-perature is about 78°, and during the coldest weather in January and the warmest in August, the thermometer rarely moves more than 5° or 6° in either direction. Similarly, seawater temperatures range comfortably between 74° and 80° year-round. Seeking a cooler climate? Head up to the mountains; for every thousand feet in elevation, the temperature drops about 3°.

Crucial to this luxurious semitropical environment are the trade winds that blow with welcome regularity from the northeast, providing a natural form of air conditioning. When the trades stop blowing, they are sometimes replaced by *kona* winds carrying rain and humid weather from the southwest. These are most frequent in the winter, when the Hawaiian islands receive their heaviest rainfall.

While summer showers are less frequent and shorter in duration, winter storms are sometimes quite nasty. I've seen it pour for five consecutive days, until hiking trails disappeared and city streets were awash. If you visit in winter, particularly from December to March, you're risking the chance of rain.

A wonderful factor to remember about this wet weather is that if it's raining where you are, you can often simply go someplace else. And I don't mean another part of the world, or even a different island. Since the rains generally batter the northeastern sections of each island, you can usually head over to the south or west coast for warm, sunny weather.

CALENDAR OF EVENTS

Something else to consider in planning a visit to Oahu is the amazing lineup of annual cultural events. For a thumbnail idea of what's happening when, check the calendar below. You might just find that special occasion to climax an already dynamic vacation. For a comprehensive listing with current updates, check the Hawaii Visitors & Convention Bureau website at www.gohawaii.com. Once you're on Oahu, you can pick up a free copy of *Honolulu Weekly*, which spotlights just about everything that's happening, and the Friday editions of the *Honolulu Advertiser* and the *Honolulu Star Bulletin*, the city's morning and afternoon newspapers.

Mid-January   The opening of **Hawaii's legislature** on the third Wednesday in January is marked by traditional pageantry. The week-long **Sony Open**, a full-field PGA tour event held at the Waialae Country Club, features some of the world's best golfers.

JANUARY

Mid-January or February The month-long **Narcissus Festival** begins the Chinese New Year with street parties and parades in Honolulu's Chinatown.

Late January In Waikiki, people come from throughout the islands to compete in ancient games, a quarter-mile outrigger canoe race and tug-of-war competitions at the **Ala Wai Challenge** at Ala Wai Park. The **Pipeline Bodysurfing Classic** takes place on the North Shore.

FEBRUARY

Early February The **World Bodyboarding Championships** start off the month with high-performance boogie boarding at its best. The **Pro Bowl** draws fans to Aloha Stadium for one of football's annual traditions. The **Punahou Carnival**, one of the best county fair–style events, features games, rides and events and a chance to mingle with local folks.

Late February The world's greatest female bodyboarders compete in the **Extreme Bodyboard Series** at the birthplace of the sport, the North Shore's Pipeline.

February through March The Japanese community in Honolulu celebrates the **Cherry Blossom Festival** with tea ceremonies, kabuki theater presentations, martial arts demonstrations and crafts exhibits.

MARCH

Early March On the first Saturday of the month, a small group of kite afficionados gather in Kapiolani Park for the **Oahu Kite Festival**.

Mid-March Japanese street performers, food booths, sumo wrestling and dancing celebrate Japanese culture during the **Honolulu Festival**, which also includes a major parade and an international kite festival.

March 17 The **St. Patrick's Day Parade** makes its way from Fort DeRussy to Kapiolani Park in honor of the state's large Hawaiian-Irish population.

APRIL

Early April Buddhist temples on the island mark **Buddha Day**, the Buddha's birthday, with special services. Included among the events are pageants, dances and a flower festival.

Mid-April Bed teams from Hawaii and as far away as Australia come to Honolulu to compete in the **International Bed Race Festival** that includes the race, as well as a carnival with food booths, rides, games and live entertainment. The **Asia Pacific Fest**, a street fair held on the University of Hawaii's Manoa campus, emphasizes Hawaii's unique cultural blend with food booths, activities and events.

May 1   **Lei Day** is celebrated on the island by people wearing flower leis and colorful Hawaiian garb. The Brothers Cazimero, one of Hawaii's popular singing groups, gives an annual **Lei Day Concert** at the Waikiki Shell.

Mid-May   Top dancers from Hawaii, Samoa and the mainland compete in the **World Fire Knife Dance Competition and Samoan Festival** at the Polynesian Cultural Center in Laie.

Late May to early June   The Outrigger Hotels **Hawaiian Ocean-fest** offers more than a week of watersport competitions between individuals and teams from around the world at locations along Waikiki Beach.

During June   Starting on Memorial Day and lasting for four weekends, the **50th State Fair** highlights Hawaii's agriculture, farm animals, flowers and products in Aloha Stadium. There are also rides, games and commercial booths.

Early June   A floral parade with floats and marching bands, a ceremony decorating Kamehameha's statue with leis, and an all-day festival of Hawaiian entertainment in Kapiolani Park commemorate Hawaii's first king with the **King Kamehameha Celebration**.

Mid-June to mid-July   Athletes from throughout the state come to compete in 40 various Olympic sports at 50 locations around the island as part of the **Aloha State Games**. The **Matsuri Festival** focuses on Japanese culture, with Bon dance performers in full regalia, a parade and other activities and events in Waikiki.

Late June   More than 20 hula *halaus* from around the islands and as far away as Japan compete in the **King Kamehameha Hula Competition**, an annual event that showcases chanting as well as both traditional and contemporary hula styles. The three-day **Taste of Honolulu** food and wine festival raises money for charities.

Early July   Military and high school bands interspersed with floral floats make their way through the streets of Kailua, during the city's **4th of July Weekend Parade**. The **4th of July All Star Rodeo** at the New Town & Country Stables in Waimanalo showcases professional rodeo events, with the crowd as colorful as the competing *paniolos* (Hawaiian cowboys). Oahu's biggest water-sports carnival, **BayFest**, takes place at Kaneohe Bay on the Marine Corps base, with live entertainment, food booths and a carnival, in addition to, you guessed it, watersports events.

Mid-July   The contestants in the **TransPacific Yacht Race** start arriving in Honolulu from Los Angeles to be greeted by festivities and parties at the city's marinas.

Mid- to late July   The **Hawaii All-collectors Show** at the Blaisdell Exhibition Hall provides hours of fun for browsers as well as buyers of Hawaiiana.

Late July   Dancers from all the islands come to Moanalua Gardens to participate in the **Prince Lot Hula Festival** in honor of Prince Lot. **Ocean Concepts Bayfest**, one of Oahu's biggest water carnivals, presents three days of rides, games and watersports.

AUGUST

During August   The dramatic **Haleiwa Cup**, a one-mile ocean swim from Haleiwa Beach Park to Puena Point and back, draws more than 350 swimmers. The **Wahine Bodyboard Championships** take place on designated beaches on the island. In Honolulu, dancers six to twelve years old gather to compete in the **Queen Liliuokalani Keiki Hula Festival**.

Early August   The **Hawaii Dragon Boat Festival**, held at Ala Moana Beach Park, is a colorful spin on an oriental nautical theme, with races, crafts, multicultural entertainment and food.

Mid-August   The three-day **Made in Hawaii Festival** highlights local products at the Blaisdell Exhibition Hall.

SEPTEMBER

Early September   Iolani Palace celebrates **Queen Liliuokalani's Birthday** with island entertainment. The **Queen Liliuokalani Canoe Regatta** is also staged early this month.

Mid-September and October   The highlight of Hawaii's cultural season is the **Aloha Week** festival, a series of week-long celebrations featuring parades, street parties and pageants.

Late September   The Bishop Museum hosts the annual festival of Hawaiian women's music and dance known as **Bankoh na Wahine o Hawaii**.

OCTOBER

During October   The **Honolulu Orchid Show** presents a display of thousands of orchids and other tropical plants at the Blaisdell Center.

Early October About 100 teams of the top male outrigger canoe paddlers in the world compete in the 40.8-mile Molokai-to-Oahu outrigger canoe race, the **Annual Bankoh Molokai Hoe,** which ends at Fort DeRussy Beach in Waikiki.

Late October In honor of Halloween, the Mission Houses Museum sponsors the **Spooky Stories Tour** of downtown historic sites, including the capitol, Iolani Palace, the Royal Tomb and Cemetery and the Mission Houses.

Early to mid-November The **Hawaii International Film Festival** provides a showcase of 100 foreign, independent, short and premiere films, seminars and workshops. The **Kaneohe Bay Fall Craft and Plant Fair** takes place at the Kaneohe Marine Corps Base on the Windward Coast.

NOVEMBER

Mid-November Sail out to snorkel with over 200 Hawaiian spinner dolphins during the **Dolphin Rendezvous.**

November through December The world's greatest surfers compete on the North Shore in a series of contests, including the **Triple Crown of Surfing.**

During December Honolulu City Lights at City Hall marks the start of the Christmas season with a tree-lighting ceremony, a parade and a wreath exhibit. **A Candlelight Christmas** at Mission Houses is an old-fashioned celebration of the season. The two-day **Festival of Art & Fine Crafts** at Thomas Square Park features over 110 arts and crafts vendors.

DECEMBER

Early December Buddha's enlightenment is commemorated with **Bodhi Day** ceremonies and religious services. Runners by the thousands turn out for the **Honolulu Marathon.**

Late December Christmas day brings a football double-header to Aloha Stadium, with fans of college football treated to the **Aloha Bowl,** followed by the all-pro **Oahu Bowl.**

The **Hawaii Visitors & Convention Bureau,** a state-run agency, is a valuable resource from which to obtain free information on Oahu. The Bureau can help plan your trip and then offer advice once you reach the island. ~ 2270 Kalakaua Avenue, Room 801, Honolulu, HI 96815; 808-923-1811; www.gohawaii.com.

▾▾▾▾▾▾▾▾▾▾▾
Before You Go

VISITORS CENTERS

Another excellent resource is the **Hawaii State Public Library System**. With a network of libraries, this government agency provides facilities for residents and non-residents alike. The libraries are good places to find light beach-reading material as well as books on Hawaii. Visitors can check out books by simply applying for a library card with a valid identification card. ~ www.librarieshawaii.org.

PACKAGE TOURS

In planning a Hawaiian sojourn, one potential moneysaver is the package tour, which combines air transportation with a hotel room and other amenities. Generally, it is a style of travel that I avoid. However, if you can find a package that provides air transportation, a hotel or condominium accommodation and a rental car, all at one low price—it might be worth considering. Just try to avoid the packages that preplan your entire visit, dragging you around on air-conditioned tour buses. Look for the package that provides only the bare necessities, namely transportation and lodging, while allowing you the greatest freedom.

However you decide to go, be sure to consult a travel agent. They are professionals in the field, possessing the latest information on rates and facilities, and their service to you is usually free.

PACKING

When I get ready to pack for a trip, I sit down and make a list of everything I'll need. It's a very slow, exact procedure: I look in closets, drawers and shelves, and run through in my mind the activities in which I'll participate, determining which items are required for each. After all the planning is complete and when I have the entire inventory collected in one long list, I sit for a minute or two, basking in my wisdom and forethought.

Then I tear the hell out of the list, cut out the ridiculous items I'll never use, halve the number of spares among the necessary items, and reduce the entire contents of my suitcase to the bare essentials.

Before I developed this packing technique, I once traveled overland from London to New Delhi carrying two suitcases and a knapsack. I lugged those damned bundles onto trains, buses, jitneys, taxis and rickshaws. When I reached Turkey, I started shipping things home, but by then I was buying so many market goods that it was all I could do to keep even.

Vacation Rentals on Oahu

Aston
800-922-7866
e-mail info@astonhotels.com

Condo Rentals of Waikiki
800-927-0555
www.waikikirentals.com

CyberRentals
www.cyberrentals.com

Gold Coast Real Estate, Inc.
808-926-7525
www.goldcoasthawaii.com

Hawaiian Condo Resorts
800-487-4505
www.hawaiicondo.com

Hawaiian Islands Bed & Breakfast
800-258-7895
www.lanikaibeachrentals.com

Marc Resorts
800-535-0085
www.marcresorts.com

Marina Hawaii Vacations
808-951-8315
www.marinahawaiivacations.com

Pacific Realty
808-941-5247
e-mail prce.hawaii@verizon.net

Tropical Villa Vacations
888-875-2818
www.tropicalvillavacations.com

VacationHosts.com
800-754-0905
www.vacationhosts.com

Luxury Vacation Homes
800-262-9013
www.luxuryvacationhomes.com

Waikiki Vacation Rentals
800-543-5663
e-mail corasinc@aol.com

I ended up carrying so much crap that one day, when I was sardined in a crowd pushing its way onto an Indian train, someone managed to pick my pocket. When I felt the wallet slipping out, not only was I unable to chase the culprit—I was so weighted down with baggage that I couldn't even turn around to see who was robbing me!

I'll never travel that way again, and neither should you. Particularly when visiting Oahu, where the weather is mild, you should pack very light. The airlines permit two suitcases and a carry-on bag; try to take one suitcase and maybe an accessory bag that can double as a beach bag. Dress styles are very informal here, and laundromats are frequent, so you don't need a broad range of clothing items. Donning aloha attire—aloha shirts and muumuus—on Friday is a custom even the most staid businessperson generally follows.

Remember, you're packing for a semitropical climate. Take along a sweater or light jacket for the mountains, and a poncho to protect against rain. But otherwise, all that travelers on Oahu require are shorts, bathing suits, lightweight slacks, short-sleeved shirts and blouses, and summer dresses or muumuus. Rarely do visitors require sport jackets or formal dresses. Wash-and-wear fabrics are the most convenient.

For footwear, I suggest soft, comfortable shoes. Low-cut hiking boots or walking shoes are preferable for hiking; for beachgoing, there's nothing as good as sandals.

There are several other items to squeeze in the corners of your suitcase—sunscreen, sunglasses, a towel and, of course, your copy of *Hidden Oahu*. You might also consider packing a mask, fins and snorkel, and possibly a camera.

If you plan on camping, you'll need most of the equipment required for mainland overnighting. On Oahu, you can get along quite comfortably with a lightweight tent and sleeping bag. You'll also need a knapsack, canteen, camp stove and fuel, mess kit, first-aid kit (with insect repellent, water purification tablets and Chapstick), toilet kit, a pocket knife, hat, waterproof matches, flashlight and ground cloth.

LODGING   Accommodations on Oahu range from funky cottages to bed-and-breakfast inns to highrise condos. You'll find inexpensive family-run hotels, middle-class tourist facilities and world-class resorts. Generally, the farther a hotel is from the beach, the less it costs.

Whichever you choose, there are a few guidelines to help save money. Try to visit during the off-season, avoiding the high-rate periods during the summer and from Christmas to Easter. If you must travel around Christmas and during the summer high season, it's wise to book reservations as far in advance as possible. Rooms with mountain views are less expensive than oceanview accommodations. Another way to economize is by reserving a room with a kitchen. In any case, try to reserve far in advance.

A photography hint: Buy your film in the islands and have it developed before you leave to avoid X-ray damage. Never carry undeveloped film in your checked luggage.

To help you decide on a place to stay, I've described the accommodations not only by area but also according to price (prices listed are for double occupancy during the high season; prices may decrease in low season). *Budget* hotels are generally less than $60 per night for two people; the rooms are clean and comfortable, but lack luxury. The *moderately* priced hotels run $60 to $120, and provide larger rooms, plusher furniture and more attractive surroundings. At *deluxe*-priced accommodations you can expect to spend between $120 and $180 for a homey bed and breakfast or a double in a hotel or resort. You'll check into a spacious, well-appointed room with modern facilities; downstairs the lobby will be a fashionable affair, and you'll usually see a restaurant, lounge and a cluster of shops. If you want to spend your time (and money) in the island's very finest hotels, try an *ultra-deluxe* facility, which will include all the amenities and price well above $180.

BED-AND-BREAKFAST INNS The bed-and-breakfast business on Oahu becomes more diverse and sophisticated every year. Today there are several referral services that can find you lodging. Claiming to be the biggest clearinghouse in the state, **Bed & Breakfast Honolulu (Statewide)** represents over 400 properties on Oahu. ~ 3242 Kaohinani Drive, Honolulu, HI 96817; 808-595-7533, 800-288-4666, fax 808-595-2030; www.hawaiibnb.com.

The original association, **Bed & Breakfast Hawaii**, claims about 200 locations on Oahu. Founded in 1979, this Kauai-based service is well known throughout Hawaii. ~ P.O. Box 449, Kapaa, HI 96746; 808-822-7771, 800-733-1632, fax 808-822-2723; www.bandb-hawaii.com.

For other possibilities contact **Hawaiian Islands Bed & Breakfast**. ~ 808-261-7895, 800-258-7895, fax 808-262-2181; www.

lanikaibeachrentals.com. You can also try **Affordable Accommodations**, which is based on Maui and has 20 listings on Oahu. ~ 2825 Kauhale Street, Kihei, HI 96753; 808-879-7865, 888-333-9747, fax 808-874-0831; www.affordablemaui.com. Or call **All-Islands. com**, an Oahu-based reservation service that represents more than 250 bed and breakfasts on the island. ~ 808-263-2342, 800-542-0344, fax 808-263-0308; www.all-islands.com, e-mail inquiries@all-islands.com.

When traveling around Christmas, Easter and during the summer high season, it's wise to book reservations as far in advance as possible.

While the properties represented by these agencies range widely in price, **Hawaii's Best Bed & Breakfasts** specializes in small, upscale accommodations. With about 100 establishments to choose from, it places guests in a variety of privately owned facilities; most are deluxe priced. ~ P.O. Box 758, Volcano, HI 96785; 808-985-7488, 800-262-9912, fax 808-967-8610; www. bestbnb.com, e-mail reservations@bestbnb.com.

CONDOS

Many people visiting Hawaii, especially those traveling with families, find that condominiums are often cheaper than hotels. While some hotel rooms come with kitchenettes, few provide all the amenities of condominiums. A condo, in essence, is an apartment away from home. Designed as studio, one-, two- or three-bedroom apartments, they come equipped with full kitchen facilities and complete kitchenware collections. Many also feature washer/dryers, dishwashers, air conditioning, color televisions, telephones, lanais and community swimming pools.

Utilizing the kitchen will save considerably on your food bill; by sharing the accommodations among several people, you'll also cut your lodging bill. While the best way to see Oahu is obviously by hiking and camping, when you're ready to come in from the wilds, consider reserving a place that provides more than a bed and a night table.

DINING

A few guidelines will help you chart a course through Oahu's countless dining places. Within a particular chapter, the restaurants are categorized geographically, with each restaurant entry describing the establishment as budget, moderate, deluxe or ultra-deluxe in price.

To establish a pattern for Oahu's parade of dining places, I've described not only the cuisine but also the ambience of each establishment. Restaurants listed offer lunch and dinner unless otherwise noted.

Dinner entrées at *budget* restaurants usually cost $8 or less. The ambience is informal café style and the crowd is often a local one. *Moderately* priced restaurants range between $8 and $16 at dinner and offer pleasant surroundings, a more varied menu and a slower pace. *Deluxe* establishments tab their entrées above $16, featuring sophisticated cuisines, plush decor and more personalized service. *Ultra-deluxe* restaurants generally price above $24.

Breakfast and lunch menus vary less in price from restaurant to restaurant. Even deluxe-priced kitchens usually offer light breakfasts and lunch sandwiches, which place them within a few dollars of their budget-minded competitors. These early meals can be a good time to test expensive restaurants.

Oahu is an ideal vacation spot for family holidays. The pace is slow, the atmosphere casual. A few guidelines will help ensure that your trip to the islands brings out the joys rather than the strains of parenting, allowing everyone to get into the aloha spirit.

TRAVELING WITH CHILDREN

Use a travel agent to help with arrangements; they can reserve spacious bulkhead seats on airlines and determine which flights are least crowded. They can also seek out the best deals on inexpensive condominiums, saving you money on both room and board.

Planning the trip with your kids stimulates their imagination. Books about travel, airplane rides, beaches, whales, volcanoes and Hawaiiana help prepare even a two-year-old for an adventure. This preparation makes the "getting there" part of the trip more exciting for children of all ages.

And "getting there" means a long-distance flight. Plan to bring everything you need on board the plane—diapers, food, toys, books and extra clothing for kids and parents alike. I found it helpful to carry a few new toys and books as treats to distract my son and daughter when they got bored. I also packed extra snacks.

Allow extra time to get places. Book reservations in advance and make sure that the hotel or condominium has the extra crib, cot or bed you require. It's smart to ask for a room at the end of the hall to cut down on noise. Some resorts and hotels have daily programs for kids during the summer and holiday seasons. Hula lessons, lei making, storytelling, sandcastle building and various sports activities keep *keikis* (kids) over six happy while also giving Mom and Dad a break. As an added bonus, these resorts offer family plans, providing discounts for extra rooms or permitting children to share a room with their parents at no extra charge. Check with your travel agent.

When reserving a rental car, inquire to see if they provide car seats and if there is an added charge. Hawaii has a strictly enforced car seat law. Besides the car seat you may have to bring along, also pack shorts and T-shirts, a sweater, sun hat, sundresses and waterproof sandals. A stroller with sunshade for little ones helps on sightseeing sojourns; a shovel and pail are essential for sandcastle building. Most importantly, remember to bring a good sunblock. The quickest way to ruin a family vacation is with a bad sunburn. Also plan to bring indoor activities such as books and games for evenings and rainy days.

Most towns have stores that carry diapers, food and other essentials. However, prices are much higher on Oahu than on the mainland. To economize, some people take along an extra suitcase filled with diapers and wipes, baby food, peanut butter and jelly, etc. If you're staying in Waikiki, **ABC stores** carry a limited selection of disposables and baby food. Shopping outside Waikiki in local supermarkets will save you a considerable sum: **Star Market** is open from 5 a.m. to 2 a.m. ~ 2470 South King Street, Honolulu; 808-973-1666.

A first-aid kit is always a good idea. Also check with your pediatrician for special medicines and dosages for colds and diarrhea. If your child does become sick or injured in the Honolulu area, contact **Kapiolani Medical Center** at 808-983-6000. On the Windward Coast, call **Castle Medical Center** ~ 808-263-5500; on the North Shore, **Kahuku Hospital** ~ 808-293-9221; and on the leeward side, **Wahiawa General Hospital** ~ 808-621-8411. There's also a **Hawaii Poison Center** in Honolulu. ~ 808-941-4411.

Hotels often provide access to babysitters. **Aloha Babysitting Service** is a bonded babysitting agency. ~ 808-732-2029, fax 808-735-1958.

There are plenty of places to take kids who tire of the beach. The Honolulu Zoo, the Waikiki Aquarium, Hawaii Children's Discovery Center, The Polynesian Cultural Center and Sea Life Park are a few that come to mind, but there are many, many more. Be sure to look in the local paper for events that are occurring while you are there such as luaus, *hukilaus* and island entertainment.

Time Out for Parents

When parents vacationing at the major resorts want to relax in a spa, golf, shop or simply have a little down time, they can send the kids to Keiki Camp. These half- or full-day programs will keep the little ones entertained. Ask your travel agent about special family packages with discounts and freebies on meals, activities and hotel rates.

The **Hilton Hawaiian Village** has the most extensive *keiki* program. The year-round Rainbow Express Keiki Club runs from 8:30 a.m. to 3 p.m. for ages 5 to 12; $22 to $50, with discounts for a second child. Activities include Hawaiian crafts, hula, seashell hunts, sandcastle building, fishing and trips to Waikiki attractions. Kids also can use a lending library of books, games and toys, join the King's Jubilee Keiki Parade on Friday nights or take a wildlife and ecology tour. Reservations are required. ~ 2005 Kalia Road; 808-949-4321, 800-774-1500.

The **Sheraton Waikiki Hotel**'s year-round Keiki Aloha Children's Program runs from 9 a.m. to 6 p.m. It's open to children ages 5 to 12 staying at any Sheraton in Waikiki. Activities include visiting the Waikiki Aquarium, Bishop Museum, Honolulu Zoo, Sea Life Park and Hawaii Army Museum, boogieboarding, hula, lei making, surfing, bamboo pole fishing, catamaran sailing and volcano making. Parents can join many of the activities. Free shuttle service is available for Moana Surfrider and Princess Kaiulani guests. Fees range from $20 to $30 and $10 for each parent; reservations required. ~ 2255 Kalakaua Avenue; 808-922-4422 ext. 79105.

At the **Kahala Mandarin Oriental**, kids ages 5 to 12 can attend sessions from 9 a.m. to 4 p.m. The year-round program features reef walking, snorkeling, storytelling, bamboo pole fishing, lei making, hula, crabbing and Hawaiian art. Fees range from $30 to $50. ~ 5000 Kahala Avenue; 808-739-8608.

The **Turtle Bay Resort** offers its daily Keiki Turtle Club from late May to early September for kids ages 5 to 12. The sessions run from 9 a.m. to 3 p.m. and feature lei making, coconut frond weaving, hula, sponge painting, beading, sandcastle building and shell collecting. Fee of $29 includes lunch, supplies, T-shirt and backpack. ~ 57-091 Kamehameha Highway, Kahuku; 808-239-8811.

JW Marriott Ihilani Resort & Spa (92-1001 Olani Street, Kapolei; 808-679-0079) and **Waikiki Beach Marriott Resort** (2552 Kalakaua Avenue; 808-922-6611) offer children's programs from June through September. The Waikiki Beach's Keiki Kamp and Ihilani's Keiki Beachcomber Club run from 9 a.m. to 3 p.m for kids ages 4 to 12. Activities include treasure hunts, hula dancing, lei making, karaoke, sports and crafts. Register before 6 p.m. the day before. Fees range from $30 to $55 and include lunch and a T-shirt.

WOMEN TRAVELING ALONE

Traveling solo grants an independence and freedom different from that of traveling with a partner, but single travelers are more vulnerable to crime and should take additional precautions.

It's unwise to hitchhike and probably best to avoid inexpensive accommodations on the outskirts of Honolulu; the money saved does not outweigh the risk. Bed and breakfasts, youth hostels and YWCAs are generally your safest bet for lodging, and they also foster an environment ideal for bonding with fellow travelers. There are several YWCAs on Oahu; check specific lodging sections for other options. On the Windward Coast, call the YWCA–Camp Kokokahi. ~ 45-035 Kaneohe Bay Drive; 808-247-2124.

Keep all valuables well-hidden and hold on to cameras and purses. Avoid late-night treks or strolls anywhere, even beaches, and especially through undesirable parts of town, but if you find yourself in this situation, continue walking with a confident air until you reach a safe haven. A fierce scowl never hurts.

These hints should by no means deter you from seeking out adventure. Wherever you go, stay alert, use your common sense and trust your instincts. If you are hassled or threatened in some way, never be afraid to scream for assistance. It's a good idea to carry change for a phone call. In case of emergency, contact the **Sex Abuse Treatment Center**. ~ 808-524-7273.

For more helpful hints, get a copy of *Safety and Security for Women Who Travel* (Travelers' Tales).

A CIRCLE OF ALOHA

The lei. A symbol of Hawaii, along with grass skirts and shimmering palm trees. If you are fortunate enough to be met at the airport by someone you know, chances are you will be wreathed in fragrant blossoms and kissed on both cheeks. But if you come to the island as a stranger, give yourself this aromatic gift. At some point venture downtown to Maunakea Street where you will find a row of small shops selling a variety of flower leis, including the fragrant plumeria or ginger leis. Lei-giving is a tradition that dates back to ancient times, when they were used as head wreaths as well as flower necklaces in religious ceremonies and were presented to the *alii*. And as in ancient times, the craft of lei-making is thriving today. You can still find leis that incorporate ferns, *pukiawe* (red berries), *lehua* blossoms and *maile* leaves into intricate works of art, some having hundreds of blossoms and all made with aloha.

The Gay & Lesbian Community Center, specializing in support groups and community outreach, supplies Oahu visitors with gay-relevant information. Stop by during office hours to pick up lesbian and gay newspapers and brochures. It's located in the YWCA; call for office hours. ~ 2424 Beretania Street; 808-951-7000, fax 808-951-7001; www.glcc-hawaii.org.

GAY & LESBIAN TRAVELERS

For monthly updates on the gay and lesbian scene on Oahu, pick up a copy of *Da Kine* at bars and clubs in Waikiki, the main library and the Academy of Arts Theater. Along with coverage of news and entertainment, it provides a calendar of events and a listing of services. ~ 2410 Cleghorn Street #2302, Honolulu, HI 96815; 808-923-7378, fax 808-922-6124; e-mail ha@gte.net.

The *Pocket Guide to Hawaii*, published by Pacific Ocean Holidays, is also helpful for gay travelers. It comes out three times a year and lists the best and hottest establishments and beaches that Hawaii has to offer. Send $5 per copy (via mail only) if ordering from the mainland; otherwise, it's distributed free by local gay businesses. This outfit can also help book vacation packages. ~ P.O. Box 88245, Honolulu, HI 96830-8245; 808-923-2400, reservations only 800-735-6600; www.gayhawaii.com.

Hawaiinet Tour & Travel Services Network, Inc. offers special tour packages to both gays and straights. They can help decide on hotels, condos and restaurants. ~ P.O. Box 15671, Honolulu, HI 96830-5671; 808-545-1119, fax 808-524-9572; www.hawaiinet.com.

For further information, be sure to look under "gay-friendly travel" in the index at the end of the book.

Oahu is a hospitable place for senior citizens to visit. Countless museums, historic sights and even restaurants and hotels offer senior discounts that can cut a substantial chunk off vacation costs. Be sure to check out the early-bird specials for discount dining.

SENIOR TRAVELERS

The American Association of Retired Persons (AARP) offers membership to anyone over 50. AARP's benefits include travel discounts with a number of firms. ~ 601 E Street NW, Washington, DC 20049; 800-424-3410; www.aarp.org.

Elderhostel offers reasonably priced, all-inclusive educational programs in a variety of locations throughout the year. ~ 11 Avenue de Lafayette, Boston, MA 02111; 877-426-8056, fax 617-426-0701; www.elderhostel.org.

Be extra careful about health matters. Consider carrying a medical record with you—including your medical history and current medical status as well as your doctor's name, phone number and address. Make sure your insurance covers you while you are away from home.

DISABLED TRAVELERS   The **Commission on Persons with Disabilities** publishes a survey of the city, county, state and federal parks in Hawaii that are accessible to travelers with disabilities. ~ 919 Ala Moana Boulevard, Room 101, Honolulu, HI 96814; 808-586-8121, fax 808-586-8129; e-mail accesshi@aloha.net.

The Commission on Persons with Disabilities provides "Aloha Guides to Accessibility," which covers Oahu and gives information on various hotels, shopping centers, and restaurants that are accessible.

The **Society for Accessible Travel & Hospitality** offers information for travelers with disabilities. ~ 347 5th Avenue, Suite 610, New York, NY 10016; 212-447-7284, fax 212-725-8253; www.sath.org. **Travelin' Talk**, a network of people and organizations, also provides assistance. ~ P.O. Box 1796, Wheat Ridge, CO 80034; 303-232-2979; www.travelintalk.net.

Be sure to check in advance when making room reservations. Some hotels feature facilities for those in wheelchairs.

FOREIGN TRAVELERS   **Passports and Visas**   Most foreign visitors are required to obtain a passport and tourist visa to enter the United States. Contact your nearest United States Embassy or Consulate well in advance to obtain a visa and to check on any other entry requirements.

Customs Requirements   Foreign travelers are allowed to carry in the following: 200 cigarettes (1 carton), 50 cigars or 2 kilograms (4.4 pounds) of smoking tobacco; one liter of alcohol for personal use only (you must be 21 years of age to bring in alcohol); and US$100 worth of duty-free gifts that include an additional quantity of 100 cigars. You may bring in any amount of currency, but must fill out a form if you bring in over US$10,000. Carry any prescription drugs in clearly marked containers. (You may have to produce a written prescription or doctor's statement for the customs officer.) Meat or meat products, seeds, plants, fruits and narcotics are not allowed to be brought into the United States. Contact the **United States Customs Service** for further information. ~ 1301 Constitution

Avenue NW, Washington, DC 20229; 202-927-6724; www. customs.treas.gov.

Driving   If you plan to rent a car, an international driver's license should be obtained prior to arrival. Some rental car companies require both a foreign license and an international driver's license. Many car rental agencies require that the lessee be at least 25 years of age; all require a major credit card. Seat belts are mandatory for the driver and all passengers. Children under the age of 5 or weighing less than 40 pounds should be in the back seat in approved child safety restraints.

Currency   United States money is based on the dollar. Bills come in six denominations: $1, $5, $10, $20, $50 and $100. Every dollar is divided into 100 cents. Coins are the penny (1 cent), nickel (5 cents), dime (10 cents), quarter (25 cents), half-dollar (50 cents) and dollar (100 cents).

You may not use foreign currency to purchase goods and services in the United States. Consider buying traveler's checks in dollar amounts. You may also use credit cards affiliated with an American company such as Interbank, Barclay Card, VISA, Master Card and American Express.

Electricity and Electronics   Electric outlets use currents of 110 volts, 60 cycles. For appliances made for other electrical systems, you need a transformer or adapter. Travelers who use laptop computers for telecommunication should be aware that modem configurations for U.S. telephone systems may be different from their European counterparts. Similarly, the U.S. format for videotapes is different from that in Europe; U.S. Park Service visitors centers and other stores that sell souvenir videos often have them available in European format.

Weights and Measurements   The United States uses the English system of weights and measures. American units and their metric equivalents are as follows: 1 inch = 2.5 centimeters; 1 foot (12 inches) = 0.3 meter; 1 yard (3 feet) = 0.9 meter; 1 mile (5280 feet) = 1.6 kilometers; 1 ounce = 28 grams; 1 pound (16 ounces) = 0.45 kilogram; 1 quart (liquid) = 0.9 liter.

MAIL

If you're staying in a particular establishment during your visit, you can usually have personal mail sent there. Otherwise, for cardholders, **American Express** will hold letters for no charge at its Honolulu office for 30 days, and will provide forwarding services. If you decide to use their facilities, have mail addressed to American Express, Client Mail, 2424 Kalakaua Avenue, Honolulu, HI 96815. ~ 808-922-4718. If you don't use this service, your only other recourse is to have mail sent to a particular post office in care of general delivery.

Transportation

AIR

During the 19th century, sleek clipper ships sailed from the West Coast to Hawaii in about 11 days. Today, you'll be traveling by a less romantic but far swifter conveyance—the jet plane. Rather than days at sea, it will be about five hours in the air from California, nine hours from Chicago, or around 11 hours if you're coming from New York.

There's really nothing more invigorating than stepping off a plane in Hawaii. Several major airlines—**Aloha, United, Northwest, Hawaiian, Continental, American** and **Delta**—fly regular schedules to Honolulu.

A vigorous agricultural inspection keeps unwanted pests out of Hawaii. If you forgot that apple tucked into your backpack, a sniffing dog inspector may tag you.

Whichever carrier you choose, ask for the economy or excursion fare, and try to fly during the week; weekend flights are generally higher in price. To qualify for the lower price fares, it is sometimes necessary to book your flight two weeks in advance and to stay in the islands at least one week. Generally, however, the restrictions are minimal. Children under two years of age can fly for free, but they will not have a seat of their own. Each passenger is permitted two large pieces of luggage plus a carry-on bag. Shipping a bike or surfboard will cost extra. (There is a size restriction on surf boards—longboarders will have to rent them on the island.)

There's one airport on Oahu and it's a behemoth. **Honolulu International Airport** is a Pacific crossroads, an essential link between North America and Asia. Honolulu International includes all the comforts of a major airport. You can check your bags; fuel up at a restaurant, coffee shop or cocktail lounge; shop at several stores; or shower.

GROUND TRANSPORT

To cover the eight or so miles into Waikiki, it's possible to hire a cab for $25 to $30. For $8 (roundtrip $13), **Robert's Hawaii** will take you to your Waikiki hotel or condominium. ~ 808-539-9400, 800-831-5541; www.robertshawaii.com.

City buses #19 and #20 travel through Downtown Honolulu and Waikiki. This is the cheapest transportation, but you're only allowed to carry on baggage that fits on your lap. So, unless you're traveling very light, you'll have to use another conveyance.

If you decide to venture off Oahu, you have a few options. Since cruise ships are the only commercial boats serving all six Hawaiian islands, most of the transportation is by plane. **Aloha Airlines** and **Hawaiian Airlines**, the state's major carriers, provide frequent interisland jet service. If you're looking for smooth, rapid, comfortable service, this is certainly it. You'll be buckled into your seat, offered a low-cost cocktail and whisked to your destination within 20 to 40 minutes.

GETTING BETWEEN ISLANDS

Without doubt, the best service aboard any interisland carrier is on Aloha Airlines. They have an excellent reputation for flying on time and offer various travel passes for island-hopping travelers. I give them my top recommendation.

Now that you know how to fly quickly and comfortably, let me tell you about the most exciting way to get between islands. **IslandAir** flies twin-engine propeller planes. These small airplanes travel at low altitudes and moderate speeds over the islands. Next to chartering a helicopter, they are one of the finest ways to see the islands from the air.

The service is very personalized; often the pilot will point out landmarks along the route, and sometimes he'll fly out of his way to show you points of particular interest. I often fly this way when I'm in the islands and highly recommend these small planes to anyone with a sense of adventure.

Let me describe a typical flight I took between Honolulu and Kona. So that I'd get a better view, the captain suggested that I sit up front in the copilot's seat. After taking off in a wide arc around Honolulu, we passed close enough to Diamond Head to gaze down into the crater, then headed across the Kaiwi Channel to Molokai. Since we had to pick up passengers at Molokai's lonely airstrip, the pilot gave us a tour of the island. We paralleled the island's rugged north face, where sharp cliffs laced with waterfalls drop thousands of feet to the sea. Then we swept in toward Maui for a view of Haleakala Crater, and continued past the Big Island's snowtipped volcanoes before touching down in Kona. All for the price of an airline ticket!

Rates for these twin-engine propeller planes are very competitive when compared with the interisland jets. Coupled with the fact that your ticket on the smaller carriers is worth a guided tour as well as a trip between islands, you really can't do better than booking your flights on these sturdy little planes.

CAR RENTALS

Renting a car is as easy on Oahu as anywhere. Several rental agencies compete fiercely with one another in price and quality of service. So before renting, shop around: check the listings in this book, and also look for the special temporary offers that many rental companies sometimes feature.

There are several facts to remember when renting a car. First of all, a major credit card is essential. Also, many agencies don't rent at all to people under 25. Regardless of your age, many companies charge several dollars a day extra for insurance. The insurance is optional and expensive, and in many cases, unnecessary (many credit cards provide the same coverage when a rental is charged to the card). Find out if you credit card company offers this coverage. Your personal insurance policy may also provide for rental cars and, if necessary, have a clause added that will include rental car protection. Check on this before you leave home. But remember, whether you have insurance or not, you are liable for the first several thousand dollars in accident damage.

Oahu's environment is fragile. Part of its natural beauty comes from its geographic isolation from alien ecosystems. Bringing in plants, produce or animals can introduce pests and non-endemic species that could eventually undermine the ecosystem.

Rates fluctuate with the season; slack tourist seasons are great times for good deals. Also, three-day, weekly and monthly rates are almost always cheaper than daily rentals; cars with standard shifts are generally less than automatics; and compacts are more economical than the larger four-door models.

Of all the islands, Oahu offers the most car-rental agencies. At the Honolulu airport, **Avis Rent A Car** (808-834-5536, 800-321-3712), **Budget Rent A Car** (808-838-1111, 800-527-0700), **Dollar Rent A Car** (808-831-2330, 800-800-4000), **National Car Rental** (808-831-3800, 800-227-7368) and **Hertz** (808-831-3500, 800-654-3011) all have booths. Their convenient location helps to save time while minimizing the problem of picking up your car.

Though not at the airport, **Alamo Rent A Car** provides airport pick-up service. ~ 808-833-4585, 800-327-9633. **VIP Rental** is a cheaper outfit. ~ 234 Beachwalk; 808-922-4605.

There are many other Honolulu-based companies offering very low rates but providing limited pick-up service at the airport. I've never found the inconvenience worth the savings. There you are— newly arrived from the mainland, uncertain about your environment, anxious to check in at the hotel—and you're immediately confronted with the Catch-22 of getting to your car. Do you rent a vehicle in which to pick up your rental car? Take a bus? Hitchhike? What do you do with your bags meanwhile?

If you prefer to go in high style, book a limousine from **Cloud Nine**. ~ 808-524-7999, 800-524-7999.

JEEP RENTALS

I don't recommend renting a jeep. They're more expensive and less comfortable than automobiles, and won't get you to very many more interesting spots. In addition, the rental car collision insurance provided by most credit cards does not cover jeeps. Except in extremely wet weather when roads are muddy, all the places mentioned in this book, including the hidden locales, can be reached by car. However, if you choose to rent one, **Adventure Rentals** offers them. ~ 808-944-3131. Or try **Dollar Rent A Car**. ~ 808-831-2331. VIP **Car Rental** rents Suzuki Samurais. ~ 808-922-4605.

MOPED RENTALS

In Waikiki, **Adventure Rentals** rents mopeds and motorcycles. ~ 1946 Ala Moana Boulevard; 808-944-3131. You can also try **Blue Sky Rentals**, located on the ground floor of the Inn On The Park Hotel. ~ 1920 Ala Moana Boulevard; 808-947-0101.

PUBLIC TRANSIT

Oahu has an excellent bus system that runs regularly to points all over the island and provides convenient service throughout Honolulu. Many of the beaches, hotels, restaurants and points of interest mentioned in this chapter are just a bus ride away. It's even possible to pop your money in the fare box and ride around the entire island.

TheBus carries more than 260,000 people daily, loading them into 525 buses that rumble along city streets and country roads from 5 a.m. to 10 p.m. (though some lines run past midnight). There are also express buses traveling major highways at commuter times. Most buses are handicapped accessible and many have bike racks.

If you stay in Waikiki you'll inevitably be sardined into a #19 or #20 bus for the ride through Honolulu's tourist mecca. Many bus drivers are Hawaiian; I saw some hysterical scenes on this line when tourists waited anxiously for their stop to be called, only to realize they couldn't understand the driver's pidgin. Hysterical, that is, *after* those early days when *I* was the visitor with the furrowed brow.

But you're surely more interested in meeting local people than tourists, and you can easily do it on any of the buses outside Waikiki. They're less crowded and a lot more fun for people-watching.

For information on bus routes call TheBus at 808-848-5555 or visit www.thebus.org. And remember, the only carry-on luggage permitted is baggage small enough to fit on your lap.

AERIAL TOURS

The quickest way to see all Oahu has to offer is by taking to the air. In minutes you can experience the island's hidden waterfalls, secluded beaches and volcanic landmarks. Tranquil gliders and hovering whirlybirds all fly low and slow to make sure you see what you missed on the trip over from the mainland. You can also take extended flights that include the outer islands.

Makani Kai Helicopters offers helicopter tours of Waikiki and Honolulu, Hanauma Bay, the Koolau Mountains, China-man's Hat, Sacred Falls, Kahana Rainforest and the North Shore. They also take trips to the "Jurassic Park Valley," an area where parts of the movie were filmed. Reservations required. ~ 110 Kapalulu Place, Honolulu; 808-834-1111, fax 808-833-7406; www.makanikai.com.

A WALK ON THE CULTURAL SIDE

Chinatown's rich history and culture can be experienced in several inexpensive walking tours that make this exotic place come alive. Explore the markets to find the special ingredients that make up Thai, Vietnamese and Chinese cooking on walks hosted by **Lyon Arboretum**. ~ 808-988-0456, Learn about the past in a two-hour morning tour offered by the **Hawaii Heritage Center**. ~ 808-521-2749. Hear tidbits about the economic contributions of the Chinese on a Tuesday-morning tour by the **Chinese Chamber of Commerce of Hawaii**. ~ 808-533-3181.

To enjoy a one- or two-passenger glider trip, head out to **The Original Glider Rides** and talk to Mr. Bill. On your 20-minute trip you're likely to see fields of sugar cane, marine mammals, surfers working the North Shore and neighboring Kauai. You'll also enjoy peace and quiet while working your way down from 3000 feet. A videotape of the ride and your reactions makes a memorable souvenir. ~ Dillingham Airfield, Mokuleia; 808-677-3404; www. honolulusoaring.com.

WALKING TOURS

Oahu Nature Tours offers four different eco-tours that provide an overview of native Hawaiian birds and plants. One focuses on Oahu's volcanic coast, beginning in Diamond Head Crater, continuing through a lagoon wildlife sanctuary, then heading out to the island's southeast corner. Another tour takes you into the Hawaiian rainforest at 2000-feet elevation in the Koolau Mountains. Equipment, transportation and water are provided. Fee. ~ P.O. Box 8059, Honolulu, HI 96815; 800-924-2473; www.oahu naturetours.com.

Ready for goosebumps? Stroll through the past with a company called **Chicken Skin Tours**. Based in Honolulu they offer a number of bus and walking tours. The Ghost Hunter's Bus Tour focuses on the supernatural lore of the island. Reservations highly recommended. Fee. ~ 808-943-0371, fax 808-951-8878; www.chicken-skin.com, e-mail timewalk@pixi.com.

TWO

The Land
and Outdoor Adventures

 With its luxurious parks, mountain trails and miles of white-sand beaches, Oahu is a paradise for campers, snorkelers and hikers. Because of Oahu's varied terrain and its' microenvironments, it's possible to experience all kinds of outdoor adventures. One day you'll hike through a steaming rainforest filled with tropical flowers; the next day you'll snorkel among darting reef fish then camp on a white-sand beach beneath towering ironwood trees.

Paradise means more than physical beauty, however. It also involves an easy life and a bountiful food supply. The easy living is up to you; just slow down from the frantic pace of mainland life and you'll discover that island existence can be relaxing. As for wild food—you'll find it hanging from trees, swimming in the ocean and clinging to coral reefs. Just be sure to use the proper techniques in taking from the environment and always keep Hawaii's delicate ecosystem in mind.

In this chapter, I'll detail some of the outdoor skills necessary to camp, hike and live naturally on Oahu. This is certainly not a comprehensive study of how to survive on a Pacific island; I'm just passing along a few facts I've learned while exploring Hawaii. I don't advise that you plan to live off the land. Oahu's environment is too fragile to support you full-time. Anyway, living that way is a hell of a lot of work! I'll just give a few hints on how to supplement your provisions with a newly caught fish or a fresh fruit salad. That way, not only will you save on food bills, you'll also get a much fuller taste of the islands.

Obviously, none of these techniques were developed by me personally. In fact, most of them date back centuries to the early days, when Polynesian explorers applied the survival skills they had learned in Tahiti and the Marquesas to the newly discovered islands of Hawaii. So as you set out to fish along a coral reef, hunt for shellfish in tidepools or gather seaweed at low tide, give a prayerful thanks to the generations of savvy islanders who have come before you.

More than 25 million years ago a fissure opened along the Pacific floor. Beneath tons of sea water molten lava poured from the rift. This liquid basalt, oozing from a hot spot in the earth's center, created a crater along the ocean bottom. As the tectonic plate that comprises the ocean floor drifted over the earth's hot spot, numerous other craters appeared. Slowly, in the seemingly endless procession of geologic time, a chain of volcanic islands, now stretching almost 2000 miles, has emerged from the sea.

On the continents it was also a period of terrible upheaval. The Himalayas, Alps and Andes were rising, but these great chains would reach their peaks long before the Pacific mountains even touched sea level. Not until about 25 million years ago did the first of these underwater volcanoes, today's Kure and Midway atolls, break the surface and become islands. It was not until about five million years ago that the first of the main islands of the archipelago, Niihau and Kauai, broke the surface to become high islands.

For a couple of million more years, the mountains continued to grow. The forces of erosion cut into them, creating knife-edged cliffs and deep valleys. Then plants began germinating: mosses and ferns, springing from windblown spores, were probably first, followed by seed plants carried by migrating birds and on ocean currents. The steep-walled valleys provided natural greenhouses in which unique species evolved, while transoceanic winds swept insects and other life from the continents.

Some islands never survived this birth process: the ocean simply washed them away. The first islands that did endure, at the northwestern end of the Hawaiian chain, proved to be the smallest. Today these islands, with the exception of Midway, are barren uninhabited atolls. The volcanoes that rose last, far to the southeast, became the mountainous archipelago generally known as the Hawaiian Islands.

Many of the plants you'll see on Oahu are not indigenous. In fact, much of the lush vegetation of this tropical island found its way here from locations all over the world. Sea winds, birds and seafaring settlers brought many of the seeds, plants, flowers and trees from the islands of the South Pacific, as well as from other, more distant regions. Over time, some plants adapted to the island's unique ecosystem and climate, creating strange new lineages and evolving into a completely new ecosystem. This process has long interested scientists, who call the Hawaiian Islands one of the best natural labs for studies of plant evolution. Unfortunately, other new arrivals have become pests and invasive weeds.

Sugar cane arrived in Hawaii with the first Polynesian settlers, who appreciated its sweet juices. By the late 1800s, it was well established as a lucrative crop. The pineapple was first planted during the same century. A member of the bromeliad family, this spiky plant is actually a collection of beautiful pink, blue and purple flowers, each of which develops into a fruitlet. The pineapple is a collection of these fruitlets, grown together into a single fruit that takes 14 to 17 months to mature. Sugar cane and pineapple are still the main crops in Hawaii, although competition from other countries and environmental problems caused by pesticides have taken their toll.

Visitors to Oahu will find the island a perpetual flower show. Sweetly scented plumeria, deep red, shiny anthurium, exotic ginger, showy birds of paradise, small lavender crown flowers, highly fragrant gardenias and the brightly hued hibiscus run riot on the island and add color and fragrance to the surrounding area. Scarlet and purple bougainvillea vines, and the aromatic lantana, with its dense clusters of flowers, are also found in abundance.

Although many people equate the tropics with the swaying palm tree, Oahu is home to a variety of exotic trees. The famed banyan tree, known for pillarlike aerial roots that grow vertically downward from the branches, spreads to form a natural canopy. When the roots touch the ground, they thicken, providing support for the tree's branches to continue expanding. The state tree, the candlenut, or *kukui*, tree, originally brought to Hawaii from the South Pacific islands, is big, bushy and prized for its nuts, which can be used for oil or polished and strung together to make leis. Early Hawaiians used the oil for light and natural remedies. Covered with tiny pink blossoms, the canopied monkeypod tree has fernlike leaves that close up at night. With its cascades of bright yellow or pink flowers, the cassia tree earns its moniker— the shower tree.

Found in a variety of shapes and sizes, the ubiquitous palm does indeed sway to the breezes on white-sand beaches, but it also comes in a short, stubby form, the Samoan coconut, featuring more frond than trunk. The fruit, or nuts, of these trees are prized for their oil, which can be utilized for making everything from margarine to soap. The wood (rattan for example) is often used for making furniture.

FRUITS AND VEGETABLES   There's a lot more to Hawaii's tropical wonderland than gorgeous flowers and overgrown rainforests. The islands are also teeming with edible plants. Roots, fruits, vegetables, herbs and spices grow like weeds from the shoreline to the mountains. Following is a list of some of the more commonly found edibles.

Avocado: Covered with either a tough green or purple skin, this pear-shaped fruit sometimes weighs as much as three pounds. It grows on ten- to forty-foot-high trees, and ripens from June through November.

Oahu's island flower is the *ilima*, a small golden blossom. Parts of it are used medicinally: the buds create a mild laxative for children, while the bark is a kind of tonic.

Bamboo: The bamboo plant is actually a grass with a sweet root that is edible and a long stem frequently used for making furniture. Often exceeding eight feet in height, the most common bamboo is green until picked, when it turns a golden brown.

Banana: Polynesians use banana trees not only for food but also for clothing, medicines, dyes and even alcohol; culturally, it represents man. The fruit, which grows upside down on broad-leaved trees, can be harvested as soon as the first banana in the bunch turns yellow.

Breadfruit: This large round fruit grows on trees that reach up to 60 feet in height. Breadfruit must be boiled, baked or fried.

Coconut: The coconut tree is probably the most important plant in the entire Pacific. Every part of the towering palm is used. Most people are concerned only with the hard brown nut, which yields delicious water as well as a tasty meat. If the coconut is still green, the meat is a succulent jellylike substance. Otherwise, it's a hard but delicious white rind.

Guava: A roundish yellow fruit that grows on a small shrub or tree, guavas are extremely abundant in the wild. They ripen between June and October.

Lychee: Found hanging in bunches from the lychee tree, this popular summer fruit is encased in red, prickly skin that peels off to reveal the sweet-tasting, translucent flesh.

Mango: Known as the king of fruits, the mango grows on tall shade trees. The oblong fruit ripens in the spring and summer.

Mountain apple: This sweet fruit grows in damp, shaded valleys at an elevation of about 1800 feet. The flowers resemble fluffy crimson balls; the fruit, which ripens from July to December, is also a rich red color.

Papaya: This delicious fruit, which is picked as it begins to turn yellow, grows on unbranched trees. The sweet flesh can be bright orange or coral pink in color. Summer is the peak harvesting season.

Passion fruit: Oval in shape, this tart yellow fruit grows to a length of about two or three inches. It's produced on a vine and ripens in summer or fall.

Taro: The tuberous root of this Hawaiian staple is pounded into a grayish purple paste known as *poi.* One of the most nutritious foods, it has a rather bland taste. The plant has wide, shiny, thick leaves with reddish stems; the root is white with purple veins.

FAUNA

On Oahu, it seems there is more wildlife in the water and air than on land. A scuba diver's paradise, the ocean is also a promised land for many other creatures. Coral, colorful fish and sea turtles are only part of this underwater community. Sadly, many of the island's coral reefs have been dying mysteriously in the last several years. No one is sure why, but many believe this is partially due to runoff from pesticides used in agriculture.

Spinner dolphins are also favorites among visitors. Named for their "spinning" habit, they can revolve as many as six times dur-

A FRUIT FOR ALL SEASONS

Coconuts are one of those blessings from heaven, providing food, fuel, water, shade and building materials. The fronds were used with *pili* grass to thatch roofs, the hollowed trunks are made into *pahu,* or drums, and the fiber can be dried for fuel. It was also fashioned into ropey sandals that allowed Hawaiians to walk across razor-sharp lava. Nutritionally, the water inside is sterile and full of healthful enzymes, and the meat can be eaten or pressed into cream and oil. Most importantly, coconuts grow well close to the ocean, offering welcome shade from the harsh tropical sun.

ing one leap. They resemble the spotted dolphin, another frequenter of Hawaiian waters, but are more likely to venture closer to the shore. Dolphins have clocked in with speeds ranging from 9 to 25 mph, a feat they often achieve by propelling themselves out of the water (or even riding the bow wave of a ship). Their thick, glandless skin also contributes to this agility. The skin is kept smooth by constant renewal and sloughing (bottlenoses replace their epidermis every two hours). Playful and intelligent, dolphins are a joy to watch. Many research centers are investigating the mammals' ability to imitate, learn and communicate; some believe that dolphin intelligence may be comparable to that of humans.

One of the few mammals to live in the Hawaiian islands before the Polynesians' arrival, the Hawaiian monk seal has been hunted nearly to the point of extinction. Now protected as an endangered species, this tropical seal is found mostly on the outer islands, although it is occasionally spotted on Oahu. Closely related to the elephant seal, the monk seal is not as agile or as fond of land as other seals.

Green sea turtles are common on all of the Hawaiian islands, although this was not always the case. Due to the popularity of their shells and meat, they spent many years on the endangered species list, but are now making a comeback. Measuring three to four feet in diameter, these large reptiles frolic in saltwater only, and are often visible from the shore.

WHALES Every year, humpback whales converge in the warm waters off the island to give birth to their calves. They begin their migration in Alaska and can be spotted in Hawaiian waters from November through May. The humpback, named for its practice of showing its dorsal fin when diving, is quite easy to spy. Measuring 45 feet and weighing over 40 tons, humpbacks feed in shallow waters, usually diving for periods of no longer than 15 minutes. They often sleep on the surface and breathe fairly frequently.

Humpbacks are quite playful, and are seen leaping, splashing and flapping their 15-foot tails over their backs. The best time for whale watching is from January to April. Unlike other whales, humpbacks have the ability to sing. Loud and powerful, their songs carry above and below the water for miles. The songs change every year, yet, incredibly, all the whales always seem to know the current one.

DOLPHINS   Take an early-morning voyage on a boat on the west coast and you might just encounter one of the ocean's friendliest and most acrobatic creatures. You might suddenly find yourself in the midst of a pod of spinner dolphins who will play tag with your craft and dance above the waves like a troupe of whirling dervishes. There's nothing quite like it. Other dolphins that may be sighted in Hawaiian waters are the bottlenose, Risso's, melon-headed, rough-toothed, pygmy killers, and spotted or striped dolphins.

FISH   It'll come as no surprise to anyone that Oahu's waters literally brim with an extraordinary assortment of fish—over 400 different species, in fact.

The goatfish, with more than 50 species in its family worldwide, boasts at least ten in Oahu waters. This bottom dweller is recognized by a pair of whiskers, used as feelers for searching out food, that are attached to its lower jaw. The *moano* sports two stripes across its back and has shorter whiskers. The red-and-black banded goatfish has a multihued color scheme that also includes yellow and white markings; its light yellow whiskers are quite long. The head of the goatfish is considered poisonous and is not eaten.

Occasionally found on the sharper end of your line is the bonefish, or *oio*. One of the best game fish in the area, its head extends past its mouth to form a somewhat transparent snout. The *awa*, or milkfish, is another common catch. This silvery, fork-tailed fish can grow longer than three feet and puts up a good fight.

A kaleidoscope of brilliantly colored specimens can be viewed around the reefs of Oahu; you'll feel like you're in a technicolor movie when snorkeling. Over 20 known species of butterfly fish are found in this area. Highlighted in yellow, orange, red, blue, black and white, they swim in groups of two and three. The long, tubular body of the needlefish, or *aha*, can reach up to 40 inches in length; this greenish, silvery species is nearly translucent. The masked angelfish flits around in deeper waters on the outer edge of reefs. The imperial angelfish is distinguishable by fantastic color patterns of dark blue hues. The Hawaiian fish with the longest name, the colorful *humuhumunukunukuapuaa*, is found in the shallow waters along the outer fringes of reefs.

Sharks, unlike fish, have skeletons made of cartilage; the hardest parts of their bodies are their teeth (once used as tools by the Hawaiians). If you spend a lot of time in the water, you may spot a shark. But not to worry; Hawaiian waters are just about the safest around. The harmless, commonly seen blacktipped and white-tipped reef sharks (named for the color of their fins) are as concerned about your activities as you are about theirs. The gray reef shark (gray back, white belly with a black tail) and tiger shark, however, are predatory and aggressive, but they are rarely encountered.

Another cartilaginous creature you might see in shallow water near the shoreline is the manta ray, a "winged" plankton feeder with two appendages on either side of its head that work to direct food into its mouth. The eagle ray, a bottom dweller featuring "wings" and a tail longer than its body, feeds in shallow coastal waters. When it's not feeding, it lies on the ocean floor and covers itself with a light layer of sand. Since some eagle rays have stingers, take precautions by shuffling the sand as you walk. Not only will you not be impaled, you will also be less likely to squash smaller, unsuspecting sea creatures.

While on Oahu, you'll inevitably see fish out of water as well —on your plate. The purple-blue-green-hued mahimahi, or dolphin fish, can reach six feet and 70 pounds. The *opakapaka* is another common dish and resides in the deeper, offshore waters beyond the reef. This small-scaled snapper is a reddish-olive color and can grow up to four feet long. Elongated with a sharply pointed head, the *ono* (also known as the wahoo) is a carnivorous, savage striped fish with dark blue and silver coloring. Perhaps the most ubiquitous fish is the ahi, or tuna, often used for sashimi.

BIRDS The island is also home to many rare and endangered birds. Like the flora, the birds in the Hawaiian islands are highly specialized. The state bird, the nene, or Hawaiian goose, is a cousin

AGED SWIMMERS

Green sea turtles are commonly seen in Hawaiian waters, popping their heads up for a breath of air or sliding along rocky reefs to feed on the seaweed, or *limu*, that gives their flesh its distinctive green tint. The Hawaiians frequently ate *honu*, which was considered a delicacy. These creatures are an amazing 150 million years old, yet in the past century they were hunted so heavily by fishing crews that their population nearly crashed. Since being federally designated as a protected, threatened species, their numbers are rising. But their newest threat is a puzzling disease that causes large tumors to grow on their flesh.

to the Canadian goose and mates for life. Unless you visit the Big Island, Kauai or Haleakala, the only place you'll find a nene is at the Honolulu Zoo.

Also on the endangered species list, the Hawaiian hawk, or *io*, has had its status changed to "threatened." Existing exclusively on the Big Island, the regal *io* is found in a variety of habitats from forest to grassland, but is most often sighted on the slopes of Mauna Kea and Mauna Loa. On Oahu you'll have to view this critter at the zoo.

Known in Hawaiian mythology for its protective powers, the *pueo*, or Hawaiian owl, a brown-and-white-feathered bird is considered an endangered species on Oahu, and may be spotted in the mountainous areas of the island.

There *are* a few birds native to Hawaii that have thus far avoided the endangered species list. One of the most common birds is the yellow-green *amakihi*, but the red *iiwi*, more common on the Neighbor Islands is near extinction on Oahu, with maybe only five or so left on the island.

Other native birds that make Oahu their home are the Hawaiian stilt and the Hawaiian coot—both water birds—along with the black noddy, American plover and wedge-tailed shearwater.

One common seabird is the *iwa*, or frigate, a very large creature measuring three to four feet in length, with a wing span averaging seven feet. The males are solid black, while the females have a large white patch on their chest and tail. A predatory bird, they're easy to spot raiding the nesting colonies of other birds along the offshore rocks. Legend says they portend a storm.

CALL OF THE TREE FROG

They weigh less than a seeded grape. They're often smaller than the face of a quarter. But these adorable creatures are threatening the peace of Oahu. The mating call of the male tree frog has raised a battle cry among sleep-deprived Oahu residents. Researchers suspect the frogs may originate from Puerto Rico, perhaps hitchhiking over on imported house plants. With no known enemies, the tree frog's presence remains assured unless the Department of Land and Natural Resources accomplishes its goal of catching them by hand. Meanwhile, if you hear the telltale co-KEE! Co-KEE!, turn on the air conditioner or the TV and resign yourself to a nap on the beach tomorrow.

No doubt you will encounter the noisy black myna birds with their beady yellow eyes and shiny black feathers. They seem to be as numerous and sassy as the tourists on Waikiki's beach.

Not many wild four-footed creatures roam the island. Feral goats and pigs were brought here early on and have found a home in the island's forests. And some good news for people fearful of snakes: There is nary a serpent (or a sea serpent) on Oahu, although lizards such as skinks and geckos abound.

One can only hope that with the renewed interest in Hawaiian culture, and growing environmental awareness, Hawaii's plants and animals will continue to exist as they have for centuries.

▼ ▼ ▼ ▼ ▼ ▼ ▼ ▼ ▼ ▼ ▼ ▼ ▼

Outdoor Adventures

CAMPING

Camping on Oahu usually means pitching a tent. There are a few secluded spots and hidden beaches, plus numerous county, state and federal parks where you can set up camp. However, before you set out on your camping trip, there are a few very important matters that I want to explain more fully. First, bring a campstove: firewood is scarce in most areas and soaking wet in others. You should also be careful to purify all of your drinking water. And be extremely cautious near streambeds as flash-flooding sometimes occurs, particularly on the windward coast. This is particularly true during the winter months, when heavy storms from the northeast lash the island.

Another problem that you're actually more likely to encounter are those nasty varmints that buzz your ear just as you're falling asleep—mosquitoes. Oahu contains neither snakes nor poison ivy, but it has plenty of these dive-bombing pests. Like me, you probably consider that it's always open season on the little bastards.

With most of the archipelago's other species, however, you'll have to be a careful conservationist. You'll be sharing the wilderness with pigs, goats, tropical birds, deer and mongooses, as well as a spectacular array of exotic and indigenous plants. They exist in one of the world's most delicate ecological balances. There are more endangered species in Hawaii than in all the rest of the United States. So keep in mind the maxim that the Hawaiians try to follow. *Ua mau ke ea o ka aina i ka pono:* The life of the land is perpetual in righteousness.

Along with its traffic and crowds, Oahu has numerous parks. Unfortunately, these disparate elements overlap, and you may sometimes find you've escaped from Honolulu's urban jungle and landed in a swamp of weekend beachgoers. So it's best to plan outdoor adventures far in advance and to schedule them for weekdays if possible.

Currently, camping is allowed at 12 beach parks operated by the City and County of Honolulu. Six of these parks are on the island's windward side and four on the leeward side. Another two are on the North Shore. Bellows Field Beach Park at Waimanalo on the Windward Coast, only allows camping at its 50 campsites on the weekends. Swanzy Beach Park at Kaaawa on the windward side is also a weekend-only campground. The others permit tent camping every night except Wednesday and Thursday. There are no trailer hookups.

Camping at **county parks** requires a permit. The free permits can be obtained from the Department of Parks and Recreation. ~ Honolulu Municipal Building, 650 South King Street, ground floor, Honolulu, HI 96813; 808-523-4527. They are also available at any of the "satellite city halls" around the island.

State parks allow camping for up to five days, depending on the park. It's first-come, first-served on the first day, but after that visitors may reserve spaces. The Division of State Parks issues the free permits. ~ 1151 Punchbowl Street, Room 131, Honolulu, HI 96813; 808-587-0300. You can also write in advance for permits.

There are four state parks on Oahu with camping facilities. **Malaekahana State Recreation Area** on the Windward Coast between Laie and Kahuku offers both tent camping and housekeeping cabins. Also on the Windward Coast, Oahu's largest state park **Kahana Valley State Park,** located between Kaaawa and Punaluu, has campsites. Tent camping is available at **Sand Island State Recreation Area** on Sand Island in Honolulu, as well as at **Keaiwa Heiau State Recreation Area** in the hills above Honolulu.

The **Hoomaluhia Botanical Gardens** allows camping on their grounds Friday through Sunday. There is no fee, but a permit is required and no hookups are available. ~ 808-233-7323.

Remember when planning your trip, rainfall is heaviest on the Windward Coast, a little lighter on the North Shore and lightest of all on the Leeward Coast.

You might also want to obtain some hiking maps; they are available from **Hawaii Geographic Maps & Books**. The camping equipment you'll require is listed in the "Packing" section of the

Oahu
Campsites

HONOLULU COUNTY CAMPSITES

Bellows Field Beach Park, Waimanalo	50 campsites
Hauula Beach Park, Hauula	15 campsites
Kaiaka Bay Beach Park, Haleiwa	7 campsites
Keaau Beach Park, Makaha	25 campsites
Kokololio Beach Park, Laie	5 campsites
Kualoa "B" Regional Park, Kualoa	30 campsites
Lualaualei Beach Park #1, Waianae (summer only)	6 campsites
Mokuleia Beach Park, Waialua	15 campsites
Nanakuli Beach Park, Nanakuli	12 campsites
Swanzy Beach Park, Kaaawa	9 campsites
Waimanalo Bay Beach Park	10 campsites
Waimanalo Beach Park	20 campsites

For more information call 808-523-4525

STATE OF HAWAII CAMPSITES

Malaekahana State Recreation Beach, Kahuku	37 campsites
Sand Island State Recreation Center, Honolulu	34 campsites
Kahana Valley State Park, Kahana	10 campsites
Keaiwa Heiau Recreation Area, Aiea	10 campsites

For more information call 808-587-0300

preceding chapter. ~ 49 South Hotel Street #215, Honolulu, HI 96806; 808-538-3952, 800-538-3950.

The Bike Shop rents backpacks and two-person tents and has for sale a comprehensive line of camping equipment, from clothing and sleeping bags to tents and stoves. ~ 1149 South King Street; 808-596-0588.

For rentals and sales in central Oahu, try **Omar the Tent Man**. Closed Sunday. ~ 94-158 Leoole Street, Waipahu; 808-677-8785.

FISHING

While you're exploring the island, the sea will be your prime food source. Fishing on Oahu is good year-round, and the offshore waters are crowded with many varieties of edible fish. For deep-sea fishing you'll have to charter a boat, and freshwater angling requires a license; so I'll concentrate on surf-casting. It costs nothing to fish this way.

The ancient Hawaiians used pearl shells to attract the fish, and hooks, some made from human bones, to snare them. Your friends will probably be quite content to see you angling with store-bought artificial lures. The easiest, most economical way to fish is with a hand-held line. Just get a 50- to 100-foot line, and attach a hook and a ten-ounce sinker. Wind the line loosely around a smooth block of wood, then remove the wood from the center. If your coil is free from snags, you'll be able to throw-cast it easily. You can either hold the line in your hand, feeling for a strike, or tie it to the frail end of a bamboo pole.

Beaches and rocky points are generally good places to surf-cast; the best times are during the incoming and outgoing tides.

AQUACULTURE THE ANCIENT WAY

Ancient Hawaiians would have fared well on the television series *Survivor;* they had fishtrapping down pat. Using enclosed brackish water off the coast, fish were bred and maintained in fishponds through ingenious use of *makaha*, sluice gates that controlled the in- and outflow of water. Designed to allow young fish in and keep the ready-to-eat fish from escaping, the gates also helped control the growth of algae, the lowest but most vital rung on the pond food ladder. This ancient technique is still practiced in Kaneohe Bay, where the **Kualoa Ranch & Activity Club** maintains an operational pond and sells its produce. ~ Kualoa Ranch, Kaneohe; 800-231-7321; www.kualoa.com.

Popular baits include octopus, eel, lobster, crab, frozen shrimp and sea worms.

For freshwater angling head up into the Koolau Mountains to fish the **Nuuanu Reservoir** (open to the public by lottery). Another possibility is the **Wahiawa Public Fishing Area,** also known as Lake Wilson. Both of these reservoirs are good places to catch Chinese catfish. Call the Division of Aquatic Resources, Department of Land & Resources at 808-587-0110 for information on permits and seasons.

DEEP-SEA FISHING   Many visitors to Hawaii don't think of Oahu as a place to deep-sea fish and instead wait until they get to the Neighbor Islands, but that may be a mistake. Oahu is the cheapest place in Hawaii to fish, with rates about 25 percent lower than, say, Maui.

The fish caught vary depending on the time of year, although it's mostly mahimahi, especially during the winter months. In the fall and summer you are likely to catch marlin, and in summer, ahi tuna as well. Although you're not guaranteed a catch, some record-breaking fish have been caught on boats operating out of Oahu. In 1970, an 1805-pound pacific blue marlin, the largest fish ever caught anywhere in the world with a rod and reel, was the result of an Oahu-based fishing charter.

Although the boats are all charters, share charters are the norm, with a minimum of four passengers required. If there are not enough for a particular boat, the skipper may recommend a different boat or another day to go out. Keeping the fish you catch is not always part of the deal. If you would like to do so, negotiate with the boat owner or skipper beforehand.

Most of the island's fishing fleet dock at Kewalo Basin (Fisherman's Wharf) on Ala Moana Drive between Waikiki and downtown Honolulu.

Hawaii Fishing Adventures and Charters books deep-sea fishing trips that go out for blue marlin, yellowfin tuna and mahimahi. Charters leave from Kewalo Basin, and reservations are required (all equipment provided). ~ 575 Cooke Street A315; 808-396-2607, 877-388-1376; www.sportfishhawaii.com. Or consider **Sport Fishing**, which runs the *Pacific Blue* and *Ilima* out of Kewalo Basin. Equipment provided. ~ 808-596-2087. **Maggie Joe Sportfishing** does day trips as well as overnight and multiday excursions. An overnight trip to Molokai or a five-day cruise to

Kauai and Niihau are among the options. ~ 808-591-8888, 877-806-3474; www.maggiejoe.com.

TORCHFISHING & SPEARFISHING   The old Hawaiians often fished at night by torchlight. They fashioned torches by inserting nuts from the *kukui* tree into the hollow end of a bamboo pole, then lighting the flammable nuts. When fish swam like moths to the flame, the Hawaiians speared, clubbed or netted them.

Today, it's easier to use a lantern and spear. (In fact, it's all *too* easy and tempting to take advantage of this willing prey: Take only edible fish and only what you will eat. Also, follow state rules on size and season limits for some species.) It's also handy to bring a facemask or a glass-bottomed box to aid in seeing underwater. The best time for torchfishing is a dark night when the sea is calm and the tide low.

During daylight hours, the best place to spearfish is along coral reefs and in areas where the bottom is a mixture of sand and rock. Equipped with speargun, mask, fins and snorkel, you can explore underwater grottoes and spectacular coral formations while seeking your evening meal. Spearguns can be purchased inexpensively throughout the island.

For information on seasons, licenses and official regulations, check with the **Aquatic Resources Division of the State Department of Land & Natural Resources**. ~ 808-587-0100.

CRABBING   For the hungry adventurer, there are several important crab species in Hawaii. The most sought-after are the Kona and Samoan varieties. The Kona crabs are found in relatively deep water, and can usually be caught only from a boat. Samoan crabs inhabit sandy and muddy areas in bays and near river mouths. All you need to catch them are a boat and a net fastened to a round wire hoop secured by a string. The net is lowered to the bottom; then, after a crab has gone for the bait, the entire contraption is raised to the surface.

SQUIDDING   Between June and December, squidding is another popular sport. Actually, the term is a misnomer: squid inhabit deep water and are not usually hunted. What you'll really be after are octopuses. There are two varieties here, both of which are commonly found in water three or four feet deep: the *hee*, a greyish-brown animal

Ocean Safety

For swimming, surfing and scuba diving, there's no place quite like Oahu. With endless miles of white-sand beach, the island attracts aquatic enthusiasts worldwide. They come to enjoy Oahu's colorful coral reefs and matchless surf conditions. Many water lovers, however, don't realize how dangerous the sea can be. Particularly on Oahu, where waves can reach 30-foot heights and currents flow unobstructed for thousands of miles, the ocean is sometimes as treacherous as it is spectacular. Dozens of people drown every year in Hawaii, many others are dragged from the crushing surf with broken backs, and countless numbers sustain minor cuts and bruises.

These accidents can be avoided if you approach the ocean with a respect for its power as well as an appreciation of its beauty. Just heed a few simple guidelines. First, never turn your back on the sea. Waves come in sets: one group may be small and quite harmless, but the next could be large enough to sweep you out to sea. Never swim alone.

Don't try to surf, or bodysurf, until you're familiar with the sports' techniques and precautionary measures. Be careful when the surf is high.

If you get caught in a rip current, don't swim against it: swim across it, parallel to the shore. These currents, running from the shore out to sea, can often be spotted by their ragged-looking surface water and foamy edges.

Around coral reefs, wear something to protect your feet against cuts. Recommended are inexpensive Japanese *tabis*, or reef slippers. If you do get a coral cut, clean it with hydrogen peroxide, then apply an antiseptic or antibiotic substance.

When stung by a Portuguese man-of-war or a jellyfish, rinse the affected area with sea water to remove any tentacles. Use gloves or towels—not your bare fingers—to remove remaining tentacles. For jellyfish stings only, you might also try vinegar or isopropyl alcohol.

If you step on the sharp, painful spines of a sea urchin, soak the affected area in very hot water for 15 to 90 minutes. Another remedy calls for applying urine or undiluted vinegar. If the pain persists for more than a day, or you notice swelling or other signs of infection, consult a doctor.

Oh, one last thing. The chances of encountering a shark are about as likely as sighting a UFO. But should you meet one of these ominous creatures, stay calm. Simply swim quietly to shore. By the time you make it back to terra firma, you'll have one hell of a story to tell.

that changes color like a chameleon, and the *puloa*, a red-colored mollusk with white stripes on its head.

Both are nocturnal and live in holes along coral reefs. At night by torchlight you can spot them sitting exposed on the bottom. During the day, they crawl inside the holes, covering the entrances with shells and loose coral.

The Hawaiians used to pick the octopus up, letting it cling to their chest and shoulders. When they were ready to bag their prize, they'd dispatch the creature by biting it between the eyes. You'll probably feel more comfortable spearing the beast.

SHELLFISH GATHERING Other excellent food sources are the shellfish that inhabit coastal waters. Oysters and clams, which use their muscular feet to burrow into sand and soft mud, can be collected along the bottom of Oahu's bays. Spiny lobsters, rarely found in Hawaiian waters, are illegal to spear, but can be taken in season with short poles to which cable leaders and baited hooks are attached. You may also just grab them with a gloved hand but be careful—spiny lobsters live up to their name. You can also gather limpets, though I don't recommend it. These tiny black shellfish, locally known as *opihi*, cling tenaciously to rocks in the tidal zone. In areas of very rough surf, the Hawaiians gather them by leaping into the water after one set of waves breaks, then jumping out before the next set arrives. Being a coward myself, I simply order them in Hawaiian restaurants.

HELP PROTECT THE REEF

Exploring underwater in Oahu is one of the most wonderful experiences available in the islands. But we must protect that environment while we enjoy it. Did you know that coral reefs are living animals that live in large colonies? They are also home to hundreds of creatures, including colorful reef fish. It takes years and years for coral reefs to regenerate themselves when damaged, and if they are badly damaged they die. We can help protect the reefs by not touching them (they are protected by Hawaiian law—it is illegal to take live coral from their beds); not walking or standing on them; and not feeding the fish that inhabit them, which upsets the eco-balance.

There are still some people who don't think of seaweed as food, **SEAWEED** but it's very popular among Japanese, and it once served as an **GATHERING** integral part of the Hawaiian diet. It's extremely nutritious, easy to gather and very plentiful. Rocky shores are the best places to find the edible species of seaweed. Some of them float in to shore and can be picked up; other species cling stubbornly to rocks and must be freed with a knife; still others grow in sand or mud. Low tide is the best time to collect seaweed: more plants are exposed, and some can be taken without even getting wet.

One of the great myths about Oahu is that you need to go far off **DIVING** the beaten track to discover its secret treasures. The fact is that within half an hour of Waikiki are excellent snorkeling and diving opportunities. Only an hour away are excellent reefs easily reached by dive boats. From popular Hanauma Bay, just a short ride from the heart of Honolulu, to Kahe Point on the Leeward Coast, there are snorkeling and diving opportunities for beginners and certified pros alike.

Although the most popular snorkeling locale on the island is Hanauma Bay, and most people go there, other possible spots are Shark Cove on the North Shore and Electric Beach on Kahe Point on the northwest Coast. Or you can snorkel at Makua Beach, located between Makaha and Yokohama Bay on the Leeward Coast, and swim with the dolphins.

The best diving in Oahu depends on the season. In the summertime the north and west shores are best, but during winter the waves are too big to dive there. The North Shore's outstanding dive sites are Shark's Cove, known for its lava tubes, and Haleiwa, with its 100-foot sheer drop wall. There's also the Leeward Coast's Kahe Point, which has an artificial reef. During the winter months divers head for Magic Island, which is accessible by land from Ala Moana Beach. One of Oahu's most exciting dive spots is Turtle Canyon, one-and-a-half miles offshore (accessed by boat), where you can swim with sea turtles.

Off the Leeward Coast is the *Mahi* shipwreck, which *Skin Diver* magazine ranked as the fifth best wreck dive in the world. There's also a shipwreck of sorts in front of Waikiki, where a YO257 World War II oil tanker has been brought in to create an artificial reef.

Because conditions vary, I strongly recommend seeking instruction and advice from local diving experts before setting out.

HONOLULU   **South Seas Aquatics** features dives off a custom 38-foot dive boat. They sell diving equipment. ~ 2155 Kalakaua Avenue, Suite 112, Honolulu, HI 96815; 808-922-0852, fax 808-922-0853; www.ssahawaii.com.

Waikiki Diving Center takes divers to different sites around Oahu, depending on the time of year and the weather. The company offers two- to three-day PADI and NAUI courses and sells, rents and repairs diving equipment. It will also take nondivers out on an inexpensive introductory scuba charter so they can see what the sport is all about. ~ 424 Nahua Street, Honolulu; 808-922-2121; www.waikiki.com.

Clark's Divemaster Tours includes Waikiki as one of its dive options. ~ 234 Beach Block Avenue, Suite 2C, Honolulu; 808-923-5595.

SOUTHEAST OAHU   **Aloha Dive Shop** runs day trips for certified divers and lesson packages for students at Maunalua Bay in the southeast corner of the island. ~ Hawaii Kai Shopping Center, 377 Kehole Street, Hawaii Kai; 808-395-5922.

LEEWARD COAST   **Hawaii Sea Adventures** heads to the west side of Oahu and dives the *Mahi* shipwreck. They feature lessons as well as half- and full-day trips and charters. ~ 98-718 Moanalua Road, Pearl City; 808-487-7515.

Bojac Aquatic has daily boat dives to such southside sites as the Sea Tiger and Rainbow Reef, as well as the *Mahi* shipwreck off the west coast. It also conducts three-day and two-week PADI and NAUI courses. ~ 24 Sand Island Access Road; 808-671-0311.

WINDWARD COAST   At **Aaron's Dive Shop** you can choose between beach and boat dives, as well as special night trips. ~ 307 Hahani Street, Kailua; 808-261-1211.

NORTH SHORE   Depending on the season, the **Haleiwa Surf Center** teaches such sports as snorkeling, surfing, swimming, lifesaving, windsurfing and sailing. This county agency is also an excellent source of information on the island's water sports and facilities. ~ Haleiwa Alii Beach Park, Haleiwa; 808-637-5051. **Surf N' Sea** offers half-day beach and boat dives on the North Shore and Leeward Coast including the *Mahi* shipwreck. ~ 62-595 Kamehameha Highway, Haleiwa; 808-637-9887.

SNUBA

Somewhere between snorkeling and scuba diving is Snuba, a relatively new watersport that's catching on in resort areas around the world. You don't need certification, and it's so safe even an eight-year-old can do it.

Snuba was created for those who would like to take snorkeling a step further but may not be quite ready for scuba diving. It's a shallow-water dive system that allows underwater breathing. Basically this is how it works. Swimmers wear a breathing device (the same one used in scuba diving) that is connected to a built-in scuba tank that floats on a raft. They also wear a weight belt, mask and fins. The air comes through a 20-foot tube connected to the raft, which follows the swimmer. Groups of six participants are taken out with a guide. They can dive up to 20 feet.

Snuba of Oahu offers Snuba tours at Hanauma Bay, Maunalua Bay and Ko Olina. The Ko Olina trip leaves from Ihilani Resort and involves a two-and-a-half-hour sail out to sea; lunch is included. Common sightings include an array of fish, eels, dolphins and turtles. The company will pick you up in Waikiki or you can meet the group at the Snuba site. ~ Koko Marina Shopping Center, 7192 Kalanianaole Highway, Hawaii Kai; 808-306-0322.

SURFING

Surfing, a sport pioneered centuries ago by Hawaiian royalty, is synonymous with Oahu. Stars bring their boards from all over the world to join international competitions that take advantage of

SNORKELING SAFETY TIPS

Don't miss out on an opportunity to explore the depths of Oahu's busy ocean life (even if you only venture a few feet down). You're apt to find fish and coral in a dazzling array of colors, sizes and shapes. But take the following precautions before you dip into the water:
- always snorkel with someone else
- avoid big waves, surfers and windy conditions
- bring a flotation device like an inner tube, noodle or life jacket, especially if you are with kids or are a beginning swimmer
- don't poke your hands into crevices in a reef (a favorite eel hangout)
- look up now and again to watch the weather conditions—if you're having trouble getting back to shore because the waves are too high, wait for the set to break
- wear lots of waterproof sunscreen (and perhaps a T-shirt) because your back will be lobster red if you don't!

ideal surf and wind conditions. From the 30-foot winter rollers on the North Shore to beginner lessons off Waikiki, this is beach boy and girl territory. The Surf News Network operates **Surfline**, a call-in recorded message information service that updates surf information for surfers and windsurfers several times a day. ~ 808-596-7873; www.surf-news.com.

WAIKIKI For everything "on the water, in the water and under the water" see **Prime Time Rentals** near Fort DeRussy Beach. They offer beach accessories, equipment sales and rentals, lessons and plenty of friendly advice. Private and group surfing lessons have a "stand and surf" guarantee. ~ Kalia Road; 808-949-8952. The **Aloha Beach Service**, in front of the Sheraton Moana Surfrider Hotel, offers lessons and rents long boards. ~ 808-922-3111.

A number of stores located in different parts of the island also rent boards. Near downtown, go to **Local Motion** for surfboard rentals. Check out there selection of beachwear, boards and equipment for sale. ~ 1958 Kalakaua Avenue; 808-979-7873. In the Diamond Head area, **Downing Hawaii** rents boards. Closed Sunday. ~ 3021 Waialae Avenue; 808-737-9696.

NORTH SHORE A resource for both the participatory and spectator aspects of surfing is the **Haleiwa Surf Center**. Surf lessons normally run September to early May. ~ Haleiwa Alii Beach Park, Haleiwa; 808-637-5051. In the same area surfing lessons and rentals are also available from **Surf N' Sea**. Lessons last two to three hours; price includes all gear. ~ 62-595 Kamehameha Highway, Haleiwa; 808-637-9887.

WIND-SURFING Windsurfing is becoming almost as popular as surfing these days, and few places are better to try this sport than on Oahu. If you're

---

STAYING DRY WHILE EXPLORING THE DEPTHS

If you are not interested in Snuba or scuba diving but do want to see what's down under, try one of the two submarine adventures in Waikiki, **Atlantis Submarine** (808-973-9811, 800-548-6262; www.goatlantis.com) or **Voyager** (808-539-9495). You'll descend to 100 feet in air-conditioned hi-tech subs and explore an artificial reef complete with sunken ships and airplanes, created to bring back marine life to the area. It's not cheap, though.

just starting out or are at an intermediate level, the bedroom community of Kailua on the Windward Coast, about a half-hour drive from Honolulu, is the place to go. This is the best place in Hawaii for all but the most advanced sailors. There's a protective reef and no breakers, and on-shore trades provide just the right winds for the sport year-round. The quiet town has also become a sort of windsurfing resort, with scores of bed and breakfasts offering accommodations at reasonable rates.

The northern end of Sunset Beach, Sunset Point (also known as Backyards) is where the top windsurfers on the island hang out. It has the most challenging waves for windsurfing. Beginners should beware of the strong currents and reef.

WINDWARD COAST Kailua Sailboard and Kayak Company will teach you the tricks of the trade or help you brush up on your technique. You can also rent sailboards, boogieboards, long boards, kayaks and snorkeling equipment here. ~ 130 Kailua Road, Kailua; 808-262-2555. In the same area, **Naish Hawaii** offers lessons and rentals. This company manufactures its own boards and also operates a shop filled with the latest in sailboarding apparel and accessories, as well as long boards. ~ 155-A Hamakua Drive, Kailua; 808-261-6067.

NORTH SHORE For classes and information check out the **Haleiwa Surf Center**. Lessons are generally given from May to early September. ~ Haleiwa Alii Beach Park, Haleiwa; 808-637-5051.

The latest craze to hit the water is kitesurfing. Following principles similar to paragliding, windsurfing and even snowboarding, you're strapped to a light board and pulled across the water by, well, a big kite. Most folks in decent physical condition pick up the sport quickly, especially if they've had experience with a related activity. After some concentrated study, you'll graduate to bigger kites and speeds of up to 40 m.p.h. Kitesurfers have been known to jump 30 feet off the water. You'll find plenty of ideal kitesurfing spots on Oahu: look for an area clear of trees and powerlines, preferably an uncrowded beach. If a 30-foot leap seems like a little too much excitement, you'll still enjoy watching the riders jump, jibe and "kite the surfzone." Lessons and rentals are provided by **Kailua Sailboards & Kayaks, Inc.**, along with hotel transportation. ~ 130 Kailua Road, Kailua; 808-262-2555; e-mail watersports@aloha.net.

KITE-SURFING

SAILING   One of the best ways to enjoy Oahu is aboard a sailboat. From brief cruises off Honolulu to a day-long charter along the North Shore, this is the perfect antidote to the tourist crowds. It's also surprisingly affordable.

Ko Olina Ocean Adventures operates the *Lanikila*, a motorized catamaran that takes up to 13 people from one of Ko Olina's sheltered lagoons to sightsee and open-water snorkel along the Waianae Coast. Departures are at 2 p.m. daily, except Sunday. The two-hour trip often includes dolphin and flying fish sightings en route. A light lunch is served. ~ 808-396-2068; www.koolinaoceanadventures.com.

If you're eager to charter your own yacht, contact **The Yacht Connection**. The company charters all sizes of vessels ranging from fishing boats to luxury yachts. ~ 1750 Kalakaua Avenue, Suite 3138, Honolulu; 808-523-1383; www.hawaiiyachts.com.

Above Heaven's Gate operates charter group cruises to the Diamond Head reef area aboard a 56-foot teakwood pirate ship. You can also take a guided Hobie-cat tour off the Windward Coast to undiscovered islands most tourists miss (by appointment only). Along the way you'll enjoy Waimanalo, Kaneohe, Lanikai and Kailua Bay. You can also learn how to sail this swift 16-foot craft. ~ 41-1010 Laumilo Street, Waimanalo Bay; 808-259-5429, 800-800-2933, fax 808-259-5633; www.hawaiiwed dings.com.

Those staying around Haleiwa may be interested in sailing with **North Shore Catamaran Charters**, which has daily trips aboard its 40-foot catamaran that carries up to 25 passengers. From the end of December through April, there are two-and-a-half-hour whale-watching trips, from May to September, four-hour snorkel/picnic cruises, and sunset sails twice a week throughout the year. ~ 59740 Alapio Road, Haleiwa; 808-638-8279, 888-638-8279.

KAYAKING   A sport well suited for Oahu, kayaking is an ideal way to explore the island's protected bays, islands and inland rivers. It seems that kayakers are popping up everywhere, particularly around the southeast coast of the island and up the Waimea River. To rent or purchase kayaks and equipment, or to sign up for lessons and tours, consider **Go Bananas** just outside Waikiki. ~ 799 Kapahulu

The New Travel

Travel has become a personal art form. A destination no longer serves as just a place to relax: It's also a point of encounter. To many, this new wave in travel customs is labeled "adventure travel" and involves trekking glaciers or dusting the cliffs in a hang glider; to others, it connotes nothing more daring than a restful spell in a secluded resort. Actually, it's a state of mind, a willingness not only to accept but seek out the uncommon and unique. It is also a chance to give, not just to take.

Few places in the world are more conducive to this imaginative new travel than Hawaii. Several organizations in the islands cater specifically to people who want to add local customs and unusual adventures to their vacation itineraries.

The **Nature Conservancy of Hawaii**, a nonprofit conservation organization, conducts several hikes and work trips each month for members at the organization's Honouliuli Preserve in the southern Waianae Mountains of western Oahu. To request a yearly hiking schedule contact the organization by letter or fax. ~ P.O. Box 1716, Makawao, HI 96768; 808-537-4508, fax 808-545-2019; www.tnc.org/hawaii.

The **Hawaii Nature Center** offers hikes throughout Oahu two or three times a month. It also offers talks by naturalists on such subjects as geology, birdlife, native flora and taro cultivation. There are hikes and activities for the little ones, too, with activities aimed for explorers as young as three years old. ~ 2131 Makiki Heights Drive, Honolulu, HI 96822; 808-955-0100, fax 808-955-011; www.hawaiinaturecenter.org..

The **Sierra Club** sponsors weekly hikes on Oahu, as well as trail building and other projects aimed at helping to preserve the island's natural heritage. The club has a recorded message line that lists weekly weekend outings. ~ P.O. Box 2577, Honolulu, HI 96803; 808-538-6616; www.hi.sierraclub.org.

In existence since 1910, the **Hawaiian Trail and Mountain Club** maintains a clubhouse for members in Waimanalo and sponsors hikes every weekend. Unlike the other environmental organizations listed here, this one is run entirely by volunteers and does not have an office. To become a member you must go on three hikes. Call ahead since some of the hikes are members only. ~ 808-674-1459, 808-377-5442; www.aditl.com/htmc.

Avenue; 808-737-9514. For kayak rentals and lessons contact **Kailua Sailboard and Kayak Company**. ~ 130 Kailua Road, Kailua; 808-262-2555.

WATER-SKIING

Near Koko Head, **Wakeboard & Waterski Center** offers instruction every day. A beginning class is 30 minutes, but you can also ski for 15 or 45 minutes or an hour. ~ Koko Marina Shopping Center, 7192 Kalanianaole Highway, Hawaii Kai; 808-395-3773; www.hisports.com.

PARA-SAILING

Vacations offer a time for new adventures, to try a sport you've never attempted before, like parasailing. **Aloha Parasail** offers ten-minute flights. You'll share a boat with other fliers, so the entire trip takes about two hours from the time you leave your hotel and return. ~ P.O. Box 90846, Honolulu, HI 96835; 808-521-2446.

Seabreeze Parasail provides Waikiki pick-ups for a flight above tropically blue Moanalua Bay. You can also tie in a fling on a waverunner jet ski as well as scuba diving. Minimum weight is 60 pounds. ~ Koko Marina Shopping Center, 7192 Kalanianaole Highway, Hawaii Kai; 808-396-0100.

SKYDIVING & HANG GLIDING

You can learn to skydive and participate in a tandem dive with **Skydive Hawaii** at Dillingham Airfield on the North Shore. Upon arrival you'll watch a video and participate in a 20-minute training session. A tandem master trains students how to put on the equipment, what to do in the plane, how to get out and how to deploy the parachute. Once 13,005 feet in the air, the excitement begins. You'll free fall at about 120 mph for a minute, then open the parachute at 5500 feet for a six-minute ride at a smooth

---

SAILS IN THE SUNSET

Ever dream of sailing off into the sunset, wind blowing in your hair? Snorkeling trips, swimming in the ocean off Diamond Head, a sunset cruise or a whale-watching venture can all be arranged with **Honolulu Sailing Company**. You can even get married at sea by your licensed and uniformed captain. This personable outfit will sail to meet your needs. ~ 47-335 Lulani Street, Honolulu; 808-239-3900; www.honsail.com.

12 mph after that. They also provide round-trip transportation from Waikiki. ~ 68-760 Farrington Highway; 808-637-9700.

Another skydiving operation at Dillingham Field is **Pacific International Skydiving Center**. ~ 68-760 Farrington Highway; 808-637-7472.

North Shore Hang Gliding offers daily ultralight airplane and tandem hang-gliding instruction at Dillingham Field. Call the company, and they'll also give you information on hang gliding in the area. ~ 328 Ilihau Street, Kailua; 808-637-3178.

JOGGING

Jogging is very big on Oahu. There are several popular spots, and though they are never quite deserted, the crowds rarely become unmanageable. **Ala Moana Regional Park** is a good area for a run; the paved road fronts the beach, and the cool ocean breezes are welcome. **Kapiolani Park** is another jogger's mecca. **Ala Wai Canal** is a less-recommended road; it's along a main drag and can get chaotic. Oahu also hosts endless races and marathons. For information on participation, pick up a free copy of *Hawaii Race Magazine*, available in most newsstands, or check them out online at www.hawaiirace.com.

RIDING STABLES

It's not the Wild West, but Oahu is *paniolo* country. To explore its beaches, valleys and pasturelands, contact the following listings.

Located on the Windward Coast across from Chinaman's Hat, **Kualoa Ranch & Activity Center** leads one- and two-hour rides that provide startling views of the ocean and surrounding mountains. Special lessons for kids ages three through nine are also available. They also offer many other activities including a trip to Secret Island and snorkeling tours. Don't forget your swimsuit. ~ 49-560 Kamehameha Highway, Kaaawa; 808-237-8515; www.kualoa.com.

The **Turtle Bay Resort** on the North Shore has riding programs for the general public. They offer 45-minute guided tours for beginning riders, as well as 30-minute rides for advanced equestrians. These, and a one-and-one-half-hour evening ride, all take place on the grounds of the hotel, with trails along the beach and through a lovely wooded area. ~ 808-293-8811.

Happy Trails Ranch on the North Shore conducts one- to two-hour trail rides through a rainforest valley and pastureland. Riders stop at tropical orchards to sample whatever fruit is in season.

The ranch also has peacocks, chickens, a wild boar and six species of ducks. Children will love this place, and they can ride if they are six years or older. ~ P.O. Box 461, Kahuku, HI 96731; 808-638-7433.

GOLF   Even before Tiger Woods, golf has been a very popular sport among visitors in Hawaii, and no other island has more golf courses than Oahu. With more than 30 to choose from, there's one to suit every level of play. And the scenery is spectacular.

HONOLULU   For a round of golf in Honolulu, try the **Ala Wai Golf Course**, Hawaii's first municipal course. ~ 404 Kapahulu Avenue; 808-733-7387. **Hawaii Kai Golf Course** is a popular spot with both tourists and *kamaainas* and features two 18-hole courses—one beginner and one championship. ~ 8902 Kalanianaole Highway; 808-395-2358.

WINDWARD COAST   The lush **Olomana Golf Links** has an 18-hole course. ~ 41-1801 Kalanianaole Highway, Waimanalo; 808-259-7926. For an inexpensive round of golf visit the **Bay View Golf Park**. ~ 45-285 Kaneohe Bay Drive, Kaneohe; 808-247-0451. Located below the Nuuanu Pali Lookout, the **Pali Golf Course** affords sweeping views of the rugged Koolaus and the windward coastline. ~ 45-050 Kamehameha Highway, Kaneohe; 808-266-7612. If you want to play a casual game, try the nine-hole **Kahuku Golf Course**. ~ Kahuku; 808-293-5842. The **Koolau Golf Course** has been declared the most challenging course in America by the United States Golf Association. ~ 45-550 Kionaole Road, Kaneohe; 808-236-4653.

NORTH SHORE   The **Links at Kuilima**, on the grounds of the Turtle Bay Resort, was created around an existing 100-acre wetland preserve, which serves as home to several endangered Hawaiian birds. The 18-hole course was designed by golf professional Arnold Palmer. There's also an 18-hole course. ~ Kahuku; 808-293-8811.

LEEWARD COAST AND CENTRAL OAHU   Set amid fields of sugarcane and pineapple along the Leilehua Plateau in the center of Oahu, the **Hawaii Country Club** is a bit rundown, but offers some challenging holes on an 18-hole, par-72 course. ~ 94-1211 Kunia Road, Wahiawa; 808-622-1744. The **Mililani Golf Club**, though not particularly demanding, provides lovely views of the

Koolau and Waianae ranges. ~ 95-176 Kuahelani Avenue, Mililani; 808-623-2254. The flat **Ted Makalena Golf Course** is not well-maintained, but is still popular with local golfers. ~ 93-059 Waipio Point Access Road, Waipahu; 808-675-6052.

The *Guinness Book of World Records* named the Ala Wai Golf Course the busiest in the world.

At the **Ko Olina Golf Club** on the leeward coast, golfers must drive their carts under a waterfall to get to the twelfth hole of this championship course. They will also enjoy the series of lakes, brooks and waterfalls that meanders through the 18-hole course. ~ 92-1220 Aliinui Drive, Kapolei; 808-676-5309.

Especially beautiful is the **Makaha Golf Club** in the Makaha Valley, where sheer volcanic cliffs tower 1500 feet above lush greens, and golfers share the course with birds and peacocks. ~ 84-626 Makaha Valley Road, Makaha; 808-695-9544.

TENNIS

Many Oahu resorts offer complete tennis facilities. But don't despair if your hotel lacks nets. There are dozens of public tennis courts in 47 locations around the island. These courts are easily accessible, and it's a great way to meet local players. You may even be able to pick up a game.

Honolulu's public courts are crowded, especially on weekends and in the evening after work, but don't despair. All courts have a 45-minute rule. If someone is waiting to play, those on the court have to quit after 45 minutes, so you never have to wait too long. Most of the courts are also lighted, allowing you to hang out at the beach until after sunset and play tennis in the cool of the evening.

HONOLULU In the Waikiki area, try **Kapiolani Park**. ~ Kalakaua Avenue. **Diamond Head Tennis Center** is another option in the area. ~ Paki Avenue. There are courts across from Ala Moana Center at **Ala Moana Tennis Center**. ~ Ala Moana Regional Park, Ala Moana Boulevard.

In Greater Honolulu you can serve and volley at **Keehi Lagoon**. ~ Off the Nimitz Highway. Or opt for a set in the lush Manoa Valley at **Manoa Valley District Park**. ~ 2721 Kaaipu Avenue.

WINDWARD COAST For your tennis needs on the Windward Coast, try **Kailua District Park**. ~ 21 South Kainalu Drive, Kailua. Or visit **Kaneohe District Park**. ~ 45-660 Keaahala Road, Kaneohe.

NORTH SHORE AND LEEWARD COAST   Sunset Beach Neighborhood Park has two lighted courts. ~ 59-360 Kamehameha Highway, Haleiwa.

Lighted courts are also available at **Waianae District Park**. ~ 85-601 Farrington Highway, Waianae.

Call the County Department of Parks and Recreation for more information on public courts. ~ 808-971-7150. The Hawaii Visitors & Convention Bureau has information on private courts. ~ 808-923-1811.

BIKING   Oahu is blessed with excellent roads, well-paved and usually flat, and cursed with heavy traffic. About three-quarters of Hawaii's population lives here, and it sometimes seems like every person owns a car. It's certainly possible to bike through Central Oahu. **Kamehameha Highway** is an option, although it is dotted with steep grades and sections that aren't too bike-friendly.

Honolulu can be a cyclist's nightmare, but outside the city the traffic is somewhat lighter. And Oahu drivers, accustomed to tourists driving mopeds, are relatively conscious of bicyclists.

If you'd really like to get away from it all, try mountain biking. Oahu's most popular mountain bike trail is **Mauna Wili** on the windward side. It starts from the Pali lookout and goes all the way to Waimanalo. In Waimea Bay, the **Ke Ala Pupukea bike path** goes through Sunset Beach Park and Waimea Bay Beach Park. It also conveniently passes a supermarket.

Keep in mind that the Windward Coast and the North Shore are the wet sides, and the south and west coasts are the driest of all. And remember, rip-offs are a frequent fact of life on Oahu. Leaving your bike unlocked is asking for a long walk back.

ON WHEELS

Riders may cruise the Kalanianaole Highway, past Kapiolani Park and around Diamond Head to Hanauma Bay, pedal along the Waianae Coast or zip across the interior from Waialua to Pearl City. Other coastal rides cover the area between Haleiwa and Kahuku and the stretch between Waimanalo Beach and Kaaawa. If you'd like a little two-wheeled company, check out the **Hawaii Bicycling League**, which regularly sponsors weekend bike rides and free annual events. ~ P. O. Box 4403, Honolulu, HI 96812; phone/fax 808-735-5756; e-mail bicycle@pixi.com.

The Department of Transportation offers a free "Bike Oahu" map that lists detailed routes, road grades and where along the way you can find water and food. The entire brochure is also on their website. ~ 808-527-5044; www.state.hi.us/dot/highways/bike/oahu.

If you'd like a little two-wheeled company, check out the **Hawaii Bicycling League**, which regularly sponsors bike rides. ~ P.O. Box 4403, Honolulu, HI 96812; phone/fax 808-735-5756.

Bike Rentals   In Waikiki, **Coconut Cruisers** rents beach cruisers and mountain bikes. ~ 2301 Kalakaua Avenue; 808-924-1644. **Blue Sky Rentals** has mountain, road and tandem bikes. ~ 1920 Ala Moana Boulevard; 808-947-0101.

Bike Repairs   In addition to doing repair work, **Eki Cyclery** sells accessories and mountain bikes. ~ 1603 Dillingham Boulevard, Honolulu; 808-847-2005. With mountain, road and triathlon bikes for sale, **The Bike Shop** also does repair work. ~ 1149 South King Street, Honolulu; 808-596-0588. **Island Triathlon & Bike** repairs and sells bikes. ~ 569 Kapahulu Avenue; 808-732-7227.

There are numerous hiking trails within easy driving distance of Honolulu. I have listed these as well as trails in the Windward Coast and North Shore areas. Unfortunately, many Oahu treks require special permission from the state, the armed services or private owners. But you should find that the hikes suggested here, none of which require official sanction, will provide you with ample adventure.

HIKING

To hike with a group or to obtain further information on hiking Oahu, contact the **Sierra Club**. ~ P.O. Box 2577, Honolulu, HI 96803; 808-538-6616; www.hi.sierraclub.org. Another agency that also has regular weekend hikes is the **Hawaii Trail and Mountain Club**. Call ahead; some hikes are for members only. ~ P.O. Box 2238, Honolulu, HI 96804. The **Hawaii Nature Center** offers guided hikes two or three times a month. Call ahead to make a reservation. You can also get free maps and general trail information. ~ 2131 Makiki Heights Drive; 808-955-0100; www.hawaiinaturecenter.org.

All distances listed for hiking trails are one way unless otherwise noted.

GREATER HONOLULU   If you're staying in Waikiki, the most easily accessible hike is the short jaunt up **Diamond Head** crater.

There's a sweeping view of Honolulu from atop this famous landmark. The trail begins inside the crater, so take Diamond Head Road around to the inland side of Diamond Head, then follow the tunnel leading into the crater.

In the Koolau Mountains above Diamond Head there is a trail that climbs almost 2000 feet and affords excellent panoramas of the Windward Coast. To get to the **Lanipo Trail** (3 miles), take Waialae Avenue off of Route H-1. Then turn up Wilhelmina Rise and follow until it reaches Maunalani Circle and the trailhead.

For spectacular vistas overlooking the lush Palolo and Manoa valleys, you can hike **Waahila Ridge Trail** (2 miles). To get there, take St. Louis Heights Drive (near the University of Hawaii campus) and then follow connecting roads up to Waahila Ridge State Recreation Area.

The following trails can be combined for longer hikes. **Manoa Falls Trail** (0.8 mile) goes through Manoa Valley. This is a pleasant jaunt that follows Waihi Stream through a densely vegetated area to a charming waterfall. **Manoa Cliffs Trail** (3.4 miles) a pleasant family hike, follows a precipice along the west side of Manoa Valley. And **Puu Ohia Trail** (.75 mile), which crosses Manoa Cliffs Trail, provides splendid views of the Manoa and Nuuanu valleys. Both trails begin from Tantalus Drive in the hills above Honolulu. **Makiki Loop Trail** (2.5 miles roundtrip) begins near Tantalus Drive. Composed of three interlinking trails, this loop passes stands of eucalyptus and bamboo trees and offers some postcard views of Honolulu. Another loop trail, **Judd Memorial** (.75 mile), crosses Nuuanu Stream and traverses bamboo, eucalyptus and Norfolk pine groves en route to the Jackass Ginger Pool. To get there, take the Pali Highway (Route 61) several miles north from Honolulu. Turn onto Nuuanu Pali Drive and follow it about a mile to Reservoir Number Two spillway.

You can access a two-mile-long portion of the Old Pali Road directly to the right of the Pali Lookout. The narrow paved roadway provides easy hikes that are perfect for family excursions and reward with sweeping panoramas of the Windward Coast. For those with a more strenuous hike in mind, the **Koolaupoko Trail** (9 miles) departs from the Pali Lookout parking lot for magnificent rainforest, valley and ocean views. In places the trail is quite steep and occasionally demanding.

In the mountains above Pearl Harbor, at Keaiwa Heiau State Recreation Area, you will find the **Aiea Loop Trail** (4.8 miles). Set in a heavily forested area, this hike passes the wreckage of a World War II cargo plane. It provides an excellent chance to see some of the native Hawaiian trees—*lehua*, *ohia* and *koa*—used by local woodworkers. (For directions to Keaiwa Heiau State Recreation Area, see the "Greater Honolulu Beaches & Parks" section in this book.)

Another hike is along **Waimano Trail** (7 miles), which climbs 1600 feet to an astonishing vista point above Oahu's Windward Coast. There are swimming holes en route to the vista point. To get there, take Kamehameha Highway (Route 90) west to Waimano Home Road (Route 730). Turn right and go two and a half miles to a point along the road where you'll see a building on the right and an irrigation ditch on the left. The trail follows the ditch.

SOUTHEAST OAHU There are several excellent hikes along this shore. The first few are within ten miles of Waikiki, near **Hanauma Bay**. From the beach at Hanauma you can hike two miles along the coast and cliffs to the Halona Blowhole. This trek passes the Toilet Bowl, a unique tidepool with a hole in the bottom that causes it to fill and then flush with the wave action. Waves sometimes wash the rocks along this path, so be prepared to get wet (and be careful!).

At the intersection where the short road leading down toward Hanauma Bay branches from Kalanianaole Highway (Route 72), there are two other trails. **Koko Head Trail** (1 mile), a hike to the top of a volcanic cone, starts on the ocean side of the highway.

◆◆

WALK SOFTLY AND SAFELY

Most trails you'll be hiking are composed of volcanic rock. Since this is a very crumbly substance, be extremely cautious when climbing any rock faces. In fact, you should avoid steep climbs if possible. It's advisable to wear long pants when hiking in order to protect your legs from rock outcroppings, insects and spiny plants. Stay on the trails: Oahu's dense undergrowth makes it very easy to get lost. If you get lost at night, stay where you are. Because of the low latitude, night descends rapidly here; there's practically no twilight. Once darkness falls, it can be very dangerous to move around.

This trek features some startling views of Hanauma Bay, Diamond Head and the Koolau Range. Another hike, along **Koko Crater Trail** (1 mile), leads from the highway up to a 1208-foot peak. The views from this crow's nest are equally spectacular.

WINDWARD COAST There are several other particularly pretty hikes much farther north, near the village of Hauula. In Hauula, if you turn off of Kamehameha Highway and head inland for about a quarter-mile up Hauula Homestead Road, you'll come to Maakua Road. Walk up Maakua Road, which leads into the woods. About 300 yards after entering the woods, the road forks. Maakua Gulch Trail branches to the left. If you continue straight ahead you'll be on Hauula Trail, but if you veer left onto Maakua Gulch Trail, you'll encounter yet another trail branching off to the left in about 150 yards. This is Papali Trail (also known as Maakua Trail).

Maakua Gulch Trail (3 miles), en route to a small waterfall, traverses a rugged canyon with extremely steep walls. Part of the trail lies along the stream bed, so be ready to get wet. **Hauula Trail** (2.5 miles) ascends along two ridges and provides fine vistas of the Koolau Range and the Windward Coast. **Papali Trail** (2.5 miles) drops into Papali Gulch, then climbs high along a ridge from which you can view the surrounding countryside.

NORTH SHORE AND LEEWARD COAST You can approach the trail to **Kaena Point** either from the North Shore or the Leeward Coast. It's a dry, rock-strewn path that leads to Oahu's western-most tip. There are tidepools and swimming spots en route, plus spectacular views of a rugged, uninhabited coastline. If you're lucky you may sight nesting albatross or rare Hawaiian Monk seals. Keep your distance as both are protected species and a portion of the point is a wildlife preserve. In ancient times, this was sacred land; it was believed the souls of the dead departed from Kaena to the afterworld, called *Po*, the realm of the spirits. To get to the trailhead, just drive to the end of the paved portion of Route 930 on the North Shore or Route 93 on the Leeward Coast. Then follow the trail out to Kaena Point. It's about two miles via the Leeward Coast, and a half-mile via the North Shore.

THREE

History and Culture

POLYNESIAN ARRIVAL The island of Hawaii, the Big Island, was the last land mass created in the ongoing dramatic geologic upheaval that formed the Hawaiian islands. But it was most likely the first Hawaiian island to be inhabited by humans. Perhaps as early as the third century, Polynesians sailing from the Marquesas Islands, and then later from Tahiti, landed on Hawaii's southern tip. The boats were formidable structures, catamaran-like vessels with a cabin built on the platform between the wooden hulls. The sails were woven from *hala* (pandanus) leaves. Some of the vessels were a hundred feet long and could do 20 knots, making the trip to Hawaii in a month.

The Polynesians had originally come from the coast of Asia about 3000 years before. They had migrated through Indonesia, then pressed inexorably eastward, leapfrogging across archipelagoes until they finally reached the last chain, the most remote—Hawaii.

These Pacific migrants were undoubtedly the greatest sailors of their day, and stand among the finest in history. When close to land they could smell it, taste it in the seawater, see it in a lagoon's turquoise reflection on the clouds above an island. They knew 150 stars. From the color of the water they determined ocean depths and current directions. They had no charts, no compasses, no sextants; sailing directions were simply recorded in legends and chants. Yet Polynesians discovered the Pacific, from Indonesia to Easter Island, from New Zealand to Hawaii. They made the Vikings and Phoenicians look like landlubbers.

CAPTAIN COOK They were high islands, rising in the northeast as the sun broke across the Pacific. First one, then a second and, finally, as the tall-masted ships drifted west, a third island loomed before them. Landfall! The British crew was ecstatic. It meant fresh water, tropical fruits, solid ground on which to set their boots and a chance to carouse with the native women. For their captain, James Cook, it was another in an amazing career of discoveries. The man whom many call history's greatest explorer was about to land in one of the last spots on earth to be discovered by the West.

He would name the place for his patron, the British earl who became famous by pressing a meal between two crusts of bread. The Sandwich Islands. Later they would be called Owhyhee, and eventually, as the Western tongue glided around the uncharted edges of a foreign language, Hawaii.

It was January 1778, a time when the British Empire was still basking in a sun that never set. The Pacific had been opened to Western powers over two centuries before, when a Portuguese sailor named Magellan crossed it. Since then, the British, French, Dutch and Spanish had tracked through in search of future colonies.

They happened upon Samoa, Fiji, Tahiti and the other islands that spread across this third of the globe, but somehow they had never sighted Hawaii. Even when Cook finally spied it, he little realized how important a find he had made. Hawaii, quite literally, was a jewel in the ocean, rich in fragrant sandalwood, ripe for agricultural exploitation and crowded with sea life. But it was the archipelago's isolation that would prove to be its greatest resource. Strategically situated between Asia and North America, it was the only place for thousands of miles to which whalers, merchants and bluejackets could repair for provisions and rest.

Cook was 49 years old when he shattered Hawaii's quiescence. The Englishman hadn't expected to find islands north of Tahiti. Quite frankly, he wasn't even trying. It was his third Pacific voyage and Cook was hunting bigger game, the fabled Northwest Passage that would link this ocean with the Atlantic.

But these mountainous islands were still an interesting find. He could see by the canoes venturing out to meet his ships that the lands were inhabited; when he finally put ashore on Kauai, Cook discovered a Polynesian society. He saw irrigated fields, domestic animals and high-towered temples. The women were bare-breasted, the men wore loincloths. As his crew bartered for pigs, fowls and bananas, he learned that the natives knew about metal and coveted iron like gold.

If iron was gold to these "Indians," then Cook was a god. He soon realized that his arrival had somehow been miraculously

timed, coinciding with the Makahiki festival, a months-long celebration highlighted by sporting competitions, feasting, hula and
exaltation of the ruling chiefs. Even war ceased during this gala
affair. Makahiki honored the roving deity Lono, whose return to
Hawaii on "trees that would move over seas" was foretold in ancient legend. Cook was a strange white man sailing tall-masted
ships—obviously he was Lono. The Hawaiians gave him gifts, fell
in his path and rose only at his insistence.

But even among religious crowds, fame is often fickle. After
leaving Hawaii, Cook sailed north to the Arctic Sea, where he failed
to discover the Northwest Passage. He returned the next year to
Kealakekua Bay on the Big Island, arriving at the tail end of another exhausting Makahiki festival. By then the Hawaiians had
tired of his constant demands for provisions and were suffering
from a new disease that was obviously carried by Lono's arch-
angelic crew—syphilis. This Lono was proving something of a
freeloader.

Tensions ran high. The Hawaiians stole a boat. Cook retali-
ated with gunfire. A scuffle broke out on the beach and in a sudden violent outburst, which surprised the islanders as much as
the interlopers, the Hawaiians discovered that their god could
bleed. The world's finest mariner lay face down in foot-deep water,
stabbed and bludgeoned to death.

Cook's end marked the beginning of an era. He had put the
Pacific on the map, his map, probing its expanses and defining its
fringes. In Hawaii he ended a thousand years of solitude. The
archipelago's geographic isolation, which has always played a crucial role in Hawaii's development, had finally failed to protect it,
and a second theme had come into play—the islands' vulnerability. Together with the region's "backwardness," these conditions

SAILORS EXTRAORDINAIRE

Centuries before Columbus happened upon the New World, and during a
time when European mariners were rarely venturing outside the Mediterranean Sea, entire families of Polynesians were crossing 2500 miles of un-
tracked ocean in hand-carved canoes. They navigated by the stars and
carried the plants and animals they would need to start a new life. In
recent years, their perilous journey has been reenacted by crews
aboard outrigger canoes painstakingly constructed in the old style.

would now mold Hawaii's history. All in turn would be shaped by another factor, one which James Cook had added to Hawaii's historic equation: the West.

KAMEHAMEHA AND KAAHUMANU   The next man whose star would rise above Hawaii was present at Cook's death. Some say he struck the Englishman, others that he took a lock of the great leader's hair and used its residual power, its *mana*, to become king of all Hawaii.

While British sailors were discovering Hawaii, the English army was battling a ragtag band of revolutionaries for control of the American colonies.

Kamehameha was a tall, muscular, unattractive man with a furrowed face, a lesser chief on the powerful island of Hawaii. When he began his career of conquest a few years after Cook's death, he was a mere upstart, an ambitious, arrogant young chief. But he fought with a general's skill and a warrior's cunning, often plunging into the midst of a melee. He had an astute sense of technology, an intuition that these new Western metals and firearms could make him a king.

In Kamehameha's early years, the Hawaiian islands were composed of many fiefdoms. Several kings or great chiefs, continually warring among themselves, ruled individual islands. At times, a few kings would carve up one island or a lone king might seize several. Never had one monarch controlled all the islands.

But fresh players had entered the field: Westerners with ample firepower and awesome ships. During the decade following Cook, only a handful had arrived, mostly Englishmen and Americans, and they had not yet won the influence they soon would wield. However, even a few foreigners were enough to upset the balance of power. They sold weapons and hardware to the great chiefs, making several of them more powerful than any of the others had ever been. War was imminent.

Kamehameha stood in the center of the hurricane. Like any leader suddenly caught up in the terrible momentum of history, he never quite realized where he was going or how fast he was moving. And he cared little that he was being carried in part by Westerners who would eventually want something for the ride. Kamehameha was no fool. If political expedience meant Western intrusion, then so be it. He had enemies among chiefs on the other islands; he needed the guns.

When two white men came into his camp in 1790, he had the military advisers to complement a fast expanding arsenal. Within months he cannonaded Maui. In 1792, Kamehameha seized the Big Island by inviting his main rival to a peaceful parley, then slaying the hapless chief. By 1795, he had consolidated his control of Maui, grasped Molokai and Lanai, and begun reaching greedily toward Oahu. He struck rapidly, landing near Waikiki and sweeping inland, forcing his enemies to their deaths over the precipitous cliffs of the Nuuanu Pali.

The warrior had become a conqueror, controlling all the islands except Kauai, which he finally gained in 1810 by peaceful negotiation. Kamehameha proved to be as able a bureaucrat as he had been a general. He became a benevolent despot who, with the aid of an ever-increasing number of Western advisers, expanded Hawaii's commerce, brought peace to the islands and moved his people inexorably toward the modern age.

He came to be called Kamehameha the Great, and history first cast him as the George Washington of Hawaii, a wise and resolute leader who gathered a wartorn archipelago into a kingdom. Kamehameha I. But with the revisionist history of the 1960s and 1970s, as Third World people questioned both the Western version of events and the virtues of progress, Kamehameha began to resemble Benedict Arnold. He was seen as an opportunist, a megalomaniac who permitted the Western powers their initial foothold in Hawaii. He used their technology and then, in the manner of great men who depend on stronger allies, was eventually used by them.

As long a shadow as Kamehameha cast across the islands, the event that most dramatically transformed Hawaiian society occurred after his death in 1819. The kingdom had passed to Kamehameha's son Liholiho, but Kamehameha's favorite wife, Kaahumanu, usurped the power. Liholiho was a prodigal son, dissolute, lacking self-certainty, a drunk. Kaahumanu was a woman for all seasons, a canny politician who combined brilliance with boldness, the feminist of her day. She had infuriated Kamehameha by eating forbidden foods and sleeping with other chiefs, even when he placed a taboo on her body and executed her lovers. She drank liquor, ran away, proved completely uncontrollable and won Kamehameha's love.

It was only natural that when he died, she would take his *mana*, or so she reckoned. Kaahumanu gravitated toward power with the drive of someone whom fate has unwisely denied. She carved her own destiny, announcing that Kamehameha's wish had been to give her a governmental voice. There would be a new post and she would fill it, becoming in a sense Hawaii's first prime minister.

And if the power, then the motion. Kaahumanu immediately marched against Hawaii's belief system, trying to topple the old idols. For years she had bristled under a polytheistic religion regulated by taboos, or *kapus*, which severely restricted women's rights. Now Kaahumanu urged the new king, Liholiho, to break a very strict *kapu* by sharing a meal with women.

Since the act might help consolidate Liholiho's position, it had a certain appeal to the king. Anyway, the *kapus* were weakening: these white men, coming now in ever greater numbers, defied them with impunity. Liholiho vacillated, went on a two-day drunk before gaining courage, then finally sat down to eat. It was a last supper, shattering an ancient creed and opening the way for a radically new divinity. As Kaahumanu had willed, the old order collapsed, taking away a vital part of island life and leaving the Hawaiians more exposed than ever to foreign influence.

Already Western practices were gaining hold. Commerce from Honolulu, Lahaina and other ports was booming. There was a fortune to be made dealing sandalwood to China-bound merchants, and the chiefs were forcing the common people to strip Hawaii's forests. The grueling labor might make the chiefs rich, but it gained the commoners little more than a barren landscape. Western diseases struck virulently. The Polynesians in Hawaii, who numbered 300,000 in Cook's time, were extremely susceptible. By 1866, their population had dwindled to less than 60,000. It was a difficult time for the Hawaiian people.

MISSIONARIES AND MERCHANTS   Hawaii was not long without religion. The same year that Kaahumanu shattered tradition, a group of New England missionaries boarded the brig *Thaddeus* for a voyage around Cape Horn. It was a young company—many were in their twenties or thirties—and included a doctor, a printer and several teachers. They were all strict Calvinists, fearful that the second coming was at hand and possessed of a mission. They were bound for a strange land called Hawaii, 18,000 miles away.

Hawaii, of course, was a lost paradise, a hellhole of sin and savagery where men slept with several wives and women neglected to wear dresses. To the missionaries, it mattered little that the Hawaiians had lived this way for centuries. The churchmen would save these heathens from hell's everlasting fire whether they liked it or not.

The delegation arrived in Kailua on the Big Island in 1820 and then spread out, establishing important missions in Honolulu and Lahaina. Soon they were building schools and churches, conducting services in Hawaiian and converting the natives to Christianity.

The missionaries rapidly became an integral part of Hawaii, despite the fact that they were a walking contradiction to everything Hawaiian. They were a contentious, self-righteous, fanatical people whose arrogance toward the Hawaiians blinded them to the beauty and wisdom of island lifestyles. Where the natives lived in thatch homes open to the soothing trade winds, the missionaries built airless clapboard houses with New England–style fireplaces. While the Polynesians swam and surfed frequently, the new arrivals, living near the world's finest beaches, stank from not bathing. In a region where the thermometer rarely drops much below 70°, they wore long-sleeved woolens, ankle-length dresses and claw-hammer coats. At dinner they preferred salt pork to fresh beef, dried meat to fresh fish. They considered coconuts an abomination and were loath to eat bananas.

HISTORY OF HONOLULU

When Captain Brown sailed into Honolulu Harbor in 1794, he was the first known foreigner to arrive in the paradise. He named the area Fair Harbor. Eventually the name Honolulu (meaning "sheltered harbor") gained precedence. King Kamehameha I settled here in 1809 after conquering Oahu, and Honolulu gained financial status when it flourished as a major shipping port. Although the town traded extensively in pineapple and sugar, and served as a supply port for whalers, its main claim to fame was sandalwood. Honolulu's sandalwood trade enjoyed a brief but brilliant boom. The islanders exported the wood to China in exchange for silk and porcelain, which was then shipped to New England. The ships returned to Honolulu with New England goods. Environmental protection policies were not in place at this time in history, and the forests were soon depleted. Nonetheless, Honolulu remained an important port; in 1850, King Kamehameha III declared the area the capital of his kingdom.

And yet the missionaries were a brave people, selfless and God-fearing. Their dangerous voyage from the Atlantic had brought them into a very alien land. Many would die from disease and overwork; most would never see their homeland again. Bigoted though they were, the Calvinists committed their lives to the Hawaiian people. They developed the Hawaiian alphabet, rendered Hawaiian into a written language and, of course, translated the Bible. Theirs was the first printing press west of the Rockies. They introduced Western medicine throughout the islands and created such an effective school system that, by the mid-19th century, 80 percent of the Hawaiian population was literate. Unlike almost all the other white people who came to Hawaii, they not only took from the islanders, they also gave.

But to these missionaries, *giving* meant ripping away everything repugnant to God and substituting it with Christianity. They would have to destroy Hawaiian culture in order to save it. Though instructed by their church elders not to meddle in island politics, the missionaries soon realized that heavenly wars had to be fought on earthly battlefields. Politics it would be. After all, wasn't government just another expression of God's bounty?

They allied with Kaahumanu and found it increasingly difficult to separate church from state. Kaahumanu converted to Christianity, while the missionaries became government advisers and helped pass laws protecting the sanctity of the Sabbath. Disgusting practices such as hula dancing were prohibited.

Politics can be a dangerous world for a man of the cloth. The missionaries were soon pitted against other foreigners who were quite willing to let the clerics sing hymns, but were damned opposed to permitting them a voice in government. Hawaii in the 1820s had become a favorite way station for the whaling fleet. As the sandalwood forests were decimated, the island merchants began looking for other industries. By the 1840s, when over 500 ships a year anchored in Hawaiian ports, whaling had become the islands' economic lifeblood. During the heyday of the whaling industry, more American ships visited Hawaii than any other port in the world.

Like the missionaries, the whalers were Yankees, shipping out from bustling New England ports. But they were a hell of a different cut of Yankee. These were rough, crude, boisterous men who loved rum and music, and thought a lot more of fornicating

with island women than saving them. After the churchmen forced
the passage of laws prohibiting prostitution, the sailors rioted along
the waterfront and fired cannons at the
mission homes. When the smoke cleared,
the whalers still had their women.

Religion simply could not compete with
commerce, and other Westerners were continu-
ously stimulating more business in the islands.
By the 1840s, as Hawaii adopted a parliamentary
form of government, American and British fortune
hunters were replacing missionaries as government
advisers. It was a time when anyone, regardless of
ability or morality, could travel to the islands and become a political powerhouse literally overnight. A consumptive American,
fleeing the mainland for reasons of health, became chief justice of
the Hawaiian Supreme Court while still in his twenties. Another
lawyer, shadowed from the East Coast by a checkered past, became attorney general two weeks after arriving.

> Hawaii is the only state in the
> union to have been ruled by a
> monarchy—from Kamehameha
> the Great in 1758 until
> Liliuokalani's overthrow in
> 1893. In all, eight monarchs
> reigned over the kingdom.

The situation was no different internationally. Hawaii was
subject to the whims and terrors of gunboat diplomacy. The archipelago was solitary and exposed, and Western powers were
beginning to eye it covetously. In 1843, a maverick British naval
officer actually annexed Hawaii to the Crown, but the London
government later countermanded his actions. Then, in the early
1850s, the threat of American annexation arose. Restless Cali-
fornians, fresh from the gold fields and hungry for revolution,
plotted unsuccessfully in Honolulu. Even the French periodically
sent gunboats in to protect their small Catholic minority.

Finally, the three powers officially stated that they wanted to
maintain Hawaii's national integrity. But independence seemed
increasingly unlikely. European countries had already begun claiming other Pacific islands, and with the influx of Yankee missionaries and whalers, Hawaii was being steadily drawn into the
American orbit.

THE SUGAR PLANTERS There is an old Hawaiian saying that
describes the 19th century: The missionaries came to do good,
and they did very well. Actually the early evangelists, few of whom
profited from their work, lived out only half the maxim. Their sons
would give the saying its full meaning.

This second generation, quite willing to sacrifice glory for gain, fit neatly into the commercial society that had rendered their fathers irrelevant. They were shrewd, farsighted young Christians who had grown up in Hawaii and knew both the islands' pitfalls and potentials. They realized that the missionaries had never quite found Hawaii's pulse, and they watched uneasily as whaling became the lifeblood of the islands. Certainly it brought wealth, but whaling was too tenuous—there was always a threat that it might dry up entirely. A one-industry economy would never do; the mission boys wanted more. Agriculture was the obvious answer, and eventually they determined to bind their providence to a plant that grew wild in the islands—sugar cane.

The first sugar plantation was started on Kauai in 1835, but not until the 1870s did the new industry blossom. By then, the Civil War had wreaked havoc with the whaling fleet, and a devastating winter in the Arctic whaling grounds practically destroyed it. The mission boys, who had prophesied the storm, weathered it quite comfortably. They had already begun fomenting an agricultural revolution.

THE GREAT MAHELE Agriculture, of course, means land, and until the 19th century all Hawaii's acreage was held by chiefs. So in 1848, the mission sons, together with other white entrepreneurs, pushed through the Great Mahele, one of the slickest real estate laws in history. Rationalizing that it would grant chiefs the liberty to sell land to Hawaiian commoners and white men, the mission sons established a western system of private property.

The Hawaiians, who had shared their chiefs' lands communally for centuries, had absolutely no concept of deeds and leases. What resulted was the old $24-worth-of-beads story. The benevolent Westerners wound up with the land, while the lucky Hawaiians got practically nothing. Large tracts were purchased for cases of whiskey; others went for the cost of a hollow promise. The entire island of Niihau, which is still owned by the same family, sold for $10,000. It was a bloodless coup, staged more than 40 years before the revolution that would topple Hawaii's monarchy. In a sense it made the 1893 uprising anticlimactic. By then Hawaii's future would already be determined: white interlopers would own four times as much land as Hawaiian commoners.

Following the Great Mahele, the mission boys, along with other businessmen, were ready to become sugar planters. The *mana* once again was passing into new hands. Obviously, there was money to be made in cane, a lot of it, and now that they had land, all they needed was labor. The Hawaiians would never do. Cook might have recognized them as industrious, hardworking people, but the sugar planters considered them shiftless. Disease was killing them off anyway, and the Hawaiians who survived seemed to lose the will to live. Many made appointments with death, stating that in a week they would die; seven days later they were dead.

Before the Great Mahele, Hawaiians flourished because they had the rights of access and were able to use the resources of both land and sea. Their traditions were based on sharing and common use.

Foreign labor was the only answer. In 1850, the Masters and Servants Act was passed, establishing an immigration board to import plantation workers. Cheap Asian labor would be brought over. It was a crucial decision, one that would ramify forever through Hawaiian history and change the very substance of island society. Between 1850 and 1930, 180,000 Japanese, 125,000 Filipinos, 50,000 Chinese, and 20,000 Portuguese immigrated. Eventually they transformed Hawaii from a chain of Polynesian islands into one of the world's most varied and dynamic locales, a meeting place of East and West.

The Chinese were the first to come, arriving in 1852 and soon outnumbering the white population. Initially, with their long pigtails and uncommon habits, the Chinese were a joke around the islands. They were poor people from southern China whose lives were directed by clan loyalty. They built schools and worked hard so that one day they could return to their native villages in glory. They were ambitious, industrious and—ultimately—successful.

Too successful, according to the sugar planters, who found it almost impossible to keep the coolies down on the farm. The Chinese came to Hawaii under labor contracts, which forced them to work for five years. After their indentureship, rather than re-enlisting as the sugar bosses had planned, the Chinese moved to the city and became merchants. Worse yet, they married Hawaiian women and were assimilated into the society.

These coolies, the planters decided, were too uppity, too ready to fill social roles that were really the business of white men. So in the 1880s, they began importing Portuguese. But the Portuguese thought they already *were* white men, while any self-respecting American or Englishman of the time knew they weren't.

The Portuguese spelled trouble, and in 1886 the sugar planters turned to Japan, with its restricted land mass and burgeoning population. The new immigrants were peasants from Japan's southern islands, raised in an authoritarian, hierarchical culture in which the father was a family dictator and the family was strictly defined by its social status. Like the Chinese, they built schools to protect their heritage and dreamed of returning home someday; but unlike their Asian neighbors, they only married other Japanese. They sent home for "picture brides," worshipped their ancestors and Emperor and paid ultimate loyalty to Japan, not Hawaii.

Queen Liliuokalani authored a number of songs, the best known being "Aloha Oe." The words to the song are preserved on a plaque set in a boulder at Washington Place, where she resided after her overthrow.

The Japanese, it soon became evident, were too proud to work long hours for low pay. Plantation conditions were atrocious; workers were housed in hovels and frequently beaten. The Japanese simply did not adapt. Worst of all, they not only bitched, they organized, striking in 1909.

So in 1910, the sugar planters turned to the Philippines for labor. For two decades the Filipinos arrived, seeking their fortunes and leaving their wives behind. They worked not only with sugar cane but also with pineapples, which were becoming a big business in the 20th century. They were a boisterous, fun-loving people, hated by the immigrants who preceded them and used by the whites who hired them. The Filipinos were given the most menial jobs, the worst working conditions and the shoddiest housing. In time, another side of their character began to show— a despondency, a hopeless sense of their own plight, their inability to raise passage money back home. They became the untouchables of Hawaii.

REVOLUTIONARIES AND ROYALISTS Sugar, by the late 19th century, was king. It had become the center of island economy, the principal fact of life for most islanders. Like the earlier whaling industry, it was drawing Hawaii ever closer to the American sphere. The sugar planters were selling the bulk of their crops in California; having already signed several tariff treaties to protect their American market, they were eager to further strengthen mainland ties. Besides, many sugar planters were second-, third- and fourth-generation descendants of the New England missionaries; they had a natural affinity for the United States.

There was, however, one group that shared neither their love for sugar nor their ties to America. To the Hawaiian people, David Kalakaua was king, and America was the nemesis that had long threatened their independence. The whites might own the land, but the Hawaiians, through their monarch, still held substantial political power. During Kalakaua's rule in the 1870s and 1880s, anticolonialism was rampant.

The sugar planters were growing impatient. Kalakaua was proving very antagonistic; his nationalist drumbeating was becoming louder in their ears. How could the sugar merchants convince the United States to annex Hawaii when all these silly Hawaiian royalists were running around pretending to be the Pacific's answer to the British Isles? They had tolerated this long enough. The Hawaiians were obviously unfit to rule, and the planters soon joined with other businessmen to form a secret revolutionary organization. Backed by a force of well-armed followers, they pushed through the "Bayonet Constitution" of 1887, a self-serving document that weakened the king and strengthened the white landowners. If Hawaii was to remain a monarchy, it would have a Magna Carta.

But Hawaii would not be a monarchy long. Once revolution is in the air, it's often difficult to clear the smoke. By 1893, Kalakaua was dead and his sister, Liliuokalani, had succeeded to the throne. She was an audacious leader, proud of her heritage, quick to defend it and prone to let immediate passions carry her onto dangerous ground. At a time when she should have hung fire, she charged, proclaiming publicly that she would abrogate the new constitution and reestablish a strong monarchy. The revolutionaries had the excuse they needed. They struck in January, seized government buildings and, with four boatloads of American marines and the support of the American minister, secured Honolulu. Liliuokalani surrendered.

It was a highly illegal coup; legitimate government had been stolen from the Hawaiian people. But given an island chain as isolated and vulnerable as Hawaii, the revolutionaries reasoned, how much did it really matter? It would be weeks before word reached Washington of what a few Americans had done without official sanction, then several more months before a new American president, Grover Cleveland, denounced the renegade action. By then the revolutionaries would already be forming a republic. They chose as their first president Sanford Dole, a missionary's son whose name eventually became synonymous with pineapples.

Not even revolution could rock Hawaii into the modern age. For years, an unstable monarchy had reigned; now an oligarchy composed of the revolution's leaders would rule. Officially, Hawaii was a democracy; in truth, the Chinese and Japanese were hindered from voting, and the Hawaiians were encouraged not to bother. Hawaii, reckoned its new leaders, was simply not ready for democracy. Even when the islands were finally annexed by the United States in 1898 and granted territorial status, they remained a colony.

More than ever before, the sugar planters, alias revolutionaries, held sway. By the early 20th century, they had linked their plantations into a cartel, the Big Five. It was a tidy monopoly composed of five companies that owned not only the sugar and pineapple industries, but the docks, shipping companies and many of the stores, as well. Most of these holdings, happily, were the property of a few interlocking, intermarrying mission families—the Doles, Thurstons, Alexanders, Baldwins, Castles, Cookes and others—who had found heaven right here on earth. They golfed together and dined together, sent their daughters to Wellesley and their sons to Yale. All were proud of their roots, and as blindly paternalistic as their forefathers. It was their destiny to control Hawaii, and they made very certain, by refusing to sell land or provide services, that mainland firms did not gain a foothold in their domain.

What was good for the Big Five was good for Hawaii. Competition was obviously not good for Hawaii. Although the Chinese and Japanese were establishing successful businesses in Honolulu and some Chinese were even growing rich, they posed no immediate threat to the Big Five. And the Hawaiians had never been good at capitalism. By the early 20th century, they had become one of the world's most urbanized groups. But rather than competing with white businessmen in Honolulu, unemployed Hawaiians were forced to live in hovels and packing crates, cooking their poi on stoves fashioned from empty oil cans.

Political competition was also unhealthy. Hawaii was ruled by the Big Five, so naturally it should be run by the Republican Party. After all, the mission families were Republicans. Back on the mainland, the Democrats had always been cool to the sugar planters, and it was a Republican president, William McKinley, who eventually annexed Hawaii. The Republicans, quite simply, were good for business.

The Big Five set out very deliberately to overwhelm any political opposition. When the Hawaiians created a home-rule party around the turn of the century, the Big Five shrewdly co-opted it by running a beloved descendant of Hawaii's royal family as the Republican candidate. On the plantations they pitted one ethnic group against another to prevent the Asian workers from organizing. Then, when labor unions finally formed, the Big Five attacked them savagely. In 1924, police killed 16 strikers on Kauai. Fourteen years later, in an incident known as the "Hilo massacre," the police wounded 50 picketers.

The Big Five crushed the Democratic Party by intimidation. Polling booths were rigged. It was dangerous to vote Democratic —workers could lose their jobs, and if they were plantation workers, that meant losing their houses as well. Conducting Democratic meetings on the plantations was about as easy as holding a hula dance in an old missionary church. The Democrats went underground.

Those were halcyon days for both the Big Five and the Republican Party. In 1900, only five percent of Hawaii's population was white. The rest was composed of races that rarely benefitted from Republican policies. But for the next several decades, even during the Depression, the Big Five kept the Republicans in power.

While the New Deal swept the mainland, Hawaii clung to its Colonial heritage. The islands were still a generation behind the

A SLICE OF THE PIE

In ancient Hawaii, the chiefs used an *ahupuaa* system to divide and manage the islands. The pie-shaped wedges of land varied in size, depending on a chief's status, but each ran from the mountains to the sea, providing the residents with all the resources they needed to exist. Those who lived in the uplands traded food they raised with their *ohana* (family) that resided by the sea. People rarely ventured beyond their own *ahupuaa*, and while they might trade with neighboring *ahupuaa*, they would never hunt or harvest outside their own boundaries. Even today, folks in Hawaii tend to stick close to home in deference to the old system.

rest of the United States—the Big Five enjoyed it that way. There was nothing like the status quo when you were already in power. Other factors that had long shaped Hawaii's history also played into the hands of the Big Five. The islands' vulnerability, which had always favored the rule of a small elite, permitted the Big Five to establish an awesome cartel. Hawaii's isolation, its distance from the mainland, helped protect their monopoly.

THE JAPANESE AND THE MODERN WORLD   All that ended on December 7, 1941. On what would afterwards be known as the "Day of Infamy," a flotilla of six aircraft carriers carrying over 400 planes unleashed a devastating assault on Pearl Harbor. Attacking the Pacific Fleet on a Sunday morning, when most of the American ships were unwisely anchored side by side, the Japanese sank or badly damaged six battleships, three destroyers and several other vessels. Over 2400 Americans were killed.

The Japanese bombers that attacked Pearl Harbor sent shock waves through Hawaii that are still rumbling today. World War II changed all the rules of the game, upsetting the conditions that had determined island history for centuries.

Ironically, no group in Hawaii would feel the shift more thoroughly than the Japanese. On the mainland, Japanese Americans were rounded up and herded into relocation camps. But in Hawaii that was impossible; there were simply too many, and they comprised too large a part of the labor force.

Many were second-generation Japanese, *nisei*, who had been educated in American schools and assimilated into Western society. Unlike their immigrant parents, the *issei*, they felt few ties to Japan. Their loyalties lay with America, and when war broke out they determined to prove it. They joined the U.S. armed forces and formed a regiment, the 442nd, which became the most frequently decorated outfit of the war. The Japanese were heroes, and when the war ended many heroes came home to the United States and ran for political office. Men like Daniel Inouye and Spark Matsunaga began winning elections and would eventually become United States senators.

By the time the 442nd returned to the home front, Hawaii was changing dramatically. The Democrats were coming to power. Leftist labor unions won crucial strikes in 1941 and 1946. Jack Burns, a former cop who dressed in tattered clothes and drove around Honolulu in a beat-up car, was creating a new Democratic coalition.

Burns, who would eventually become governor, recognized the potential power of Hawaii's ethnic groups. Money was flowing into the islands—first military expenditures and then tourist dollars, and non-whites were rapidly becoming a new middle class. The Filipinos still constituted a large part of the plantation force, and the Hawaiians remained disenchanted, but the Japanese and Chinese were moving up fast. Together they formed a majority of Hawaii's voters.

Burns organized them, creating a multiracial movement and thrusting the Japanese forward as candidates. By 1954, the Democrats controlled the legislature, with the Japanese filling one out of every two seats in the capital. Then, when Hawaii attained statehood five years later, the voters elected the first Japanese ever to serve in Congress. Today one of the state's U.S. senators and a congressman are Japanese. On every level of government, from municipal to federal, the Japanese predominate. They have arrived. The *mana*, that legendary power coveted by the Hawaiian chiefs and then lost to the sugar barons, has passed once again—to a people who came as immigrant farm-workers and stayed to become the leaders of the 50th state.

HAWAIIAN SOVEREIGNTY

Over the past few decades since the advent of Hawaiian Renaissance, there has been a loud call for Hawaiian sovereignty. A bitter feeling of mistrust is held by many Hawaiians against the U.S. government because the monarchy was overthrown by a band of U.S. merchant renegades. Hawaiians have been outspoken in their demand for righting the wrong that was done to them. However, there is confusion among various Hawaiian groups as to what should be done. Some activists see the sovereignty movement as a struggle to elevate the native Hawaiian people to a higher place *within* the structure of the United States of America. Others believe that Hawaii should be moved *out* of the United States—with the monarchy reinstated, giving Hawaii an independent status. Many think something in between should be done. Some activists demand that reparations should be inclusive of all the people of Hawaii, others think it should include only the native Hawaiian people. It is a movement marked with passion and ambiguity.

The Japanese and the Democrats were on the move, but in the period from World War II until the present day, everything was in motion. Hawaii was in upheaval. Jet travel and a population boom shattered the islands' solitude. While in 1939 about 500 people flew to Hawaii, now about seven million visitors land every year. The military population escalated as Oahu became a key base not only during World War II but throughout the Cold War and the Vietnam War, as well. Hawaii's overall population exploded from about a half-million just after World War II to over one million at the present time.

No longer did the islands lag behind the mainland; they rapidly acquired the dubious quality of modernity. Hawaii became America's 50th state in 1959, Honolulu grew into a bustling high-rise city, and hotels and condominiums mushroomed along the beaches of Maui, a neighboring island. Outside investors swallowed up two of the Big Five corporations, and several partners in the old monopoly began conducting most of their business outside Hawaii. Everything became too big and moved too fast for Hawaii to be entirely vulnerable to a small interest group. Now, like the rest of the world, it would be prey to multinational corporations.

By the 1980s, it would also be of significant interest to investors from Japan. In a few short years they succeeded in buying up a majority of the state's luxury resorts, including every major beachfront hotel in Waikiki, sending real estate prices into an upward spiral that did not level off until the early 1990s. During the rest of the decade, the economy was stagnant, with real estate prices dropping, agriculture declining and tourism leveling off at seven million visitors annually.

One element that did not plateau during the last decade was the Native Hawaiian movement. Nativist sentiments were spurred in January 1993 by the 100th anniversary of the American overthrow of the Hawaiian monarchy. Over 15,000 people turned out to mark the illegal coup. Later that year, President Clinton signed a statement issued by Congress formally apologizing to the Hawaiian people. In 1994, the United States Navy returned the island of Kahoolawe to the state of Hawaii. Long a rallying symbol for the Native Hawaiian movement, the unoccupied island had been used for decades as a naval bombing target. By 1996, efforts to clean away bomb debris and make the island habitable were well under way, although completion of the clean-up is still years off.

Then in 1998, the issue of Hawaii's monarchy arose again when demonstrators marched around the entire island of Oahu and staged rallies to protest the 100th anniversary of the United States' annexation of Hawaii.

Today, numerous perspectives remain to be reconciled, with grassroots movements working to secure a degree of autonomy for Hawaii's native people. The most common goal seems to be a status similar to that accorded the American Indians by the federal government, although there are still those who seek a return to an independent Hawaii, either as a restored monarchy or along democratic lines. Also pending resolution is the distribution of land to Native Hawaiians with documented claims, as well as a financial settlement with the state government. It's a complex situation involving the setting right of injustices of a century past.

Hawaiian Culture

Hawaii, according to Polynesian legend, was discovered by Hawaii-loa, an adventurous sailor who often disappeared on long fishing trips. On one voyage, urged along by his navigator, Hawaii-loa sailed toward the planet Jupiter. He crossed the "many-colored ocean," passed over the "deep-colored sea," and eventually came upon "flaming Hawaii," a mountainous island chain that spewed smoke and lava.

History is less romantic. The Polynesians who found Hawaii were probably driven from their home islands by war or some similar calamity. They traveled in groups, not as lone rangers, and shared their canoes with dogs, pigs and chickens, with which they planned to stock new lands. Agricultural plants such as coconuts, yams, taro, sugar cane, bananas and breadfruit were also stowed on board.

Most important, they transported their culture, an intricate system of beliefs and practices developed in the South Seas. After undergoing the stresses and demands of pioneer life, this traditional lifestyle was transformed into a new and uniquely Hawaiian culture.

It was based on a caste system that placed the *alii* or chiefs at the top and the slaves, *kauwas*, on the bottom. Between these two groups were the priests, *kahunas* and the common people or *makaainanas*. The chiefs, much like feudal lords, controlled all the land and collected taxes from the commoners who farmed it.

Life centered around the *kapu*, a complex group of regulations that dictated what was sacred or profane. For example, women were not permitted to eat pork or bananas; commoners had to prostrate themselves in the presence of a chief. These strictures were vital to Hawaiian religion; *kapu* breakers were directly violating the will of the gods and could be executed for their actions. And there were a lot of gods to watch out for, many quite vindictive. The four central gods were *Kane*, the creator; *Lono*, the god of agriculture; *Ku*, the war god; and *Kanaloa*, lord of the underworld. They had been born from the sky father and earth mother, and had in turn created many lesser gods and demigods who controlled various aspects of nature.

Don't get confused—that's not the British Union Jack you see flying but the state flag of Hawaii.

It was, in the uncompromising terminology of the West, a stone-age civilization. Though the Hawaiians lacked metal tools, the wheel and a writing system, they managed to include within their inventory of cultural goods everything necessary to sustain a large population on a chain of small islands. They fashioned fish nets from native *olona* fiber, made hooks out of bone, shell and ivory, and raised fish in rock-bound ponds. The men used irrigation in their farming. The women made clothing by pounding mulberry bark into a soft cloth called *tapa*, dyeing elaborate patterns into the fabric. They built peak-roofed thatch huts from native *pili* grass and *hala* leaves. The men fought wars with spears, slings, clubs and daggers. The women used mortars and pestles to pound the roots of the taro plant into poi, the islanders' staple food. Breadfruit, yam and coconut were other menu standards.

The West labeled these early Hawaiians "noble savages." Actually, they often lacked nobility. The Hawaiians were cannibals who practiced human sacrifice during religious ceremonies and often used human bone to fashion fish hooks. They constantly warred among themselves and would mercilessly pursue a retreating army, murdering as many of the vanquished soldiers as possible.

But they weren't savages either. The Hawaiians developed a rich oral tradition of genealogical chants and created beautiful lilting songs to accompany their hula dancing. Their musicians mastered several instruments including the *ukeke* (a single-stringed device resembling a bow), an *ohe hano ihu* or nose flute, rattles and drums made from gourds, coconut shells or logs. Their craftsmen produced the world's finest featherwork, tying thousands of tiny feathers onto netting to produce golden cloaks and ceremonial helmets. The Hawaiians helped develop the sport of surfing. They also swam, boxed, bowled and devised an intriguing game called *konane*, a cross between checkers and the Japanese game of go. They built networks of trails across lava flows, and created an elemental art form in the images—petroglyphs—that they carved into lava rock along the trails.

They also achieved something far more outstanding than their varied arts and crafts, something that the West, with its awesome knowledge and advanced technology, has never duplicated. The Hawaiians created a balance with nature. They practiced conservation, establishing closed seasons on certain fish species and carefully guarding their plant and animal resources. They led a simple life, without the complexities the outside world would eventually thrust upon them. It was a good life: food was plentiful, people were healthy and the population increased. For a thousand years, the Hawaiians lived in delicate harmony with the elements. It was not until the West entered the realm, transforming everything, that the fragile balance was destroyed. But that is another story entirely.

PEOPLE

The most isolated population center on earth, Hawaii is 2390 miles from the mainland United States and 4900 miles from China. Because of its unique history and isolated geography, Hawaii is truly a cultural melting pot. It's one of the few states in the union in which caucasians are a minority group. Whites, or haoles as they're called in the islands, comprise only about 22 percent of Hawaii's 1.2 million population. Japanese constitute 18 percent, Filipinos 13 percent, Hawaiians and part-Hawaiians account for 21 percent, Chinese about 3 percent and other racial groups 23 percent. Three out of every four Hawaii residents live on the island of Oahu, and almost half reside in Honolulu.

It's a very vital society. One-fifth of the people were born of racially mixed parents.

One trait characterizing many of these people is Hawaii's famous spirit of *aloha*, a genuine friendliness, an openness to strangers, a willingness to give freely. Undoubtedly, it is one of the finest qualities any people has ever demonstrated. *Aloha* originated with the Polynesians and played an important role in ancient Hawaiian civilization.

The aloha spirit is alive and well in the islands, although bad attitudes toward *haoles*, the pejorative term used for whites, are not unknown. All parties, however, seem to understand the crucial role tourism has come to play in Hawaii's economy, which means you're not likely to experience unpleasantness from the locals you'll meet—unless you behave unpleasantly. A smile goes a long way.

CUISINE Nowhere is the influence of Hawaii's melting pot population stronger than in the kitchen. While in the islands, you'll probably eat not only with a fork, but with chopsticks and fingers, as well. You'll sample a wonderfully varied cuisine. In addition to standard American fare, hundreds of restaurants serve Hawaiian, Japanese, Chinese, Korean, Portuguese and Filipino dishes. There are also fresh fruits aplenty—pineapples, papayas, mangoes, bananas and tangerines—plus local fish such as mahimahi, marlin and snapper.

The mainstay of the traditional Hawaiian diet is poi, a purplish paste pounded from baked or steamed taro tubers. It's pretty bland fare, but it does make a good side dish with *imu*-cooked pork or tripe stew. You should also try *laulau*, a combination of fish, pork and taro leaves wrapped in a *ti* leaf and steamed. And don't neglect to taste baked *ulu* (breadfruit) and *opihi* (limpets). Among the other Hawaiian culinary traditions are *kalua* pig, a shredded pork dish baked in an *imu* (underground oven); *lomi-lomi* salmon, which is salted and mixed with onions and tomatoes; and chicken *luau*, prepared in taro leaves and coconut milk.

SOUNDS FISHY

What are all those strange-sounding fish dishes on the menu? A quick translation will help you when choosing a seafood platter from Hawaiian waters. Firm-textured with a light taste, the most popular fish is *mahimahi*, or dolphin fish (no, it's not one of those amazing creatures that do fancy tricks on the waves); its English equivalent is dorado. *Ahi* is yellowfin tuna and is especially delicious as sashimi (raw) or blackened. *Opakapaka* is pink snapper and is a staple of Pacific Rim cuisine. Other snappers include *uku* (gray snapper), *onaga* (ruby snapper) and *ehu* (red snapper). *Ono* (which means "delicious" in Hawaiian) is king mackerel, a white fish that lives up to its name.

A good way to try all these dishes at one sitting is to attend a luau. I've always found the tourist luaus too commercial, but you might watch the newspapers for one of the special luaus sponsored by civic organizations.

Japanese dishes include sushi, sukiyaki, teriyaki and tempura, plus an island favorite—sashimi, or raw fish. On most any menu, including McDonald's, you'll find *saimin*, a noodle soup filled with meat, vegetables and *kamaboko* (fishcake).

You can count on the Koreans for *kim chi*, a spicy salad of pickled cabbage and *kalbi*, barbecued beef short ribs prepared with soy and sesame oil. The Portuguese serve up some delicious sweets including *malasadas* (donuts minus the holes) and *pao doce*, or sweet bread. For Filipino fare, I recommend *adobo*, a pork or chicken dish spiced with garlic and vinegar, and *pochero*, a meat entrée cooked with bananas and several vegetables. In addition to a host of dinner dishes, the Chinese have contributed treats such as *manapua* (a steamed bun filled with barbecued pork) and oxtail soup. They also introduced crack seed to the islands. Made from dried and preserved fruit, it provides a treat as sweet as candy.

As the Hawaiians say, *"Hele mai ai."* Come and eat!

LANGUAGE

The language common to all Hawaii is English, but because of its diverse cultural heritage, the archipelago also supports several other tongues. Foremost among these are Hawaiian and pidgin. Hawaiian, closely related to other Polynesian languages, is one of the most fluid and melodious languages in the world. It's composed of only twelve letters: five vowels—*a, e, i, o, u* and seven consonants—*h, k, l, m, n, p, w*. The glottal stop ('), when used, counts as a thirteenth letter.

At first glance, the language appears formidable: how the hell do you pronounce *humuhumunukunukuapuaa*? But actually it's quite simple. After you've mastered a few rules of pronunciation, you can take on any word in the language.

The first thing to remember is that every syllable ends with a vowel, and the next to last syllable usually receives the accent.

The next rule to keep in mind is that all the letters in Hawaiian are pronounced. Consonants are pronounced the same as in English (except for the *w*, which is pronounced as a *v* when it introduces the last syllable of a word—as in *ewa* or *awa*. Vowels are pronounced the same as in Spanish: *a* as in *among*, *e* as in *they*, *i* as in *machine*, *o* as in *no* and *u* as in *too*. Hawaiian has four vowel combinations or diphthongs: *au*, pronounced *ow*; *ae* and *ai*, which sound like *eye*; and *ei*, pronounced *ay*. As noted above, the glottal stop (') occasionally provides a thirteenth letter.

By now, you're probably wondering what I could possibly have meant when I said Hawaiian was simple. I think the glossary that follows will simplify everything while helping you pronounce common words and place names. Just go through the list, starting with words like aloha and luau that you already know. After you've practiced pronouncing familiar words, the rules will become second nature; you'll no longer be a *malihini*.

Just when you start to speak with a swagger, cocky about having learned a new language, some young Hawaiian will start talking at you in a tongue that breaks all the rules you've so carefully mastered. That's pidgin. It started in the 19th century as a lingua franca among Hawaii's many races. Pidgin speakers mix English and Hawaiian with several other tongues to produce a spicy creole. It's a fascinating language with its own vocabulary, a unique syntax and a rising inflection that's hard to mimic.

Pidgin is definitely the hip way to talk in Hawaii. A lot of young Hawaiians use it among themselves as a private language. At times they may start talking pidgin to you, acting as though they don't speak English; then if they decide you're okay, they'll break into English. When that happens, you be one *da kine brah*.

So *brah*, I take *da kine* pidgin words, put 'em together with Hawaiian, make one big list. Savvy?

aa (ah-**ah**)—a type of rough lava
ae (eye)—yes
aikane (eye-**kah**-nay)—friend, close companion
akamai (ah-kah-**my**)—wise
alii (ah-**lee**-ee)—chief
aloha (ah-**lo**-ha)—hello; greetings; love
aole (ah-**oh**-lay)—no
auwe (ow-**way**)—ouch!; oh no!
brah (bra)—friend; brother; bro'
bumby (**bum**-bye)—after a while; by and by
da kine (da kyne)—whatdyacallit; thingamajig; the best
dah makule guys (da mah-**kuh**-lay guys)—senior citizens
diamond head—in an easterly direction (Oahu only)
duh uddah time (duh **uh**-duh time)—once before

ewa (**eh**-vah)—in a westerly direction (Oahu only)

hale (**hah**-lay)—house

haole (**how**-lee)—Caucasian; white person

hapa (**hah**-pa)—half

hapa-haole (**hah**-pa **how**-lee)—half-Caucasian

heiau (hey-**yow**)—temple

hele on (**hey**-lay on)—go; move; outta here

hoaloha (ho-ah-**lo**-ha)—friend

holo holo (**ho**-low **ho**-low)—to visit

howzit? (hows-it)—how you doing? what's happening?

huhu (who-who)—angry

hukilau (**who**-key-lau)—community fishing party

hula (**who**-la)—Hawaiian dance

imu (**ee**-moo)—underground oven

ipo (**ee**-po)—sweetheart

kahuna (kah-**who**-nah)—priest; specialist or expert in any field

kai (kye)—ocean

kaka-roach (**kah**-kah roach)—ripoff; theft

kamaaina (kah-mah-**eye**-nah)—one born and raised in Hawaii; a longtime island resident

kane (**kah**-nay)—man

kapu (**kah**-poo)—taboo; forbidden

kaukau (**cow**-cow)—food; eat

keiki (**kay**-key)—child

kiawe (key-**ah**-vay)—mesquite tree

kokua (ko-**coo**-ah)—help

kona winds (**ko**-nah winds)—winds that blow against the trades

kupuna (koo-**poo**-nah)—elder

lanai (lah-**nye**)—porch; also island name

lauhala (lau-**hah**-lah) or *hala* (**hah**-lah)—a pandanus tree whose leaves are used in weaving

lei (lay)—flower garland

lolo (**low**-low)—stupid

lomilomi (**low**-me-**low**-me)—massage; salted raw salmon

luau (**loo**-ow)—Hawaiian meal

mahalo (mah-**hah**-low)—thank you

mahalo nui loa (mah-**ha**-low **new**-ee **low**-ah)—thank you very much

mahu (**mah**-who)—gay; homosexual

makai (mah-**kye**)—toward the sea

malihini (mah-lee-**hee**-nee)—newcomer; stranger

mana (**mah**-nah)—spiritual or divine power

mauka (**mau**-kah)—toward the mountains

nani (**nah**-nee)—beautiful

ohana (oh-**hah**-nah)—family
okole (oh-**ko**-lay)—rear; ass
okolemaluna (oh-ko-lay-mah-**loo**-nah)—a toast: bottoms up!
ono (**oh**-no)—tastes good
pahoehoe (pah-**hoy**-hoy)—smooth or ropy lava
pakalolo (pah-kah-**low**-low)—marijuana
pali (**pah**-lee)—cliff
paniolo (pah-nee-**oh**-low)—cowboy
pau (pow)—finished; done
pilikia (pee-lee-**key**-ah)—trouble
popakiki (poh-pah-**key**-key)—stubborn; hard head
puka (**poo**-kah)—hole
pupus (**poo**-poos)—hors d'oeuvres
shaka (**shah**-kah)—hand greeting
swell head—"big" head; egotistical
tapa (**tah**-pah) also **kapa**—fabric made from the beaten bark of mulberry shrubs
wahine (wah-**hee**-nay)—woman
wikiwiki (**wee**-key-**wee**-key)—quickly; in a hurry
you get stink ear—you don't listen well

MUSIC

Music has long been an integral part of Hawaiian life. Most families keep musical instruments in their homes, gathering to play at impromptu living room or backyard jam sessions. Hawaiian folk tunes are passed down from generation to generation. In the earliest days, it was the sound of rhythm instruments and chants that filled the air. Drums, including the *pahu hula*, were fashioned from hollowed-out gourds, coconut shells or hollowed sec-

HAWAIIAN MELODIES

Waikiki is the nightlife hotspot in the islands. Check out **Auntie Genoa Keawe**, the first lady of Hawaiian falsetto music, performing Thursday nights on the breezy Moana Terrace at the Waikiki Beach Marriott Resort. Slack key masters **George Kuo**, **Martin Pahinui** and **Aaron Mahi** play there on Sunday nights. **Olomana** is a must-see on Friday and Saturday nights at the Hilton Hawaiian Village Resort's Paradise Lounge. **Henry Kapono**, **Jonah Cummings** and **Makana** play regularly at Duke's Canoe Club in the Outrigger Waikiki Hotel. **Don Ho** does his show Sunday through Thursday at the Waikiki Beachcomber Hotel. Outside of Waikiki, **Jerry Santos** or **Robert Cazimero** perform for lucky diners at Chai's Island Bistro in the Aloha Tower Marketplace. Visitors with a classical bent will enjoy the excellent **Honolulu Symphony**.

tions of coconut palm trunks, then covered with sharkskin. Gourds and coconuts, *uliuli*, adorned with tapa cloth and feathers, were also filled with shells or pebbles to produce a rattling sound. Other instruments included the nose flute, or *ohe*, a piece of bamboo similar to a mouth flute, but played by exhaling through the nostril; the bamboo organ; and *puili*, sections of bamboo split into strips, which were struck rhythmically against the body. Stone castanets, *illili*, and *ke laau* sticks are also used as hula musical instruments.

Western musical scales and instruments were introduced by explorers and missionaries. As ancient Hawaiian music involved a radically different musical system, Hawaiians had to completely re-adapt. Actually, western music caught on quickly, and the hymns brought by missionaries fostered a popular musical style—the *himeni*, or Hawaiian church music.

Strangely enough, a Prussian bandmaster named Henry Berger had a major influence on contemporary Hawaiian music. Brought over in the 19th century by King Kalakaua to lead the Royal Hawaiian Band, Berger helped Hawaiians make the transition to Western instruments.

Hawaii has been the birthplace of several different musical instruments and styles. The ukulele, modeled on a Portuguese guitar, quickly became the most popular Hawaiian instrument. Its small size made it easy to carry, and with just four strings, it was simple to play. The ukulele is enjoying a surge of popularity on the mainland, and several craftsmen throughout the islands have begun making beautiful instruments from native woods for collectors and those who want to play in style. During the early 1900s, the steel guitar was exported to the mainland. Common in country-and-western music today, it was invented by a young man who experimented by sliding a steel bar across guitar strings.

The slack-key style of guitar playing also comes from Hawaii, where it's called *ki ho'alu*. When the guitar was first brought to Hawaii in the 1830s by Mexican and Spanish cowboys, the Hawaiians adapted the instrument to their own special breed of music. In tuning, the six (or twelve) strings are loosened so that they sound a chord when strummed and match the vocal range of the singer. Slack-key is played in a variety of ways, from plucking or slapping the strings to sliding along them. A number of different tunings exist, and many have been passed down orally through families for generations. Some of the more renowned guitarists playing today include Keola Beamer, Raymond Kane and Cyril Pahinui.

During the late 19th century, "*hapa*-haole" songs became the rage. The ukulele was instrumental in contributing to this Hawaiian fad. Written primarily in English with pseudo-Hawaiian themes, songs like "Tiny Bubbles" and "Lovely Hula Hands" were later introduced to the world via Hollywood.

The Hawaiian craze continued on the mainland with radio and television shows such as "Hawaii Calls" and "The Harry Owens Show." In the 1950s, little mainland girls donned plastic hula skirts and danced along with Hilo Hattie and Ray Kinney.

It was not until the 1970s that both the hula and music of old Hawaii made a comeback. Groups such as the Sons of Hawaii and the Makaha Sons of Niihau, along with Auntie Genoa Keawe and the late Gabby Pahinui, became popular. Before long, a new form of Hawaiian music was being heard, a combination of ancient chants and contemporary sounds, performed by such islanders as Henry Kapono, Kalapana, Olomana, the Beamer Brothers, the Peter Moon Band and the Brothers Cazimero.

Today, many of these groups, along with other notables such as the Kaau Crater Boys, Brother Nolan, Willie K., Butch Helemano, and Obrien Eselu, bring both innovation to the Hawaiian music scene and contribute to the preservation of an ancient tradition. The trend continues with hybrid infusions of reggae and rock, while performers like Kealii Reichel and groups like Kapena maintain the soft-edged sounds so well-suited to the islands.

An entire new category of music has become established in Hawaii: dubbed "Jawaiian," the sound incorporates Jamaican reggae and contemporary Hawaiian music, and is especially popular amongst the state's younger population. Pro-sovereignty groups like Sudden Rush have taken this trend one step further, laying down their message-imbued rap lyrics on reggae tunes and Hawaiian classics to create a truly unique genre.

In addition, now-deceased masters of Hawaiian song like Gabby Pahinui and Israel Kamakawiwoole have gained renewed popularity and respect for the links they created between old and contemporary Hawaiian music.

HULA

Along with palm trees, the hula—swaying hips, grass skirts, colorful leis—is linked forever in people's minds with the Hawaiian Islands. This western idea of hula is very different from what the dance has traditionally meant to native Hawaiians.

Hula is an old dance form, its origin shrouded in mystery. The ancient hula, *hula kahiko*, was more concerned with religion and spirituality than entertainment. Originally performed only by men, it was used in rituals to communicate with a deity—a connection to nature and the gods. Accompanied by drums and chants, *hula kahiko* expressed the islands' culture, mythology and history in hand and body movements. It later evolved from a strictly religious rite to a method of communicating stories and legends. Over the years, women were allowed to study the rituals and eventually became the primary dancers.

Hula *halaus* (schools) are serious business throughout the islands (and even on the mainland). Competitions bring together *halau* throughout the islands. On Oahu, the major event is The Prince Lot Hula Festival held in Moanalua Gardens every July.

When westerners arrived, the *hula kahiko* began another transformation. Explorers and sailors were more interested in its erotic element, ignoring the cultural significance. Missionaries simply found it scandalous and set out to destroy the tradition. They dressed Hawaiians in western garb and outlawed *hula kahiko*.

The hula tradition was resurrected by King David Kalakaua. Known by the moniker "Merrie Monarch," Kalakaua loved music and dance. For his coronation in 1883, he called together the kingdom's best dancers to perform the chants and hulas once again. He was also instrumental in the development of the contemporary hula, the *auwana* hula, which added new steps and movements and was accompanied by ukuleles and guitars rather than drums.

By the 1920s, modern hula had been popularized by Hollywood, westernized and introduced as kitschy tropicana. Real grass skirts gave way to cellophane versions, plastic leis replaced fragrant island garlands, and exaggerated gyrations supplanted the hypnotic movements of the traditional dance.

Fortunately, with the resurgence of Hawaiian pride in recent decades, Polynesian culture has been reclaimed and *hula kahiko* and traditional chants have made a welcome comeback.

FOUR

Waikiki

To understand the geography of Waikiki you need only know about Waikiki Beach. And to understand Waikiki Beach, you must know two things. The first is that major hotels line the beach, practically from one end to the other, and are used as landmarks by visitors and local residents alike. The other fact to remember is that to visitors Waikiki Beach is a single sandy ribbon two miles long, but to local folks it represents many beaches in one. When you park your beach towel here, consider that every few strides will carry you into another realm of Waikiki's culture and history.

Waikiki is where Hawaiian tourism began, and its reputation as a retreat dates back centuries. It is believed that the area was a favorite recreation site for the long-ago kings of Oahu and Maui, and a holy place as well. The site of the Royal Hawaiian Hotel was previously a *heiau pookanaka*, or sacrificial temple, and strictly off limits to the common people.

When Hawaii's royalty established Honolulu as their capital in the mid-1800s, Waikiki continued as a getaway, thanks to sunny shores and well-formed waves, just right for their favorite sport of surfing. The royal family would often invite well-known visitors such as Robert Louis Stevenson (who purportedly wrote several novels here) and Jack London to join them at their Waikiki retreat. And it gradually gained a reputation with not-so-well-known haoles as well. By the late 1800s, guesthouses were springing up along the strand. The first hotel, the Moana, was built at the turn of the 20th century, as was a tram line from downtown Honolulu that brought visitors and townspeople to enjoy the beach and surf at Waikiki. Their taste for "country life" did not extend to embrace the mosquitoes (deemed unsanitary and dangerous) that thrived in the wetlands; a struggle between the burgeoning tourist industry and Waikiki's farmers ensued over the local "swamps."

The area might have remained an isolated getaway surrounded by wetlands, taro patches and duck ponds if it weren't for the dredging of the Ala Wai canal in the 1920s. The wetlands were drained and filled with coral from the canal, laying the foundation for what would someday be one of the world's most famous resort areas. But not quite yet.

First there had to be more tourists—and a way to bring them to Honolulu. Matson Navigation built the 650-passenger *Mololo* in 1925, and the glory days of Hawaiian tourism began. Matson also developed the Royal Hawaiian Hotel to the tune of $2 million, an astronomical sum at the time. But the investment paid off, and Waikiki began to compete with Europe as a vacation destination for the well-heeled.

More hotels were built, and during World War II, GIs on leave soaked up the sun on Waikiki's shores, further establishing its reputation. Then in the jet age that followed, it became a highrise resort area. A motley collection of hotels, squeezed together in the small space that is Waikiki, stands as an architectural monument to the neighborhood's history and gives each section of Waikiki a different flavor.

This fabled peninsula extends two miles from the Ala Wai Yacht Harbor to Diamond Head and measures a half-mile in width from the Ala Wai Canal to the Pacific. Kalakaua Avenue, the main drag, is packed elbow to elbow with throngs of visitors. Paralleling the ocean, this broad boulevard is all at once noisy, annoying, exciting, cosmopolitan and fascinating. Today, visitors from Japan, Korea and Australia, arriving in ever-increasing numbers, add to the international atmosphere.

But the main appeal is still the district's white-sand corridor. Dotting the beach are picnic areas, restrooms, showers, concession stands and beach equipment rentals. Most of the beach is protected by coral reefs and sea walls, so the swimming is excellent, the snorkeling fair. This is also a prime area for surfing. Two- to four-foot waves, good for beginners and still challenging to experienced surfers, are common here.

That makes it a suitable spot for a statue of the legendary late Duke Kahanamoku, widely considered the ambassador of modern surfing and still revered by the current generation of wave riders. You can see his statue at Kuhio Beach Park, facing Kalakaua

Avenue. The hotels disappear at popular Kapiolani Beach Park, which has undergone a freshening up of its restrooms and other public facilities while retaining its broad oceanfront lawns and shady trees.

It's difficult to visit Waikiki and not spot the **Hilton Hawaiian Village**. The *Guinness Book of World Records* notes the massive resort for having two of the tallest mosaics in the world. The rainbow-patterned murals flank both sides of the Rainbow Tower. Even if you're staying somewhere else on the island, be sure to wander through the shops and gardens of the complex; the landscaped grounds include 22 acres of indigenous flora. ~ Hilton Hawaiian Village, 2005 Kalia Road; 808-949-4321, fax 808-947-7898; www.hiltonhawaiianvillage.com.

The western flank of Waikiki Beach sits near the Hilton Hawaiian Village. Here you will find a pretty lagoon fringed by palm trees. The curving strand nearby, fronting the resort, is called **Kahanamoku Beach**. Named for Hawaii's great surfer, Duke Kahanamoku, it features numerous facilities. Beach stands rent everything from towels, chairs and air mattresses to snorkel sets, surfboards and Hobie-cat sailboats.

Also here is Port Hilton, the pier from which the resort complex launches catamaran cruises. One of these boats will take you to what may be the only hidden attraction around Waikiki, the **Atlantis XIV**, a 64-passenger sub located just off the coast that carries visitors to the bottom for a close-up look at an artificial reef, complete with sunken ships and airplanes, created to bring back marine life to the area. In fact, the submarine experience is likely to be better than the sea life, which is often limited. Steep admission (a fleet of 48-passenger subs also make the trek at a slightly lower fee). ~ 808-973-9811, 800-548-6262, fax 808-973-2499; www.goatlantis.com.

Fort DeRussy Beach, owned by the military but open to the public, features the area's widest swath of white sand. It is also beautifully backdropped by a grove of palm trees. There are restrooms, picnic tables and barbecues, plus tennis, squash and volleyball courts.

The nearby **U.S. Army Museum of Hawaii** has every weapon from Hawaiian shark teeth blades to modern-day instruments of destruction. You can also trace the United States' unending series of military campaigns from the uniforms and equipment (ours

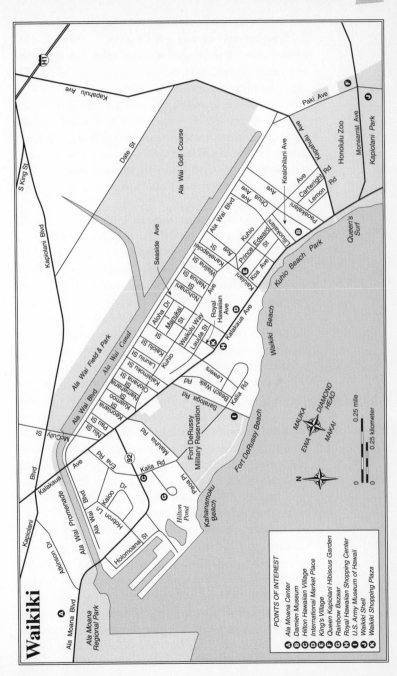

Waikiki

POINTS OF INTEREST

- Ⓐ Ala Moana Center
- Ⓑ Damien Museum
- Ⓒ Hilton Hawaiian Village
- Ⓓ International Market Place
- Ⓔ King's Village
- Ⓕ Queen Kapiolani Hibiscus Garden
- Ⓖ Rainbow Bazaar
- Ⓗ Royal Hawaiian Shopping Center
- Ⓘ U.S. Army Museum of Hawaii
- Ⓙ Waikiki Shell
- Ⓚ Waikiki Shopping Plaza

and theirs) on exhibit here. Closed Monday. ~ Kalia Road, Fort DeRussy; 808-438-2821, fax 808-438-2819.

Past Fort DeRussy Beach stretches a palisade of highrise hotels. Lining the beachfront, they provide numerous facilities for thirsty sunbathers or adventuresome athletes. Continue on and you will pass the Sheraton strip, a lengthy stretch of Waikiki Beach fronted entirely by hotels. This section marks Waikiki's center of action. The first hotel is the **Outrigger Reef on the Beach**, followed by the **Halekulani**, a pricey property that many consider Waikiki's best hotel. Next is the **Sheraton Waikiki**. A highrise structure built with two curving wings, it resembles a giant bird roosting on the beach.

The hotels here are so famous that the nearby strand is named **Royal-Moana Beach**. Stretching between the Royal Hawaiian and Moana hotels, it has been a sun-soaked gathering place for decades. That's because these two grand dames are Waikiki's oldest hotels.

The **Royal Hawaiian Hotel** is Hawaii's "Pink Palace," a Spanish Moorish–style caravansary painted shocking pink. Built in 1927, it is a labyrinth of gardens, colonnades and balconies; the old place is certainly Waikiki's most interesting edifice. ~ 2259 Kalakaua Avenue; 808-923-7311, fax 808-924-7098; www.royal-hawaiian.com.

HIDDEN ►   You can explore the hidden past of Hawaii's most popular tourist destination on the **Waikiki Historic Trail**. Just follow the surfboard-shaped markers that denote historic sights along the beach and streets. Or take the guided Queen's Tour, which covers a portion of the trail. The free and highly entertaining 90-minute tour is offered at 9 a.m. daily, except Sunday, and is led by native Hawaiian storytellers and historians. ~ It begins and ends at the Royal Hawaiian Shopping Center's Fountain Courtyard, 2233 Kalakaua Avenue; 808-737-6442.

The **Sheraton Moana Surfrider Resort**, built in 1901, was Waikiki's first resort. Its vaulted ceilings, tree-shaded courtyard and spacious accommodations reflect the days when Hawaii was a retreat for the rich. Further delving into the history of the place can be done in its Historical Room, containing interesting photographs and memorabilia dating from the hotel's conception. The **Moana Banyan tree**, planted on the grounds in 1904, stretches 150 feet across and 75 feet high. The Moana's beach is also the site of one of Waikiki's most renowned surfing spots, **Canoe's Surf**.

~ 2365 Kalakaua Avenue; 808-922-3111, fax 808-923-0308; www.starwood.com/hawaii.

Just beyond the Moana is **Kuhio Beach Park,** which runs along Kalakaua Avenue from Kaiulani to Kapahulu avenues. In addition to a broad sandy beach and a creative layout that includes a banyan tree, traditional healing stones and a cascading fountain, there are numerous facilities here—picnic areas, beach equipment rentals, showers and restrooms, as well as lifeguards. The shady pavilions in this public park also attract local folks who come to play cards and chess. Needless to say, this convenient beach is often quite crowded. Diners like it because of its proximity to many Waikiki budget restaurants; parents favor the beach for its protective sea wall, which provides a secure area where children can swim; and people-watchers find it an ideal place to check out the crowds of tourists and local residents. The park has been gussied up recently; renovations so far include broader walkways, grassy areas and artificial waterfalls and tidepools. The residence of Prince Kuhio, the park's namesake and most famous resident, was torn down in 1936 to make way for the beach. Ironic, considering he was an outspoken proponent of establishing Hawaiian homesteads. Apparently even royalty is not exempt from the effects of expansion. ~ Kalakaua Avenue.

Tucked behind St. Augustine Catholic Church, on a side street near the beach, sits the tiny **Damien Museum,** a tribute to Father ◀ HIDDEN Damien, the Belgian priest best known for his work in Kalaupaupa, the leper colony on Molokai. Father Damien established

AUTHOR FAVORITE

The **Waikiki Aquarium** is the place where you can finally discover what a *humuhumunukunukuapuaa,* that impossibly named fish, really looks like. (Don't be surprised if the name proves to be longer than the fish.) Within the aquarium's glass walls, you'll see more than 350 different species of fish originating from Hawaiian and South Pacific waters. Ranging from rainbow-hued tropical fish to blacktip reef sharks, they constitute a broad range of underwater species. Then there are Hawaiian monk seals (an endangered species) and other intriguing creatures. A biodiversity exhibit features a rotating display of creatures not native to Hawaii. Admission. ~ 2777 Kalakaua Avenue; 808-923-9741, fax 808-923-1771; www.waquarium.org.

churches throughout the islands, but his dedication to those suffering from Hansen's Disease (leprosy) is what made him a Hawaiian hero. The exhibits include his glasses, chalice and other unassuming belongings, as well as his prayer book and vestments. Photos depicting his final years on Molokai, where he, too, died of the disease, paint an evocative portrait of this selfless man. Closed weekends. ~ 130 Ohua Avenue; phone/fax 808-923-2690.

Since 1983, visitors to the **Lucoral Museum** have viewed its collection of corals, pearls and gemstones from around the world. These gems and stones appear in both raw and finished forms, as well as carved into various artworks. Lucoral offers jewelry-making classes; a re-creation of a mining cave allows a glance at freshly unearthed jade, rose quartz and other gems. Be sure to visit the third-floor artists' workshop, where local artisans help you design your own baubles and create them before your eyes. Closed weekends. ~ 2414 Kuhio Avenue; 808-922-1999, fax 808-924-6698.

HIDDEN ▶   The strand just beyond Kuhio Beach Park is called **Queen's Surf**. Here also are picnic areas, shady pavilions, restroom facilities and showers. Something of a Bohemian quarter, this pretty plot draws gays, local artists and a wide array of intriguing characters. On the weekends, conga drummers may be pounding out rhythms along the beach while other people gather to soak in the scene.

Kapiolani Park next door extends across 140 acres on both sides of Kalakaua Avenue. Hawaii's oldest park, this tree-studded playland dates back more than 100 years. Perhaps more than anything else, it has come to serve as a jogger's paradise. From dawn 'til dark, runners of all ages, colors, sizes and shapes beat a path around its perimeter. But Kapiolani offers something to just about anyone. There are tennis courts, softball and soccer fields, an archery area, and much more. To fully explore the park, you must visit each of its features in turn.

HIDDEN ▶   Across the park, the **Queen Kapiolani Hibiscus Garden**, with its colorful flowerbeds and shady pavilion, is a pretty place to stroll and picnic. Despite its proximity to the Waikiki waterfront and a busy shopping area, the little spot has maintained its peace—I'm almost hesitant to mention it here. Perhaps it has remained a secret because of its relatively small size (tour buses can't stop here). Or perhaps there are more mysterious reasons for it. According

Aloha Patrol

You'll spot them strolling, or cruising on their bikes, down the streets of Waikiki every night. They wear white shirts accented at the shoulders with Hawaiian print. They're members of the "Aloha Patrol," and they're here to help you.

Crime ranks at the top of the list of problems facing Honolulu residents. Whenever you meet the locals they're likely to talk about the rise in robberies and car break-ins. If you rent a car in Hawaii the company will warn you not to leave valuables inside, and you'll be reminded at the parks and the beaches by signs stating the same thing. Although your chances of being ripped off are probably pretty slim, as a tourist you are a prime target, so it's something to be wary of.

Tired of having crime tarnish their island's reputation, the citizens of Oahu have taken action. In late 1996, they formed the first Aloha Patrol to be a citizen's watchgroup and the eyes and ears of the police in Waikiki, as well as to be the spirit of aloha for guests. Early the next year, they expanded their work to the North Shore. Today, these "sidewalk ambassadors" have expanded to become a professional security force for the Waikiki Business Improvement District.

In Waikiki, the Aloha Patrol members walk the streets from 10 a.m. to 11 p.m. daily, answering questions, giving directions, telling people about themselves and the Aloha Patrol and, if they see any problems, alerting the police by two-way radio. On the North Shore, they patrol the beach parking lots each afternoon to prevent car break-ins. And it seems to work. Since the program began, there have been no robberies in the afternoons at the patrolled beaches and visitors to Honolulu can be assured that the streets of Waikiki are safer because of the folks in the crisp white shirts. For APO assistance, call 808-924-9740.

to legend, Tahitian *kahunas* (priests) visited the area in the 14th century and left behind more than spiritual healing. The story goes that they also imbued the stones in the garden with their powers, which now protect the park's blossoms against errant pickers. ~ Monsarrat and Paki avenues.

The **Waikiki Shell**, located in Kapiolani Park, is a great place for an evening under the stars with Diamond Head as a backdrop. General admission means lawn seating, which is the perfect way to enjoy the Honolulu Symphony backing up headliners like Michael Feinstein, local favorites like the Brothers Cazimero, or megastars like Bob Dylan. Check with the Blaisdell Center box office to see if anything is scheduled for the Shell while you're in town and plan to go. ~ 808-527-5400, 808-591-2211, fax 808-591-8072; www.blaisdellcenter.com.

The park's grandest feature is the **Honolulu Zoo**. Like city zoos everywhere, this tropical facility has a resident population of elephants, giraffes, ostriches, zebras, hippos, Sumatran tigers, lions, alligators and so on. But it also includes animals more common to the islands, creatures like the nene (a rare goose), Komodo dragons and Galápagos tortoises. Perhaps most interesting of all, there is an outstanding population of tropical birds. Admission. ~ 808-971-7171, fax 808-971-7173; www.honolulu zoo.org.

Kapiolani Park includes a stretch of beach called **Sans Souci**, a popular spot where residents and visitors share the sand and reef-sheltered waters. It's also an easy place to set out for a kayak paddle to the marine preserve off Diamond Head or to head toward Waikiki, which stands in highrise silhouette.

THE PAST UNCOVERED

In Hilton Hawaiian Village's sweeping Kalia Tower, the resort has established a satellite branch of the **Bishop Museum** with material you won't find in the main headquarters. Visitors are met with *oli* (traditional chants) and move through the exhibits to the rhythms of Hawaii's musical heritage. There are vivid life-size scenes of life in Waikiki over the past two centuries, and an impressive collection of art and photographs. ~ Hilton Hawaiian Village, 2005 Kalia Road; 808-949-4321, fax 808-947-7898; www.hiltonhawaiianvillage.com.

The beach is bordered to the west by the **Natatorium**, a salt-water pool and grandstand built in the 1920s as a monument to those Hawaiians who lost their lives in World War I. Closed in 1979 due to slipshod maintenance and deterioration, it is slated to be restored. However, legal challenges have put the start of restoration on hold pending environmental, health and best-use issues. The City continues to say it will pursue a full restoration that includes the saltwater pool as well as the landmark arch at the entrance. Opponents, however, don't believe the restoration is worth the millions of dollars it will take; they are also skeptical that the fully restored pool would be hygenic for the public.

Sans Souci is certainly not a hard place to find, since one of the world's most famous landmarks rises just behind it. More than any other place in the islands, **Diamond Head** is the trademark of Hawaii. A 760-foot crater, it is the work of a volcano that has been dead for about 100,000 years. To the Hawaiians it was known as *Leahi*. They saw in its sloping hillsides the face of an ahi, or yellowfin tuna. Then, in the 19th century, sailors mistook its volcanic glass rocks for rare gems and gave the promontory its present name. Formed 350,000 years ago, this natural landmark was a sacred place to the ancient Hawaiians. A *heiau* once graced its slopes and King Kamehameha is said to have worshiped here, offering a human sacrifice to the Polynesian war god.

It is possible to drive into the gaping maw of this old dragon. Just take Kalakaua Avenue until it meets Diamond Head Road, then follow the latter around to the inland site of the crater. From there a tunnel leads inside. Once within, there is a three-quarter-mile trail climbing to the rim of the crater. From here you can gaze along Oahu's southeast corner and back across the splendid little quarter called Waikiki.

LODGING

While it may no longer be the simple country retreat it was at the 20th century's turn, Waikiki does have one advantage: believe it or not, it's a great place to find low-rent hotels. A lot of the cozy old hostelries have been torn down and replaced with highrises, but a few have escaped the urban assault. Some of those skyscrapers, too, are cheaper than you might think. One thing to consider when staying in Waikiki is that it is not exactly quiet. Early-morning garbage trucks and late-night party-goers make considerable street noise. Streets on the outskirts (Saratoga Road) are less noisy than those in the heart of things (e.g., Lewers and Beach Walk). Ask for rooms off the street or high in the sky! Let's take a look at some of the better bargains Waikiki has to offer.

What better combination can you ask for than a place that is both a hotel *and* a hostel? At the **Island Hostel/Hotel**, located inside the Hawaiian Colony building, you can book a room with private bath or join fellow travelers in a coed dorm room. The dorm includes kitchen privileges. ~ 1946 Ala Moana Boulevard; phone/fax 808-942-8748. BUDGET.

The Polynesian Hostel Beach Club offers both private and dormitory accommodations (baths are shared in either case) in this apartment building. Each room has its own refrigerator and bathroom and sleeps up to six people. Laundry facilities and a full kitchen are available for guests, as well as a barbecue and outdoor deck area. It is the closest hostel to the beach, which is one block away. ~ 2584 Lemon Road; 808-922-1340, 877-504-2924, fax 808-262-2817; www.hostelhawaii.com, e-mail polynesian@ hostelhawaii.com. BUDGET.

An inexpensive place for both men and women in Waikiki is the YMCA **Central Branch**. It's handily situated across the street from Ala Moana Center and a block from the beach. And you're welcome to use the gym, pool, saunas, television room and coffee shop. You can also expect the usual Y ambience—long sterile hallways leading to an endless series of identical, cramped, uncarpeted rooms. You will pay several dollars more for a private bathroom, but low prices help make up for the lack of amenities. ~ 401 Atkinson Drive; 808-941-3344, fax 808-941-8821; e-mail hidomen @aol.com. BUDGET.

Budget travelers should also consider a stay at **Hostelling International—Waikiki**. This helpful facility features single-sex

CATCH A WAVE

All along Waikiki Beach, concessions offer rides on **outrigger canoes**. They are long, sleek fiberglass crafts resembling ancient Polynesian canoes. Each seats four to six passengers, plus a captain. For very cheap you can join the crew on a low-key wave-riding excursion that will have you paddling as hard and fast as you can to catch waves and ride them far into the shore.

dormitory-style accommodations and private studio units available for couples. The latter are plain cinder block rooms with private baths and mini-refrigerators. Open to both men and women, the hostel provides bedding and a common kitchen and creates a family-style atmosphere conducive to meeting other travelers. Internet access is available for a fee. Seven-day maximum stay. ~ 2417 Prince Edward Street; 808-926-8313, fax 808-922-3798; www.hiayh.com, e-mail ayaloha@lava.net. BUDGET.

The walls are still cinderblock, but the price is right at the **Waikiki Prince Hotel**. All 30 guest rooms have air conditioning and cable television; many of the units are equipped with kitchenettes (which are outfitted with microwaves, stoves and utensils). ~ 2431 Prince Edward Street; 808-922-1544, fax 808-924-3712; www.waikikiprince.com, e-mail waikikiprince@hotmail.com. BUDGET.

One economical place that I particularly recommend is small, intimate and close to the beach: **Hale Pua Nui**, a congenial home away from home. There are 22 studio apartments here, each spacious, well-furnished and cross-ventilated. The rooms are quaintly decorated, carpeted and equipped with kitchenettes, cable television and air conditioning. The personalized service you receive from the management makes the Hale Pua Nui an ideal vacation spot for budget-conscious travelers. ~ 228 Beach Walk; 808-923-9693, fax 808-923-9678. BUDGET.

A lowrise hotel tucked away in the shadow of vaulting condominiums, **The Breakers** is truly a find. Dating to the 1950s, this Waikiki original consists of 64 rooms and 15 suites surrounding a pool and landscaped patio. Shoji doors add to the ambience while kitchenettes in every room and a location one block from the beach round out the features. ~ 250 Beach Walk; 808-923-3181, 800-426-0494, fax 808-923-7174; www.breakershawaii.com, e-mail breakers@aloha.net. MODERATE.

Rising higher from the ground, while still keeping costs low, is the **Royal Grove Hotel**, a six-story, 87-unit establishment. If you can get past the garish pink exterior here, you'll find the rooms more tastefully designed. All accommodations are carpeted and comfortably furnished, and some are decorated in simple but appealing styles. There are TVs and phones in all of the rooms, plus an almond-shaped pool and spacious lobby. Rents vary according to which wing of this sprawling building your bags are parked in. Most rooms even have kitchenettes with microwaves, as well as air conditioning, so it's hard to go wrong here. ~ 151 Uluniu Avenue; 808-923-7691, 800-922-7508, fax 808-922-7508; www. royalgrovehotel.com, e-mail rghawaii@gte.net. BUDGET.

Kai Aloha Apartment Hotel offers intimacy combined with modern convenience; each guest room has air conditioning, an all-electric kitchen, radio, telephone with voice mail, cable television and carpeting. Studio apartments feature lovely rattan furniture and are attractively decorated with old drawings and paintings. The one-bedroom apartments will comfortably sleep four people. Daily maid service is provided. ~ 235 Saratoga Road; 808-923-6723, fax 808-922-7592; e-mail kai.aloha@gte.net. MODERATE.

Dominating the mid-range hotel scene in Waikiki are the Outrigger's Ohana hotels. It seems like everywhere you turn in this tourist enclave another one looms above: There are over a dozen. An easy walk from the beach is the **OHANA Royal Islander**. Each of the 101 units are equipped with air conditioning, phone, cable TV, hairdryers and lanais; some have ocean views. Note that there are no bathtubs here, only showers. Guests may use the pool at another Ohana property across the street. ~ 2164 Kalia Road; 808-922-1961, 800-462-6262, fax 808-923-4632; www. ohanahotels.com. DELUXE.

If you're willing to sacrifice intimacy, you may find that the **OHANA Coral Seas Hotel** is one of the better deals in Waikiki. This seven-story hostelry is located just a hundred yards from the beach. They have appealing accommodations with amenities such as air conditioning, telephones, wall-to-wall carpeting and small lanais. In some units you can add a kitchenette to the list of extras. There's a pool at another OHANA hotel next door that guests may use. If you want, just for the hell of it, to directly experience the Waikiki tourist scene, this is the place. The OHANA Coral Seas Hotel is at the heart of the action. ~ 250 Lewers Street; 808-923-3881, 800-462-6262, fax 808-922-2330; www. ohanahotels.com. MODERATE.

The **OHANA Village** is located on a busy street a block from the beach, but it offers rooms with or without kitchenettes at reasonable cost. You can expect street noise. The lobby contains about five different shops selling a variety of clothing and sundries. There is a pool. ~ 240 Lewers Street; 808-923-3881, 800-462-6262, fax 808-922-2330; www.ohanahotels.com. DELUXE.

Located a stone's skip from the beach, the OHANA Waikiki Tower is a 439-unit colossus. Each room comes with carpeting, telephone, TV, cable movies, refrigerator and shared lanai; many rooms also have a kitchenette. The decor is bland but the furniture comfy. Downstairs is an open-air lobby with adjoining restaurant and pool. ~ 200 Lewers Street; 808-922-6424, 800-462-6262, fax 808-923-7437; www.ohanahotels.com. DELUXE.

The Ewa Hotel has 90 rooms. Tucked away on a back street one block from the beach, this pastel-and-rattan establishment has a 1980s aura about it. Close to Kapiolani Park and offering kitchenettes in many rooms, it is particularly convenient for families. ~ 2555 Cartwright Road; 808-922-1677, 800-359-8639, fax 808-923-8538; www.ethotel.com, e-mail mail@ethotel.com. MODERATE.

About the same size is the Waikiki Hana Hotel, a 73-room place that offers a restaurant and small lobby. Quiet (for Waikiki), friendly and comfortable, its rooms are brightly decorated and trimly appointed with air conditioning and color televisions. Some have kitchenettes and lanais. ~ 2424 Koa Avenue; 808-926-8841, 800-367-5004, fax 808-924-3770. MODERATE.

The Aston Honolulu Prince Hotel was once a college dormitory. Today it's a ten-story hotel with a comfortable lobby. The standard rooms are small and blandly decorated. Located two

AUTHOR FAVORITE

The **Halekulani** ("House Befitting Heaven") is the grand dame of Oahu hotels, exuding elegance and refinement. It's gone through various incarnations since its 1907 start: the beachfront home and five bungalows were replaced in the 1920s with a plantation mansion building designed by C.W. Dickey, then later sold and heavily renovated, reopening in 1984 as a modern 456-room resort. A refurbishment that added a spa was completed in April 2003. Its signature oceanfront swimming pool boasts an orchid made from 1.25 million South African glass mosaic tiles that reflect the changing light. It's a splurge, though. ~ 2199 Kalia Road; 808-923-2311, 800-367-2343, fax 808-926-8004; www.halekulani.com. ULTRA-DELUXE.

blocks from the beach, this hotel also has one- and two-bedroom apartments available with full kitchens. ~ 415 Nahua Street; 808-922-1616, 800-922-7866, fax 808-922-6223; www.aston-hotels.com, e-mail hop@aston-hotels.com. MODERATE TO DELUXE.

Holiday Inn Waikiki, another good bargain, is easy walking distance from both Ala Moana Center and the beach. For the price, accommodations at this 17-story caravansary are relatively plush. Each room has air conditioning, television, telephone, decorations, carpeting, a shower-tub combination, a small refrigerator, a hair dryer, in-room coffee and an in-room safe. The room I saw was quite spacious and contained a king-size bed. There's also a fitness center. ~ 1830 Ala Moana Boulevard; 808-955-1111, 888-992-4545, fax 808-947-1799; www.waikiki.holiday-inn.com, e-mail holinnwk@pixi.com. MODERATE TO DELUXE.

The **Aston Waikiki Grand Hotel** is right across the street from lush Kapiolani Park. The standard rooms in this ten-story building are comfortable, pleasant places to park your bags. Downstairs there's a windswept lobby. ~ 134 Kapahulu Avenue; 808-923-1511, 800-922-7866, fax 808-922-8785; www.aston-hotels.com. MODERATE.

Leisure Resorts Honolulu is a modern, attractive complex of three low-slung buildings surrounding a garden and swimming pool. The rooms are decorated in a tropical theme with rattan furniture and come with all-electric kitchenette, telephone, TV and air conditioning. ~ 431 Nohonani Street; 808-923-7336, 800-634-6981, fax 808-923-1622; www.leisureindustries.com, e-mail rvalcourt@leisureresorts.com. MODERATE.

BABES IN TOW

Waikiki is the perfect place to vacation with your toddler. Was there ever a better sandbox for making sandcastles? For a gentle, no-wave swimming area head to **Kuhio Beach Park** (page 99) with its protected seawall. When you (or your little one) tire of the ocean, walk or take the number 4, 8, 19, 20 or 43 bus to the **Honolulu Zoo** (page 102) or the **Waikiki Aquarium** (page 99). **Kapiolani Park** (page 100) also has oodles of space to run and play tag. In the evening, you can always hire a babysitter from a bonded service (see "Traveling with Children" in Chapter One) for a night on the town.

The **Aston Coconut Plaza Hotel,** a ten-story highrise, has accommodations with kitchenettes; all guest rooms have refrigerators and microwaves; standard rooms have a wet bar. Decorated in Mexican tile and furnished with wicker, the rooms are attractively appointed. The lobby adds elements of elegance in the form of an open-air lounge and pool. Breakfast included. ~ 450 Lewers Street; 808-923-8828, 800-922-7866, fax 808-923-3473; www. aston-hotels.com, e-mail res.plz@aston-hotels.com. MODERATE.

The **Queen Kapiolani Hotel** is a 314-room facility that rises 19 stories above nearby Kapiolani Park. There's a spacious lobby, three floors of public rooms, several shops and a swimming pool here. The guest rooms are plainly decorated and modest in size. Located one block from the beach. ~ 150 Kapahulu Avenue; 808-922-1941, 800-367-2317, fax 808-922-2694; www.queenkapio lani.com, e-mail res@queenkapiolani.com. MODERATE TO ULTRA-DELUXE.

The **Hawaiiana Hotel** is an intimate, lowrise facility that offers a garden courtyard arrangement with rooms surrounding either of the hotel's two pools. Some of the rooms have a private lanai; all have wicker armoires, kitchenettes and pastel decor. ~ 260 Beach Walk; 808-923-3811, 800-367-5122, fax 808-926-5728; e-mail hawaiiana@lava.net. MODERATE TO DELUXE.

The OHANA **East** maintains a resort feel, even though it's a highrise city hotel just blocks from the beach. Many rooms are equipped with kitchenettes, including a refrigerator, sink and coffeemaker, and there's a Thai restaurant on-site. ~ 150 Kaiulani Avenue; 808-922-5353, 800-688-7444; www.ohanahotels.com. DELUXE TO ULTRA-DELUXE.

If you'd like to stay directly across the street from the beach, check into the **Aston Waikiki Circle Hotel.** This 14-story hotel-in-the-round has air-conditioned rooms at reasonable rates. Many have an ocean view, which is the main advantage here. ~ 2464 Kalakaua Avenue; 808-923-1571, 800-922-7866, fax 808-926-8024; www.aston-hotels.com. DELUXE TO ULTRA-DELUXE.

A small boutique hotel right across the street from the beach, the **Aston Waikiki Beachside Hotel** is the kind of place where the receptionist already knows your name when you first walk in the door. It's as if they were waiting for you. The rooms are small but attractively done in coordinated coral colors with Chinese screen paintings and furnishings. The ocean-facing rooms in front have a balcony with two chairs and a table, so guests can watch the parade of surfers and sun worshippers below. This place is popular with business travelers and couples. ~ 2452 Kalakaua Avenue; 808-931-2100, 800-922-7866, fax 808-931-2129; www.aston-hotels.com. ULTRA-DELUXE.

The Cabana at Waikiki is a lodging option for gay and lesbian visitors. The hotel has 15 nicely decorated one-bedroom suites, with queen beds in the bedroom and a queen sofa-bed in the living room. Rattan furnishings and Hawaiian prints convey a tropical feel. All suites have TV/VCR/stereos and microwave-equipped kitchenettes, complete with toasters and blenders. There is an eight-person jacuzzi for guest use. Continental breakfast is included. ~ 2551 Cartwright Road; 808-926-5555, 877-902-2121, fax 808-926-5566; www.cabana-waikiki.com, e-mail marlin800@aol.com. MODERATE TO DELUXE.

There are three attractive facilities on the edge of Waikiki that are removed from the crowds. The New Otani Kaimana Beach Hotel rests beside beautiful Sans Souci Beach in the shadow of Diamond Head. Its two restaurants and oceanside bar lend the feel of a big hotel, but the friendly staff and standard rooms create a family atmosphere. ~ 2863 Kalakaua Avenue; 808-923-1555, 800-356-8264, fax 808-922-9404; www.kaimana.com, e-mail rooms@kaimana.com. DELUXE.

There's a pleasantly personable feeling at W Honolulu-Diamond Head. Located at the foot of Diamond Head and Kapiolani Park, with 48 rooms spread out over 12 floors, the W will cater to your needs while allowing you privacy to enjoy their stunning views or play a quiet game of backgammon in the lobby. There's a bar and a restaurant, which serves Polynesian fare. ~ 2885 Kalakaua Avenue; 808-922-1700, 888-528-3465, fax 808-923-2249; www.starwood.com. ULTRA-DELUXE.

HIDDEN ▶ Another hotel is equally secluded from the bustle of Waikiki. Located even closer to the fabled crater, the Diamond Head Beach Hotel is an ultra-contemporary establishment. The rooms are done in a tasteful, Balinese-themed style, and many come with a kitchen. Located on the ocean, this 13-story facility is one of the most chic resting places around. ~ 2947 Kalakaua Avenue; 808-922-1928, 800-535-0085, fax 808-924-8980; www.marcresorts.com/diamondhead, e-mail marc@aloha.net. ULTRA-DELUXE.

The elegant **Magnolia at Waikiki,** formerly an apartment building, is now a quiet boutique inn about a block from the beach and surrounded by tropical gardens, fountains and a jacuzzi spa. Spacious one- and two-bedroom teak-furnished suites are available (550 square feet, not bad for a hotel suite), with balconies, living rooms, dining areas and fully-equipped kitchens. This is a place to settle in and stay awhile. ~ 2566 Cartwright Road; 808-387-6912, 888-777-9136, fax 808-926-8733; www.magnoliaat waikiki.com, e-mail info@magnoliaatwaikiki.com. ULTRA-DELUXE.

Offering over 2500 rooms, the **Hilton Hawaiian Village** is the largest resort in the islands and Waikiki's premier family hotel. The grounds provide a Disneyesque atmosphere that keeps children of all ages engaged—fireworks on Friday evening, shopping malls, restaurants and nightly entertainment, not to mention a penguin pool, flamingos, cockatoos and koi ponds. Seaside diversions include paddle boats, surfboards and sailing trips as well as numerous swimming pools to dip in, an acre of sand for sandcastle-making and an ocean of fun. Not to be overlooked, the rooms are attractively furnished and well-cared for and the service is friendly and welcoming. ~ 2005 Kalia Road; 808-949-4321, 800-221-2424, fax 808-947-7898; www.hiltonhawaiian village.com. ULTRA-DELUXE.

Waikiki was little more than a thatch-hut village when its first deluxe hotel went up in 1901. Today the **Sheraton Moana Surfrider Resort** retains the aura of those early days in its Colonial architecture and Victorian decor. Insist on a room in the main building with its traditional appointments and turn-of-the-20th-century ambience. Downstairs are restaurants, bars, a lobby filled

---

TROPICAL TREATMENTS

Papaya, Kona coffee, aloe vera gel, spirulina, *kukui* nut oil, pineapple, *noni*, seaweed and other exotic foods have left the buffet table and found their way into the Waikiki Beach Marriott Resort's spa, **Olakino Salon.** There they are used for unique massage, skin and nail treatments tenderly administered in a suitably tropical setting. You can also soak in a traditional Japanese *furo* bathtub, get your hair done by stylist Paul Brown or work out at the 24-hour gym if you can muster the energy. ~ 2552 Kalakaua Avenue; 808-922-6611, 800-367-5370; www.marriott waikiki.com.

with wicker furniture, and an ancient banyan tree beneath which Robert Louis Stevenson once wrote. A throwback to colonial times, tea is served every afternoon at the Banyan Veranda. ~ 2365 Kalakaua Avenue; 808-922-3111, 800-782-9488, fax 808-923-0308; www.starwood.com/hawaii. ULTRA-DELUXE.

The grand dame of Hawaiian hotels captures the sense of Old Hawaii. Built in 1927 and affectionately known as the "Pink Palace," the **Royal Hawaiian Hotel** is an elegant, Spanish Moorish–style building complete with colonnaded walkways and manicured grounds. This castle away from home is decorated in French provincial fashion and features a fabulous lobby bedecked with chandeliers. Adjacent to the original building is a 17-story tower that brings the room count to 675. Worth visiting even if you never check in. ~ 2259 Kalakaua Avenue; 808-923-7311, 800-782-9488, fax 808-924-7098; www.royal-hawaiian.com. ULTRA-DELUXE.

Ho hum. Another big, luxurious hotel property in Waikiki. But the **Waikiki Beach Marriott Resort**, with 1310 rooms, two swimming pools, shops and restaurants, has the ideal location, right on Waikiki Beach and within walking distance of several major attractions like the International Market Place, Diamond Head and Kapiolani Park. It also offers kids' programs, cultural activities, nightly Hawaiian entertainment and a snazzy spa with unique Polynesian treatments. ~ 2552 Kalakaua Avenue; 808-922-6611, 800-367-5370, fax 808-921-5255; www.marriott waikiki.com. ULTRA-DELUXE.

PEACEFULNESS THROUGH A BOWL OF TEA

Perhaps there's some truth in the idea that the way to the heart is through the stomach. The Japanese concept of *Chado* conveys its ideals (harmony, respect, purity and tranquility) through the practice of **tea ceremonies**. Followers of *Chado* preach that a world fraught with tension can be helped by the process of preparing the perfect cup of tea. All aspects of the preparation are important. The Way of Tea has been in existence since at least the 16th century, but only recently have the teachings gained wider acknowledgment. Hawaii hosts a branch of the Urasenke Foundation, the international society of *Chado*. They host tea ceremonies that are open to the public on Wednesday and Friday from 10 a.m. until 12 p.m. Stop by and give tea a chance. ~ 247 Saratoga Road; 808-923-3059, fax 808-923-3784.

The **Ambassador Hotel of Waikiki** is convenient and comfortable, with studios and one- to three-bedroom suites that have kitchens, although few other amenities. Off-season internet rates can run as low as $59 for a studio. ~ 2040 Kuhio Avenue; 808-941-7777, 800-923-2620, fax 808-951-3939; www.ambassador waikiki.com, e-mail reservations@ambassadorwaikiki.com. DE-LUXE TO ULTRA-DELUXE.

CONDOS

The **Royal Kuhio**, a good bet for families, is a 389-unit highrise two blocks from Waikiki Beach. One-bedroom units feature fully equipped kitchens and balconies with ocean or mountain views. Studios are $120; one-bedroom units are $140. ~ 2240 Kuhio Avenue; 808-923-0555, 800-927-0555, fax 808-923-0720; www.waikikicondos.com, e-mail info@waikikicondos.com.

Offering kitchenettes and balconies, the **Aston Pacific Monarch** has studio apartments from $155 to $175 and one-bedroom units from $185 to $225 for up to four. There is a rooftop pool, jacuzzi and sauna, and the beach is just two blocks away. ~ 2427 Kuhio Avenue; 808-923-9805, 800-922-7866, fax 808-924-3220; www.aston-hotels.com, e-mail res.pam@aston-hotels.com.

At the **Aston Waikiki Beach Tower**, all 140 units feature contemporary furniture, wetbars, kitchens and beautiful lanais. The kids will enjoy the pool and paddle tennis court. One-bedroom units begin at $540. Two-bedroom suites for up to six guests start at $640. ~ 2470 Kalakaua Avenue; 808-926-6400, 800-922-7866, fax 808-922-8785; www.aston-hotels.com, e-mail res.awt@ aston-hotels.com.

At **Winston's Waikiki Condos**, one-bedroom condos rent for $99 to $155 (lower monthly rates available) for one to four people. All suites are comfortably furnished with rattan furniture and feature lanais and full and complete kitchens. The units, just one block from the beach, are well-maintained and clean. Eight of the twenty-five units have washers and dryers. Patrick Winston offers special deals for *Hidden Oahu* readers, so make sure you call ahead and mention this book. He also offers an old-fashioned concierge and travel agency service to help you make the most of your stay. ~ 417 Nohonani Street, Suite 409; phone/fax 808-924-3332, 800-545-1948; www.winstonswaikikicondos. com, e-mail info@winstonswaikikicondos.com.

The **Outrigger Waikiki Shore** offers 107 studios and one- and two-bedroom units. These condos feature complete kitchens, washer/dryers and great views. Studios are $245 while one-bedroom units are $350. Two-bedroom units accommodating up to six cost $460 to $650. ~ 2161 Kalia Road; 808-971-4500, fax 808-971-4580; www.outrigger.com, e-mail wsr@outrigger.com.

At **Aston at the Waikiki Banyan** one-bedroom units are $215 to $260 for one to four people. These highrise ocean and mountain view units have full kitchens, rattan furniture and lanais. One block from the beach. ~ 201 Ohua Avenue; 808-922-0555, 800-922-7866, fax 808-922-0906; www.aston-hotels.com, e-mail res.ban@aston-hotels.com.

DINING

This tourist mecca is crowded with restaurants. Since the competition is so stiff, the cafés here are cheaper than anywhere else on the islands. There are numerous American restaurants serving moderately good food at modest prices, so diners looking for standard fare will have no problem. But as you're probably seeking something more exotic, I'll also list some interesting Asian, Hawaiian, health food and other offbeat restaurants.

If you decide to go to **Nick's Fishmarket**, plan on eating seafood. You have never seen such a list of fresh fish dishes. Not that much of it will seem familiar, but there is mahimahi, *opakapaka* and ahi. Or if you prefer to dine on something you recognize, how about shrimp scampi, abalone, lobster or scallops? The service is attentive. ~ 2070 Kalakaua Avenue; 808-955-6333; e-mail nick waikiki@aol.com. ULTRA-DELUXE.

Odoriko Japanese Restaurant offers traditional Japanese cuisine in a dining room that is often filled with Japanese nationals. The extensive menu, with over 100 entrées, includes sukiyaki, *shabu shabu*, *teishoku* and tempura, as well as many seafood dishes, sushi and sashimi. Early-bird specials help keep the prices down. ~ King's Village, 2400 Koa Avenue; 808-923-7368; www.kings-village.com/odoriko. MODERATE.

For a just-before-midnight snack—they close at 11:00—or to satisfy cravings for a hot bowl of noodle soup, you're never too far from an **Ezogiku**. Rub shoulders with Japanese tourists at the counter in one of these hole-in-the-wall eateries serving ramen in a variety of styles, including curry, pork and wonton. There are three locations to choose from in Waikiki. ~ 2420 Koa Avenue,

808-922-2473, fax 808-926-2207; 2546 Lemon Road, 808-923-2013; 2146 Kalakaua Avenue, 808-926-8616; www.ezogiku.com, e-mail info@ezogiku.com. BUDGET.

If you're hankering for sushi, the sushi bar at **Restaurant Suntory** is an excellent, often busy, choice. Or order traditional Japanese dishes and enjoy tableside preparation in the teppanyaki dining room. This third-floor restaurant prides itself on serving fresh island fish and locally grown organic produce; the atmosphere is charmingly authentic and elegant, but still comfortable enough for casual dining. ~ Royal Hawaiian Shopping Center, 2201 Kalakaua Avenue; 808-922-5511. MODERATE TO DELUXE.

To find an affordable meal on Kalakaua Avenue, the ocean-front strip, try the bottom floor of the **Waikiki Shopping Plaza**. Here about a dozen ethnic and American restaurants offer take-out food as well as full-course sitdown dinners. ~ 2250 Kalakaua Avenue; 808-923-1191, fax 808-922-4579. BUDGET.

The food is pretty standard fare at the Sheraton Waikiki's **Ocean Terrace** but the view deserves five stars. Set poolside next to the beach in one of the state's largest hotels, this open-air dining room provides a welcome means to dine on the water. Popular for breakfast, lunch and dinner, the evening menu centers around rotating theme buffets, such as prime rib and clam night, steak and seafood night and crab night. ~ 2255 Kalakaua Avenue; 808-922-4422 ext. 71777, fax 808-931-8530. ULTRA-DELUXE.

The **International Food Court**, tucked into the northwest corner of the International Market Place, features a cluster of food stands and a patio for dining beneath a banyan tree. Here you will

AUTHOR FAVORITE

Apart from the bustle of Waikiki but still right on the beach is the **Hau Tree Lanai**. Here beneath the interwoven branches of twin *hau* trees you can enjoy patio dining with a view that extends across Waikiki to the distant mountains. I favor the place for its breakfast (the French toast is delicious), but they also have a lunch and dinner menu that ranges from steamed vegetables to curried chicken to fresh island fish. In the evening the place is illuminated by torches, and soft breezes wisp off the water, adding to the enchantment. ~ New Otani Kaimana Beach Hotel, 2863 Kalakaua Avenue; 808-923-1555, fax 808-922-9404; www.kaimana. com. ULTRA-DELUXE.

find **Bautista's Filipino Kitchen** (808-923-7220), where the specialties include noodles, beef stew, mixed vegetables and menudo with green fish. **Peking Garden** (808-926-6060) has traditional Chinese dishes including beef and broccoli, chicken chop suey and eggplant with chicken. For Japanese and Korean food, go to **Choi's Kitchen** (808-923-5614), where *saimin* and chicken teriyaki are popular dishes. One of the better all-you-can-eat buffets is **J.R. Chinese Buffet Garden** (808-926-1488), with over 50 items representing myriad styles of Chinese cuisine, as well as salads and desserts galore. ~ 2330 Kalakaua Avenue. BUDGET.

On a balcony in the International Market Place, **Coconut Willy's Bar & Grill** has a dinner menu that includes a New York steak and shrimp platter, fish and chips, and mahimahi. There are also burgers, sandwiches and salads. Set beside the banyan tree that dominates the market, the place has a funky appeal. ~ 2330 Kalakaua Avenue; 808-923-9454, fax 808-923-0581. MODERATE.

For oceanfront dining, **The Beachwalk Cafe** is true to its name. With indoor and patio dining and a big buffet bar, it's a standard-fare American restaurant lacking in imagination but filled with beautiful views. Open for breakfast, lunch and dinner, the café serves steak, hamburgers and egg dishes, as well as offering a prime rib and crab leg dinner buffet. Ask for a table outside. ~ Sheraton Moana Surfrider Resort, 2365 Kalakaua Avenue; 808-922-3111, fax 808-924-4759; e-mail guy.villarosa@sheraton.com. DELUXE TO ULTRA-DELUXE.

Italian *and* Chinese? Sounds like an odd pairing, but **Ciao Mein's** hybrid menu is nonetheless delicious on both sides. On

CINEMA ALFRESCO

Drive-in movies are a thing of the past, but that doesn't mean you can't watch a film in the great outdoors. Few settings are more idyllic than Queen's Surf Beach, across from the Honolulu Zoo in Waikiki, where hit films are shown on a 30-foot screen several weekends each month. The Sunset on the Beach festivities start at 4 p.m. with a craft fair featuring the work of local artisans. Pick up some snacks or a plate lunch at one of the food booths and find a comfy spot on the sand or pier. Live music begins at about 4:30 p.m., followed by the movie at 6:30 p.m. Call 808-523-2489 or 808-923-1094 to find out what's playing and when.

the Chinese side try spicy kung pao chicken, Szechuan eggplant or the savory flavors of Mongolian sizzle. If you're craving Italian, start with the carpaccio followed by pasta in a light tomato basil sauce. Everything is served family style, which means shared dishes that make this a great place to go with kids or in a group. Located on the third floor of the Hyatt Regency Waikiki, the decor is Euro-chic. There is limited alfresco seating. ~ 2424 Kalakaua Avenue; 808-923-1234, fax 808-923-1025. ULTRA-DELUXE.

Fans whir overhead and a bar sits in the back; sheet music covers and old Matson oceanliner menus stand framed along the walls. Hard to believe someone would create this ambience for their restaurant, then name the place **Cheeseburger in Paradise.** But burgers it is, plus a selection of breakfast dishes for the morning. ~ 2500 Kalakaua Avenue; 808-923-3731, fax 808-923-1070; www.chzy-burger-waikiki.com, e-mail cipoahu@mauigateway.com. BUDGET TO MODERATE.

Innovative, high-quality cuisine and excellent service make the **Diamond Head Grill** one of Hawaii's best restaurants. The sesame and crab–crusted mahimahi is one of those oh-so-good dishes that makes you want to order it each time you visit. The refined and artful presentation is complemented by the eatery's New Age decor with deco highlights. Nightly jazz adds to the dining pleasure. No lunch. ~ W Honolulu hotel, 2885 Kalakaua Avenue; 808-922-3734, fax 808-791-5164; e-mail www.diamondheadgrill.com. ULTRA-DELUXE.

One of the ethnic restaurants most popular with local folks is **Keo's in Waikiki.** Fulfilling to all the senses, this intimate place is decorated with fresh flowers and tropical plants. The cuisine includes such Southeast Asian dishes as the "evil jungle prince," a sliced beef, shrimp or chicken entrée with coconut milk, fresh basil and red chili. You can choose from dozens of fish, shellfish, fowl and meat dishes. The menu offers a lot of variety, and is highly recommended. ~ 2028 Kuhio Avenue; 808-951-9355, fax 808-734-4652; www.keosthaicuisine.com, e-mail keos@keosthaicuisine.com. MODERATE TO DELUXE.

Seafood is served up in predictable but tasty ways at **Lewers Street Fish Company,** a casual, 1950s-style eatery that offers big portions and modest prices. Alongside the fish, you'll find steak, teriyaki chicken, and pasta prepared tableside. The yummy rolls and desserts come from their own bakery. This family restaurant

has a special kid's menu. ~ 247 Lewers Street; 808-971-1000.
BUDGET TO MODERATE.

Davey Jones Ribs serves pizza and pasta dishes as well as seafood and chicken. Informal and lively. ~ 250 Lewers Street; 808-923-7427, fax 808-922-7001. MODERATE.

Favored by both tourists and locals for its low prices, **Seaside Bar & Grill** has a budget-priced early-bird special nightly until 8 p.m. Choose any two items—lobster tail, crab legs, mahimahi, fried shrimp or New York steak—and they'll throw in a house salad as well. The fish is frozen and the place is actually two blocks from the "seaside," but for low-rent dining it's worth considering. Breakfast and dinner only. ~ 2256 Kuhio Avenue; 808-922-8227, fax 808-922-8166. BUDGET.

An L-shaped counter with swivel chairs is the most decor you can expect at **Fatty's Chinese Kitchen**. The prices on plate lunches and dinners are a throwback, too. With dozens of choices, including many "noodle in soup" dishes, Fatty aims to suit every palate. ~ Kuhio Mall, 2345 Kuhio Avenue; 808-922-9600. BUDGET.

The blue skies and green palms of the Caribbean never seem far away in Hawaii, and they feel even closer at **Cha Cha Cha Restaurant**. With its tropical color scheme and festive decor, this "Caribe/Mex" eatery serves up Mexican dishes such as burritos, tacos and quesadillas prepared Caribbean style with unusual spices and sauces. ~ 342 Seaside Avenue; 808-923-7797, fax 808-926-7007. BUDGET TO MODERATE.

A LITTLE CORN WITH YOUR POI

A visit to Hawaii isn't complete without attending a luau, although the tourist versions bear little resemblance to the real thing. Still, they're entertaining and a chance to try foods cooked in a traditional underground oven, or *imu*. The feast centers around a whole pig, and you'll also likely be served poi (no, it isn't like paste), *lomi* salmon, *laulau*, chicken and fish, along with modern salads and rice. The music and hula dancing is usually the energetic Tahitian style, and be prepared for some corny jokes and the chance to try hula yourself. The mai tais are usually free and strong, so go easy or you may end up with your head in the *haupia* (coconut pudding) by night's end. Germaine's Luau at the Campbell Industrial Park is a classic, or book one at the Polynesian Cultural Center or through a Waikiki resort.

A great place for breakfast, the **Waikiki Broiler** has inexpensive specials every morning. Dining is outdoors under thatched umbrellas or in a dining room with an outdoor feel. It's on a busy corner so the atmosphere is not exactly idyllic, but it's hard to match the prices—at dinner you can enjoy teriyaki steak, scallop and chicken entrées. ~ 200 Lewers Street; 808-923-8836, fax 808-924-3316. BUDGET TO DELUXE.

Perry's Smorgy, with its two locations—at the OHANA Coral Seas Hotel and on Kuhio Avenue—has an inexpensive buffet at dinner, lunch and breakfast. With an extensive salad bar, plus a host of meat and fish platters, this all-you-can-eat emporium is hard to beat. I'd suggest the OHANA branch; it's two blocks from the beach. ~ OHANA Coral Seas Hotel, 250 Lewers Street, 808-922-8814; and also at 2380 Kuhio Avenue, 808-926-0184, phone/fax 808-922-1907; www.perryshawaii.com, e-mail perrys restaurants@hotmail.com. BUDGET TO MODERATE.

Italian specialties at affordable prices draw nightly crowds to **Arancino's**. The place has the feel of a New York–style bistro, with excellent, home-style standards like eggplant parmigiana that are worth the likely 20-minute wait. The generous appetizer portions can easily become dinner. ~ 255 Beach Walk; 808-923-5557, fax 808-922-0105; www.arancino.net, e-mail info@arancino.net. BUDGET TO MODERATE.

Dishes like macadamia nut–crusted *opakapaka* and marinated rack of lamb make **Bali by the Sea** a special favorite. Plush seating, nautical lamps, fresh flowers and soft ocean breezes add to the charm of this elegant restaurant. Dress code. Closed Sunday. ~ Hilton Hawaiian Village, 2005 Kalia Road; 808-949-4321, fax 808-947-7926. ULTRA-DELUXE.

The **Shore Bird Beach Broiler** is a beachfront dining room that's a great place to enjoy a reasonably priced dinner and an ocean view. This is a cook-your-own-food facility that offers hand-carved steaks, fresh fish, teriyaki chicken and barbecued ribs. One of the best bargains on Waikiki Beach, the Shore Bird is inevitably crowded, so try to dine early. ~ Reef Hotel, 2169 Kalia Road; 808-922-2887, fax 808-923-8811. MODERATE TO DELUXE.

It's not surprising that Waikiki's most fashionable hotel, the Halekulani, contains one of the district's finest restaurants. Situated on an open-air balcony overlooking the ocean, **La Mer** has a reputation for elegant dining in intimate surroundings. French-inspired dishes include confit tomato with truffle juice and fried basil and fillet of *kumu* in a rosemary salt crust with mushrooms, vegetables and an herb butter sauce. Add the filigree woodwork and sumptuous surroundings and La Mer is one of the island's most attractive waterfront dining rooms. Formal attire required. Dinner only. ~ 2199 Kalia Road; 808-923-2311, fax 808-926-8004; www.halekulani.com. ULTRA-DELUXE.

Downstairs from La Mer is **Orchids**, serving a mix of Hawaiian and Continental cuisine like crispy *moano* on tomato confit, sautéed *onaga* filet and roasted veal chops. Orchids is open for breakfast, lunch, dinner and Sunday brunch. ~ 2199 Kalia Road; 808-923-2311, fax 808-926-8004; www.halekulani.com. ULTRA-DELUXE.

Die-hard rock-and-roll fans will enjoy eating at the **Hard Rock Cafe**, with its collection of guitars, clothes, concert posters and other memorabilia donated by rock stars decorating the walls. It's a spacious, airy place that tends to get noisy during happy hour. The food is as all-American as the decor, with burgers, barbecue ribs and chicken served until midnight. ~ 1837 Kapiolani Boulevard; 808-955-7383. BUDGET.

GROCERIES The best grocery store in Waikiki is also the biggest. Prices at **The Food Pantry** are inflated, but not as much as elsewhere in this tourist enclave. ~ 2370 Kuhio Avenue; 808-923-9831. There are also two smaller groceries: **Ala Wai Pantry** ~ 2211 Ala Wai Boulevard, 808-922-2818; and **Food Pantry** ~ 444 Hobron Lane, 808-947-3763.

ABC Discount Stores, a chain of sundry shops with branches all around Waikiki, are convenient, but have a very limited stock and even higher prices.

If you are willing and able to shop outside Waikiki, you'll generally fare much better price-wise. Try the **Foodland** supermarket in the Ala Moana Center just outside Waikiki. Cheaper than Waikiki groceries, it's still more expensive than Greater Honolulu stores. ~ 1450 Ala Moana Boulevard; 808-949-5044, fax 808-949-5869.

Also in the Ala Moana Center, **Vim N Vigor** has a variety of vitamins, supplements and health foods, as well as a juice bar and lunch counter. ~ 1450 Ala Moana Boulevard; 808-955-3600, fax 808-941-1995; www.vimnvigor.com.

This tourist mecca is a great place to look but not to buy. Browsing the busy shops is like studying a catalog of Hawaiian handicrafts. It's all here. You'll find everything but bargains. With a few noteworthy exceptions, the prices include the unofficial tourist surcharges that merchants worldwide levy against visitors. Windowshop Waikiki, but plan on spending your shopping dollars elsewhere.

SHOPPING

One Waikiki shopping area I do recommend is **Duke's Lane**. This alleyway, running from Kalakaua Avenue to Kuhio Avenue near the International Market Place, may be the best place in all Hawaii to buy jade jewelry. Either side of the lane is flanked by mobile stands selling rings, necklaces, earrings, stick pins, bracelets and more. It's a prime place to barter for tiger's eyes, opals and mother-of-pearl pieces.

The main shopping scene is in the malls. **Waikiki Shopping Plaza** has five floors of stores and restaurants. Here are jewelers, sundries and boutiques, plus specialty shops like **Waldenbooks**, with an excellent line of magazines as well as paperbacks and bestsellers. ~ 2250 Kalakaua Avenue; 808-922-4154.

The **Royal Hawaiian Shopping Center** is a four-story complex that runs for two blocks along Kalakaua Avenue, from Lewers Street to the Outrigger Waikiki. On the *makai* side (facing the ocean), it fronts the grounds of the Royal Hawaiian and the Sheraton Waikiki. It is Waikiki's largest mall and features Euro-American designer boutiques, upscale shops, numerous restaurants and fast-food kiosks, as well as an indoor shooting gallery

AUTHOR FAVORITE

If you're in the market for a ukulele, stop by **The Ukulele House**, which carries everything from children's souvenir ukes for $10–$20 to musically playable instruments ranging from $80 all the way to $2000-plus for vintage models. This world-famous supplier of vintage and unique ukuleles is also home of the world's largest ukulele. If you would like to try playing a ukulele on your visit to Hawaii, you can take free lessons here. Free lessons are also offered at the Orchid Court on the third floor of the Royal Hawaiian Shopping Center on Tuesdays and Thursdays. ~ Royal Hawaiian Shopping Center, 2233 Kalakaua Avenue; 808-923-8587, fax 808-924-8587.

and showroom. A weekly schedule of Hawaiiana and other cultural performances provides an entertaining respite from the pressures of shopping. One of Waikiki's more unique shops is in the center. Check out the **Little Hawaiian Crafts Shop** (808-926-2662, fax 808-924-7874) on the third floor, where you'll find an interesting selection of traditional and contemporary Hawaiian crafts including carved *koa* wood bowls, Niihau shell leis, Hawaiian quilts, ceramics and glassware. ~ 2233 Kalakaua Avenue.

Then there's **King's Village**, a mock Victorian town that suggests how Britain might have looked had the 19th-century English invented polyethylene. The motif may be trying to appear antiquated, but the prices are unfortunately quite contemporary. ~ 131 Kaiulani Avenue at Kalakaua Avenue.

International Market Place is my favorite browsing spot. With tiny shops and vending stands spotted around the sprawling grounds, it's a relief from the claustrophobic shopping complexes. There's an old banyan spreading across the market, plus thatched treehouses, a carp pond, brick sidewalks and woodfront stores. You won't find many bargains, but the sightseeing is priceless. ~ 2330 Kalakaua Avenue.

The **Waikiki Trade Center** is another strikingly attractive mall. With an air of Milanese splendor about it, this glass-and-steel complex is a maze of mirrors. In addition to the stained-glass windows and twinkling lights, there are several worthwhile shops. ~ Kuhio and Seaside avenues.

A nice selection of shops are located in the **Hyatt Regency Waikiki**. This triple-tiered arcade is *the* place to look when you are seeking the very best. Glamour and style are passwords around here. There are fine-art shops, designer apparel stores, gem shops

---

ISLAND SOUL

When visiting the islands, be sure to sample some of Hawaii's local talent. Many of these musicians—Keola Beamer, Kealii Reichel, Henry Kapono, Olomana and the Brothers Cazimero to name a few—may be playing at a local club. Consult the daily newspapers, or tune in to **KCCN** at 1420 on the radio dial. This all-Hawaiian station is the home of island soul.

and shops that feature made-in-Hawaii products. ~ 2424 Kalakaua Avenue.

Hilton Hawaiian Village contains the **Rainbow Bazaar**, an array of shops spread around the grounds of Hawaii's largest resort complex. This plaza contains a number of stores specializing in island fashions, plus gift shops and import emporia. The shopping center has been designed in Oriental style, with curving tile roofs and brilliantly painted roof beams. You can stroll along an Asian arcade, past lofty banyan trees and flowering gardens, to stores filled with rare art and Far Eastern antiquities. ~ 2005 Kalia Road.

Island-based **Local Motion** has opened an architecturally distinguished flagship shop for its line of logowear and sporting gear, including surfboards, body boards and backpacks. ~ 1958 Kalakaua Avenue; 808-979-7873.

Island Treasures Antique Mall has Waikiki's best selection of Hawaiiana in a multilevel complex that's home to a number of individual vendors. Fun for browsing and a purchase if you find something priced right. The shops open in the early afternoon and stay open until 10 p.m., which makes it a good tie-in with an evening stroll. Closed Monday. ~ 2145 Kuhio Avenue; 808-922-8223.

Looking for a vintage silk shirt? Those famous Hawaiian styles, like the one Montgomery Clift sported in *From Here to Eternity*, are among the alluring items at **Bailey's Antiques and Aloha Shirts**. If an original silky is beyond your means, they also have reproductions as well as collectibles like Zippo lighters. ~ 517 Kapahulu Avenue; 808-734-7628; e-mail baileysantiques@webtv.net.

Peggy's Picks ranges from Hawaiiana to an eclectic array of collectibles at affordable prices. ~ 732 Kapahulu Avenue; 808-737-3297.

Hawaii has a strong musical tradition, kept alive by excellent groups performing their own compositions as well as old Polynesian songs. I'm not talking about the "Blue Hawaii"–"Tiny Bubbles"–"Beyond the Reef" medleys that draw tourists in droves, but *real* Hawaiian music as performed by Hapa, the Brothers Cazimero, Keola and Kapono Beamer, Marlene Sai, Melveen Leed and others.

NIGHTLIFE

If you spend any time in Honolulu, don't neglect to check out such authentic sounds. One or more of these musicians will probably be playing at a local club. Consult the daily newspapers.

Over at **Nick's Fishmarket** there's live entertainment nightly. Expect to hear light rock, jazz, soul or blues while munching on half-price *pupus*. ~ 2070 Kalakaua Avenue; 808-955-6333, fax 808-946-0478; e-mail nickwaikiki@aol.com.

On Friday and Saturday nights, a contemporary Hawaiian group stars at the **Paradise Lounge**. Other forms of live entertainment are offered nightly. Choose between table or lounge seating in this carpeted club, which is decorated with Hawaiian landscapes painted by local artists. ~ Hilton Hawaiian Village, 2005 Kalia Road; 808-949-4321, fax 808-947-7926.

The **Esprit Nightclub** is a congenial spot situated right on Waikiki Beach. This cozy club features bands that play music from different eras Tuesday through Saturday, has special guests on Sunday and Monday and offers spectacular ocean views every night of the week. ~ Sheraton Waikiki Hotel, 2255 Kalakaua Avenue; 808-922-4422, fax 808-923-8785.

Two groups perform mellow Hawaiian music nightly at the **Shorebird** at the Outrigger Reef: one in the restaurant, the other in the lounge. ~ Outrigger Reef, 2169 Kalia Road; 808-922-2887.

Tired of the old nine-to-five grind? For a change of pace try **Scruples**, where the schedule is eight to four. 8 p.m. to 4 a.m. that is. Promising "dance and romance," this popular nightspot features dancing to Top-40 tunes. Cover and two-drink minimum. ~ 2310 Kuhio Avenue; 808-923-9530, fax 808-926-8804.

The first thing you'll see upon entering the Radisson Waikiki Prince Kuhio is **Cupid's Lobby Bar**. The lounge area features trop-

AUTHOR FAVORITE

Duke's Canoe Club in the Outrigger Waikiki offers a beachfront setting, a distant view of Diamond Head, and plenty of atmosphere. Duke refers to Duke Kahanamoku, the Olympic swimming champion and surfer who helped restore surfing to a position of cultural prominence. The decor documents his career with archival photography and memorabilia. It draws overflowing crowds, particularly on weekends and Sunday afternoons when Henry Kapono performs. ~ Outrigger Waikiki, 2335 Kalakaua Avenue; 808-922-2268, fax 808-923-4204.

ical palms, tapestries, rock walls and a small mirrored bar. Order drinks and *pupus* while enjoying nightly vocalists. An outdoor garden is adjacent. ~ 2500 Kuhio Avenue; 808-922-0811, fax 808-921-5583.

The Cellar specializes in dancing, with Top-40 hits spun by a deejay Tuesday through Sunday. It's a top spot for a hot night. Closed Monday, except during summer. Cover. ~ 205 Lewers Street; 808-923-9952.

Nearby, **Waikiki Broiler** has karaoke Tuesday through Sunday. ~ 200 Lewers Street at Kalia Road; 808-923-8836.

Coconut Willy's Bar & Grill, situated on a balcony in the International Market Place, has a live band that starts in the afternoon and continues on into the night. The 35-and-over crowd turns out to dance to '50s and '60s classics as well as Hawaiian and country tunes. Attractive setting. ~ 2330 Kalakaua Avenue; 808-923-9454, fax 808-923-0581.

Eurasia Night Club and Sports Bar has nightly deejays spinning hip-hop, Top-40 and R&B. The shows are broadcast live on KQMQ 93.1 FM and I94 93.9 FM on Friday and Saturday. Every night but Saturday is 18-and-over college night; Thursday is Latin night (salsa lessons are available). Cover. ~ Hawaiian Regent Hotel, 2552 Kalakaua Avenue; 808-921-5335, fax 808-926-2742.

If you like sophisticated jazz to accompany dinner or drinks, the **Diamond Head Grill** is the place to go. The vocalists and musicians are first rate, and the decibel level is suitable for either concentrating on the music, conversation or food, which is some of the best in the Islands. ~ W Honolulu hotel, 2885 Kalakaua Avenue; 808-922-3734, fax 808-791-5164; www.diamondheadgrill.com.

Cruise into **Wave Waikiki** and catch a deejay spinning hip-hop, house and dance music Sunday through Thursday nights. Rock bands take the stage Friday and Saturday. Cover after 10 p.m. ~ 1877 Kalakaua Avenue; 808-941-0424.

With room for 300 of your closest friends, **Moose McGillycuddy's** is a prime place to dance to live bands Monday through Saturday. Deejays also spin Top-40 music. Known for its weird pictures, this establishment is easily spotted. Just look for the only building on Lewers Street sporting a stuffed moose head. Occasional cover. ~ 310 Lewers Street; 808-923-0751; www.moosemcgillycuddys.com, e-mail honomoose@aol.com.

For an authentic *tourist* experience accompanied by a genuine aloha spirit, join the busloads of Waikiki visitors who are caravanned to Barbers Point for **Germaine's Luau,** the ultimate in Hawaiian kitsch. At Germaine's you'll get to witness the unearthing ceremony of a pig from its underground *imu* (oven), dine on Hawaiian-style food and watch Polynesian dancers (or join them on stage), all at a beachfront site as the sun sets on the Pacific. Closed Monday from January through April and September through December. ~ 808-949-6626, 800-367-5655, fax 808-949-4218; www.germainesluau.com.

GAY SCENE   The gay scene is centered around several clubs on Waikiki's Kuhio Avenue and in Eaton Square, near the corner of Eaton and Hobron streets, not far away.

Club goers hang in and out at **Angles Waikiki,** where a bar in the center of the room provides a place to socialize, as does the lanai outside. There are pool tables and videos, as well as a dancefloor. Every Wednesday, crowds compete for cash prizes in the Best Chest/Best Buns contest, and In-trigued, an all-male revue, entertains on Thursday and Sunday nights. ~ 2256 Kuhio Avenue; 808-926-9766; e-mail angles.waikiki@juno.com.

Fusion Waikiki is another gay club open until 4 a.m. This hot spot taking up the second and third floors of the Paradise Building features dancing to house and underground deejay music. There are male strip shows and female impersonation performances on Friday and Saturday. Cover. ~ 2260 Kuhio Avenue; 808-924-2422.

Near Diamond Head, **Hula's Bar and Lei Stand,** with an ocean view and a disco complete with strobe-lit dancefloor and videos, rocks nightly until 2 a.m. ~ Waikiki Grand Hotel, 134 Kapahulu Avenue; 808-923-0669.

Tucked away in the back of Eaton Square, a little hideaway off Ala Moana Boulevard, **P-10A,** a private coffee bar that gives gay guys an alternative place to meet. It's an alcohol- and smoke-free relaxing retreat, serving coffee and tea. For entertainment there are video games, X-rated movies and, most importantly, conversation in this low-key, quiet hangout. Although it's a private club, it costs no more than a night at a bar. Open from 6 p.m. weekdays and 24 hours from Friday to Monday morning; there's live entertainment Friday and Saturday nights. Cover. ~ Eaton Square, Hobron and Eaton streets; 808-942-8536.

Next door, the exclusively gay **Michaelangelo** serves up $2 beer and well drinks to a mix of locals and tourists. There's pool, darts and video games to pass the time at this relaxed cruise bar. ~ Eaton Square, Hobron and Eaton streets; 808-951-0008.

Dance any night of the week 'til 4 a.m. to deejay-spun house, disco and hip-hop mixes at **Venus Nightclub**. They feature a male revue and female impersonators. Cover. ~ 1349 Kapiolani Boulevard; 808-951-8671.

At a private showing in the **Douglas Simonson Studio** you can view this internationally known artist's paintings and drawings of male nudes. Call for an appointment and directions. ~ 808-737-6275.

WAIKIKI BEACH Famous all over the world, the strand in Waikiki is actually several beaches in one. Kahanamoku Beach, Fort DeRussy Beach, Royal-Moana Beach, Kuhio Beach Park and Queen's Surf form an unbroken string that runs from the Ala Wai Canal to Diamond Head Crater. Together they comprise Waikiki Beach. Since going to the beach in this busy enclave also means exploring Waikiki itself, I have placed the beach descriptions in the sightseeing section on the preceding pages.

**BEACHES
& PARKS**

FIVE

Downtown Honolulu

While the Neighbor Islands and rural Oahu still move at a leisurely, laidback pace, downtown Honolulu marches to a different drummer. As the political and commercial heart of Hawaii and the center of the only major metropolis in all of Polynesia, it plays a role far more vital than its compact size would seem to warrant.

The state, county and city government offices can all be found here, as can the headquarters of the companies that control Hawaii and whose influence reaches well beyond its shores to both the U.S. mainland and Asia. Honolulu's importance as a city has a long history, one that is partially told in its many historic buildings.

The development of Honolulu received a major boost when King Kamehameha III moved his capital from Lahaina to Honolulu in the 1840s. Although the missionaries had already established themselves in the area, it was at about this time that they began to build the church and houses that can still be seen today. As sugar developed as an agricultural industry and a cash economy took hold, the companies that were created to handle this business chose Honolulu as their headquarters.

A walk through the downtown area is a journey into the city's history. Begin at the old mission houses, now the Mission Houses Museum, and stroll past Kawaihao Church and Iolani Palace. Continue on to Merchant Street, with its 19th- and early-20th-century brick buildings, which once housed the city's financial district and headquarters for the "Big Five" companies that controlled Hawaii's economy. Wander through Chinatown past crowded restaurants adorned with ducks hanging in the windows and herbal medicine shops lined with jars and drawers of leaves, twigs, bark and flowers.

Walk down by the waterfront, where Matson Line luxury steamers delivered the first tourists and gave birth to another industry, one which still keeps Hawaii's economy thriving today. And finally, ride the elevator to the top of the Aloha Tower for a bird's-eye view of the highrise office buildings that define downtown Honolulu today.

A fitting place to begin your tour is among the oldest homes in the islands. The buildings at the **Mission Houses Museum** seem to be borrowed from a New England landscape, and in a sense they were. The Frame House, a trim white wooden structure, was cut on the East Coast and shipped around the Horn to Hawaii. That was back in 1821, when this Yankee-style building was used to house missionary families.

Like the nearby Chamberlain House and Depository and other structures here, the Frame House represents one of the missionaries' earliest centers in Hawaii. It was in 1820 that Congregationalists arrived in the islands; they immediately set out to build and proselytize. In 1831, they constructed the Chamberlain House and Depository from coral and used it as the mission store. The neighborhood's Printing Office, built of the same durable material ten years later, was used by the first press ever to print in the Hawaiian language. The Mission Houses complex tells much about the missionaries, who converted Hawaiian into a written language, then proceeded to rewrite the entire history of the islands. The museum is run by the Hawaiian Mission Children's Society. Guided tours daily. Closed Sunday and Monday. Admission. ~ 553 South King Street; 808-531-0481, fax 808-545-2280; e-mail mhm@lava.net.

Opposite, at South King and Punchbowl streets, is the **Kawaihao Church**. This imposing edifice required 14,000 coral blocks for its construction. Completed in 1842, it has been called the Westminster Abbey of Hawaii because coronations and funerals for Hawaiian kings and queens were once conducted here. Services are still performed in Hawaiian and English every Sunday at 10:30 a.m.; attending them is not only a way to view the church interior, but also provides a unique cultural perspective on contemporary Hawaiian life. Also note that the tomb of King Lunalilo rises in front of the church, and behind the church lies the cemetery where early missionaries and converted Hawaiians were buried.

Across South King Street, the brick structure with stately white pillars is the **Mission Memorial Building**, constructed in 1916 to honor those same early church leaders. The nearby Renaissance-style building with the tile roof is **Honolulu Hale,** the City Hall. You might want to venture into the central courtyard, an open-air plaza surrounded by stone columns.

As you continue walking along South King Street in a westerly direction toward the center of Honolulu, **Iolani Palace** will appear on your right. Built for King Kalakaua in 1882, this stunning Renaissance-style mansion served as a royal residence until Queen Liliuokalani was overthrown in 1893. Later the ill-starred monarch was imprisoned here; eventually, after Hawaii became a territory of the United States, the palace was used as the capitol building. Guided tours (running every half hour from 9 a.m. to 2 p.m.) lead you past the *koa* staircases, the magnificent chandeliers and the Corinthian columns that lend a touch of European grandeur to this splendid building. Cotton shoe covers are provided by docents to protect the floors (and, conveniently, to shine them as you tour the Palace). You'll be led through the crimson and gold throne room, where the original thrones reside. Royal receptions and balls were held here, as well as Queen Liliuokalani's trial in 1895. The tour winds its way through the residence, past reception areas and dining rooms, royal living quarters and guest rooms. Although the paintings, furnishings and precious Hawaiian artifacts are ample, sometimes it's the trivia that's most interesting: notice the telephone mounted on the wall of the King's Library—it's one of Honolulu's first. In fact, the Palace installed electricity several years before the White House got around to it.

The land around the Palace was significant to the Hawaiian people even before the royalty set up house. A Hawaiian temple stood here until it was probably destroyed in 1819. King Kamehameha III relocated his court from Lahaina to this location in 1845. After his residence was torn down, the current palace incarnation was constructed. Reservations are highly recommended. Closed Sunday and Monday. ~ Corner of King and Richards streets; 808-522-0832; www.iolanipalace.org.

Also located on the palace grounds are the **Iolani Barracks,** where the Royal Household Guards were stationed, and the **Coronation Pavilion,** upon which the King was crowned. You can tour the palace grounds for free, but there's an admission charge for the building. Reservations are strongly advised; children under five are not allowed. Tours are given Tuesday through Saturday.

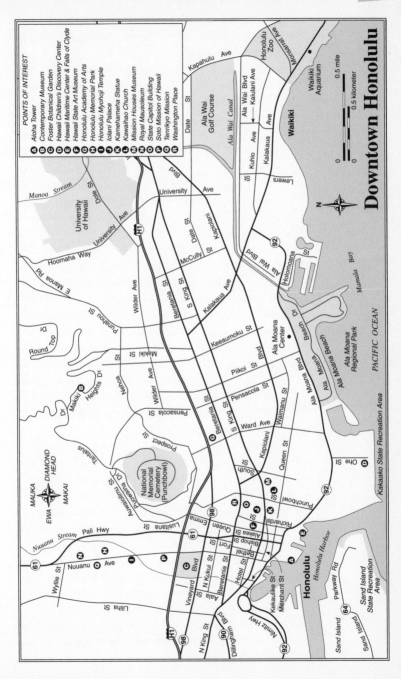

Downtown Honolulu

POINTS OF INTEREST

- Ⓐ Aloha Tower
- Ⓑ Contemporary Museum
- Ⓒ Foster Botanical Garden
- Ⓓ Hawaii Children's Discovery Center
- Ⓔ Hawaii Maritime Center & Falls of Clyde
- Ⓕ Hawaii State Art Museum
- Ⓖ Honolulu Academy of Arts
- Ⓗ Honolulu Memorial Park
- Ⓘ Honolulu Myohoji Temple
- Ⓙ Iolani Palace
- Ⓚ Kamehameha Statue
- Ⓛ Kawaiahao Church
- Ⓜ Mission Houses Museum
- Ⓝ Royal Mausoleum
- Ⓞ Soto Mission of Hawaii
- Ⓟ State Capitol Building
- Ⓠ Tenrikyo Mission
- Ⓡ Washington Place

0   0.5 mile

0   0.5 kilometer

Closed Sunday and Monday. ~ South King and Richards streets; 808-522-0832, fax 808-532-1051; www.iolanipalace.org, e-mail kanaina@iolanipalace.org.

Directly across the street rises the **Kamehameha Statue**, honoring Hawaii's first king. A huge gilt-and-bronze figure cast in Italy, it is covered with flower leis on special occasions. The spear-carrying warrior wears a feather cape and helmet. Behind him stands **Aliiolani Hale**, better known as the Judiciary Building, home to Hawaii's Supreme Court. Back in the days of the monarchy, it served as the House of Parliament. Docent-led tours of the Judiciary History Center are available Monday through Friday. ~ 808-539-4999, fax 808-539-4996; www.jhchawaii.org, e-mail jhc@aloha.net.

The Iolani Palace (*iolani* means "bird of heaven" in Hawaiian) is the only royal residence on American soil.

Behind Iolani Palace is the **State Capitol Building**. Unlike the surrounding structures, this is an ultramodern building, completed in 1969. Encircled by flared pillars that resemble palm trees, the capitol represents a variety of themes. Near the entrance there's a statue of Father Damien, who died of leprosy on Molokai Island, and Queen Liliuokalani, Hawaii's last reigning monarch. The House and Senate chambers are designed in a cone shape to resemble volcanoes, and the open-air courtyard is a commentary on the state's balmy weather. Tours of the capitol building and the legislature are given Monday through Friday. ~ Bounded by South Beretania, Richards and Punchbowl streets; 808-586-0178, fax 808-586-0046.

Since 1967 the State of Hawaii has set aside a percentage of revenues to fund the State Foundation on Culture and the Arts. The result is an art collection grown to more than 5000 pieces ranging from fabrics to paintings, glasswork to bronze sculpture. Art from the collection is exhibited in 285 buildings throughout the State. To provide a museum setting for a portion of the collection, the State purchased the historic Richard Street YMCA, a noteworthy 1920s architectural monument across the street from Iolani Palace, and created **Hawaii State Art Museum**, with three galleries on the second floor offering a total of 12,000 square feet of exhibit space. The museum opened in 2002, adding another cultural attraction to downtown Honolulu. Closed Sunday and Monday. ~ One Capitol District Building; 808-586-0307; www.state.hi.us/sfca.

Washington Place, the governor's residence, is steeped in history. Captain John Dominis began construction in 1846, but never got to live here because he died at sea (on an ill-fated journey to buy furniture) before the house was completed four years later. His famous daughter-in-law, however, made the house a palace. Queen Liliuokalani was living in Washington Place when she was overthrown, marking the end of the Hawaiian monarchy. When she was released from prison, she returned to Washington Place despite several other more comfortable living options. It has been speculated that her residence here was an act of politics and bravery: the home was cramped—at least by royal standards— but located near the new government's center of power. She did not, it would appear, wish to be forgotten. Washington Place has continued to serve its government over the years, providing living quarters for 12 governors and their families. The home has collected an eclectic assortment of furnishings, with a decor that focuses on the Queen but acknowledges the other subsequent inhabitants. ~ 320 South Beretania Street; 808-586-0240.

St. Andrews Cathedral, thought to be the only example of French-Gothic architecture in Hawaii, was erected in 1862 of stone shipped from England. The cathedral's eight bells have the names of eight Hawaiian monarchs and the dates of their reigns engraved on them, and can perform 40,320 different melodic changes. As if that wasn't enough of a claim to fame, the organ is the second largest in Hawaii. Sunday mass, including the hymns, is conducted in Hawaiian. ~ Beretania and Alakea streets; 808-524-2822, fax 808-537-4177; www.saintandrews-hi.org, e-mail standrewc001@hawaii.rr.com.

The outstanding **Honolulu Academy of Arts** often displays author James Michener's collection of woodblocks from Japan. There are also works by European, Asian and American masters, as well as important art by local painters and sculptors. A pavilion houses diverse exhibits while other galleries focus on the East meeting the West. Several elegantly landscaped courtyards add to the beauty. Closed Monday. Admission. ~ 900 South Beretania Street; 808-532-8700, fax 808-532-8787; www.honoluluacademy.org, e-mail academypr@honoluluacademy.org.

Let the kids burn off some steam at the 38,000-square-foot **Hawaii Children's Discovery Center**. Four major galleries sponsor interactive exhibits that are hands-on and educational (for example, "Fantastic You" will teach kids everything they need to know about the human body), but don't worry, they'll never catch on. You can picnic (or nap) at the park across the street. Be fore-warned: the Center does not accommodate strollers (although it is wheelchair accessible), so bring a carrier. Closed Monday. Admission. ~ 111 Ohe Street; 808-524-5437, fax 808-524-5400; www.discoverycenterhawaii.org.

WATERFRONT   For a tour of Honolulu's waterfront, head down Richards Street from the State Capitol Building toward Pier 7. Next to the **Aloha Tower Marketplace**, a festive market bazaar with shops, food and music, the imposing and historic **Falls of Clyde** lies berthed. A completely restored century-old sailing ship, the *Falls of Clyde* is reputedly the only fully rigged four-masted ship in the world. In the old days it was used to carry sugar and oil across the Pacific. Honolulu was then a harbor filled with tall-masted ships, so crowded at the dock that they bumped one an-other's gunwales. Part of this proud fleet, the *Falls of Clyde* was built in Scotland and sailed halfway round the world. For a single admission charge you can tour this marvelous piece of floating history and view the **Hokulea**, a double-hulled canoe that has sailed several times to Tahiti. A 60-foot replica of an ancient Poly-nesian craft, it follows the traditional designs of the boats used by the early Tahitians. Since 1975, this fragile craft has been sailed between Hawaii and French Polynesia by Hawaiian navigators, re-creating more than 100,000 miles of historic sea voyages. Using no modern instruments, navigating by stars and wave patterns, they traced the course of their ancestors.

From the Hawaii Maritime Center, follow the roadway along the water to **Aloha Tower** at Pier 9. You'll see it nearby, rising like a spire along the water's edge. In the early 20th century, when many visitors arrived in luxurious ocean liners, this slender struc-ture was Hawaii's answer to the Statue of Liberty. It greeted guests when they arrived and bade them farewell upon departure. Now dwarfed by the skyscrapers of Downtown Honolulu, proud Aloha Tower still commands an unusual view of the harbor and ocean. Any day between 9 a.m. and sunset you can ride an elevator to the tenth-floor observation deck for a crow's-nest view.

It's also fun to wander the nearby wharves, catching glimpses of the shops and pleasure boats that still tie up around Honolulu's historic port. You can take in the city's fishing fleet, as well as several tour boats, at **Kewalo Boat Basin**, also known as Fisherman's Wharf, midway between Waikiki and Downtown Honolulu. ~ Ala Moana Boulevard and Ward Avenue.

To see where all that delicious seafood you've been eating   ◀ *HIDDEN*
comes from, stop by the **Honolulu Fish Market**. Here auctioneers sell the day's catch. For the real experience, get there at 5:30 in the morning. Those not quite as industrious should note it's all over by noon. ~ Near the Marketplace (Pier 7).

It's not far to **Fort Street Mall**, a seven-block stretch of Downtown Honolulu that has been refurbished and converted into an attractive pedestrian thoroughfare with a few restaurants. The mall is also a good place to spend a little time shopping. Located miles from the Waikiki tourist beat, the stores here cater to local people, so you'll be able to discover objects unobtainable in kitschier quarters.

Fort Street Mall leads to **Merchant Street**, center of the old downtown section of Honolulu. The 19th- and early-20th-century buildings in this neighborhood re-create the days before Hawaii became the 50th state, when the islands were almost totally controlled by "The Big Five," an interlocking group of powerful corporations. Today the brick-rococo district remains much the same on the outside. But the interiors of the buildings have changed markedly. They now house boutiques and gourmet restaurants downstairs and multinational corporations on the upper floors.

CHINATOWN After proceeding away from the waterfront all the way to the end of Merchant Street, take a right on Nuuanu

AUTHOR FAVORITE

sights

When I'm in town I like to stop by the **Hawaii Maritime Center** (adjacent to the *Falls of Clyde*). This fascinating museum traces the archipelago's maritime history from the era of Polynesian exploration to the days of the great ocean liners and beyond. Skeletal remains of a humpback whale and an 1800-pound blue marlin are draws. Other displays focus on the old whaling trade, the invention of surfing and seaplanes. Admission. ~ Pier 7, Honolulu Harbor; 808-536-6373, fax 808-536-1519; www.bishopmuseum.org, e-mail bmoore@bishop museum.org.

Avenue, then a left on Hotel Street. As you walk along this thoroughfare, which seems to change its identity every block or two, you will pass from Honolulu's conservative financial district **HIDDEN ►** into one of its most intriguing ethnic neighborhoods, **Chinatown**.

The Chinese first arrived in Hawaii in 1852, imported as plantation workers. They quickly moved to urban areas after completing their plantation contracts, became merchants and proved very successful. Many settled right here in this weather-beaten district, which has long been a center of controversy and an integral part of Honolulu's history. When bubonic plague hit the Chinese community in 1900, the Caucasian-led government tried to contain the pestilence by burning down afflicted homes. The bumbling white fathers managed to raze most of Chinatown, destroying businesses as well as houses.

Despite the renovation of select buildings, Hotel Street, the spine of Chinatown, retains a seedy air with a sailor's port-of-call feel. Newly refurbished shops now stand cheek-by-jowl with quaint, time-worn stores. You'll still encounter the other side of Chinatown, the late-night face of the neighborhood. Strung like a neon ganglion along the thoroughfare are porno movie places, flophouses, barrooms and pool halls. This was once a booming red-light district, the haunt of a motley collection of characters.

The State's art collections, on display in public places, are highlighted in an excellent historic walking tour booklet of downtown Honolulu. It's available free from the State Foundation for Culture and the Arts. ~ 44 Merchant Street; 808-586-0304.

Chinatown is where the locals go to buy leis, with most of the lei stands located on Maunakea Street and around the corner on North Beretania. Many of these shops are family-owned and -operated, and have been open for several generations. You can watch them string leis or order garlands for special occasions or to take home.

Of course, Chinatown is also where you can eat truly authentic food, including dim sum feasts, and buy ready-made cakes, *char siu* pork, crispy roast duck and fresh *manapua*. In addition, it's also a fascinating place to shop, with unusual produce, porcelain, medicinal herbs and other exotic items for sale.

The ultimate emblem of Chinatown's revitalization is **Maunakea Marketplace**. This Amerasian shopping mall, with a statue of Confucius overlooking a brick courtyard, houses an Oriental antique shop and a Chinese art store. The most interesting feature is the produce market, a series of traditional hanging-ducks-and-live-fish stalls inside an air-conditioned building. ~ Hotel and Maunakea streets.

The best way to visit this neighborhood is on one of the **Chinatown Walking Tours** sponsored by the Chinese Chamber of Commerce. Chinatown today is an eclectic community, containing not only Chinese, but Filipinos, Hawaiians and more recent arrivals from Vietnam and Laos. To fully understand Hawaii's melting-pot population, it's important to visit this vibrant district. The walking tour is given on Tuesday mornings, and will carry you past temples and other spots all around the neighborhood. Fee. ~ 42 North King Street; 808-533-3181, fax 808-533-6967.

◀ *HIDDEN*

Continuing north along Hotel Street across Nuuanu Stream, turn right on College Walk and follow it a short distance upstream. You'll pass the **Izumo Taishakyo Mission**, a Japanese Shinto shrine. Take a minute to stop in to see the bell and gate.

Proceed farther and you will arrive at **Foster Botanical Garden**. This 14-acre plot is planted with orchids, palms, coffee trees, poisonous plants and numerous other exotic specimens. There are about 4000 species in all, dotted around a garden that was first planted over 125 years ago. You can meditate under a bo tree or wander through a "prehistoric glen," a riot of ancient ferns and unusual palms. Or you can stroll through and marvel at the universe of color crowded into this urban garden. Visitors are advised to bring insect repellent. Admission. ~ 50 North Vineyard Boulevard; 808-522-7065, fax 808-522-7050; www.co.honolulu.hi.us/parks/hbg.

When you're done enjoying Foster Botanical Garden, stop by the adjacent **Kwan Yin Temple**, where the smell of incense fills the air and Buddhist tranquility pervades. For a brief moment you'll feel like you're in China rather than Honolulu. ~ 50 North Vineyard Boulevard.

◀ *HIDDEN*

On the way back to Chinatown, walk along the other side of Nuuanu Stream and stop at the **Cultural Plaza**. This Asian-style shopping mall is bounded by Kukui, Maunakea and Beretania streets, and by the stream. You'll find porcelain, Chinese jewelry, housewares, gifts, medicinal herbs, Chinese cake shops and several restaurants. Don't miss the open-air market selling fresh vegetables, tropical fruits, fish, chicken feet, pigs' heads and other exotic items. The market entrance is in the back of the plaza.

A Hawaiian Cultural Tour

You're on the right island to get a true sense of what life was (and is) like for the Hawaiian people.

BISHOP MUSEUM   Our tour begins at the Bishop Museum (page 156), with its exceptional exhibits of Hawaiiana. Three floors of the grand hall give you a feel for Polynesian history over the centuries. Allow 1.5 hours.

IOLANI PALACE   Next, head downtown to Iolani Palace (page 130). Be sure to make reservations ahead of time if you want to see the phenomenal woodwork inside the palace. Stroll the grounds and imagine what it was like to be dressed in the long-sleeved outfits of the royal family in this heat! Most Friday afternoons the Royal Hawaiian Band plays at the Royal Bandstand. Allow 45 minutes for the tour. Stroll across the street to see the **statue** of King Kamehameha, Hawaii's first king. If you're lucky, it will be a holiday and he'll be draped in flower leis.

ROYAL MAUSOLEUM   It's about six blocks west (*ewa*) to Nuuanu Avenue. Head toward the mountains (*mauka*) and you'll arrive at the Royal Mausoleum (page 153), where Hawaii's royals are interred.

QUEEN EMMA'S SUMMER PALACE   After paying your respects, backtrack to Route H-1, head Diamond Head direction (east) and get off on

On the outskirts of Chinatown is the **Hawaii Theatre**. After years of painstaking restoration, it is again a study in neoclassical architecture. With gilded decor, Corinthian columns and striking mosaics, it has been elevated again to the grand status it enjoyed when the theater first opened in 1922. In 1929, it was the first movie theater in the islands to show movies with sound. Tours are available at this nationally registered historic place. Shows, concerts, festivals, ethnic programs and films are presented here. Closed Monday. Admission. ~ 1130 Bethel Street; 808-791-1305, 808-528-0506 (tickets), fax 808-528-1675; www.hawaii theatre.com.

If you're in the mood for a great film, head to the **Signature Theater** complex at Dole Cannery Square. Hawaii's largest cineplex with 18 screens, it also features Hawaii's best cinematic the Pali Highway (Route 61) traveling *mauka* toward Kaneohe/Kailua. You'll soon come to Queen Emma's Summer Palace (page 157). A comfortable New England–style home rather than a grand building, it was built in 1843 for the wife of King Kamehameha IV. Allow half an hour to tour her residence and lovely grounds.

NUUANU PALI LOOKOUT Continue up the highway to the Nuuanu Pali Lookout (page 157). This is where King Kamehameha I overwhelmed his enemies. The view is not to be missed.

ULUPO HEIAU You'll want to see at least one *heiau* (ancient temple) on this tour. Your best bet is to continue your drive on Route 61. As you descend into Kailua, you'll encounter Ulupo Heiau (page 185), located behind the YMCA. According to legend, this temple was built by the leprechaun-like *Menehunes*.

HEEIA STATE PARK Farther along Kaneohe Bay is Heeia State Park (page 186), where the ancient Hawaiians built one of the largest fishponds in the islands.

UNWINDING Now that you've had a day of sightseeing, round things out with an invigorating canoe ride at **Waikiki Beach** (page 104) and then dine at **Ono Hawaiian Foods** (page 169) on poi and *lomi* salmon or kalua pig. Be sure to check out the Hawaiian music scene: the Brothers Cazimero or Olomana often perform at **Chai's Island Bistro** (page 149) in Aloha Tower Marketplace.

selection, including foreign films you'll find nowhere else on the island. ~ 735-B Iwilei Road; 808-526-3456.

The **Town Inn,** on the outskirts of Chinatown, is an excellent spot to capture the local color of Honolulu's Chinese section, though the hotel itself is rather nondescript. The 26 rooms are clean, carpeted and sparsely furnished—some even have air conditioning—and all are practically devoid of decoration. First-come, first-served. ~ 250 North Beretania Street; 808-536-2377. BUDGET.

LODGING

The **Aston Executive Centre Hotel,** a highrise in the financial district, has more than 100 comfortable guest rooms. Its location and perks aimed at business folks (computer ports, conference facilities, 24-hour fitness center, daily newspaper) make this an ideal spot for a business trip. Other amenities include laundry facilities and a spa. A complimentary breakfast is included. ~ 1088 Bishop Street; 808-539-3000, fax 808-523-1088; www.astonexecutive. com, e-mail res.exc@aston-hotels. ULTRA-DELUXE.

DINING

As you get away from Waikiki you'll be dining with a more local crowd and tasting foods more representative of island cuisine, so I would certainly advise checking out some of Honolulu's eating places.

Ward Centre, situated midway between Waikiki and Downtown Honolulu, is a focus for gourmet dining. A warren of wood-paneled restaurants, it features several outstanding eateries. Particularly recommended for the price is **Scoozee's**, a "pasta, pizza, pizzazz" restaurant with entrées averaging around $10. ~ 1200 Ala Moana Boulevard; 808-597-1777, fax 808-591-1005. BUDGET TO MODERATE.

Also consider **Compadres**, upstairs in the same complex. This attractive Mexican restaurant, with oak bar and patio dining, prepares dishes from south of the border as well as salads, steaks and seafood. It specializes in tropical ambience, good food and fishbowl-size margaritas. ~ 1200 Ala Moana Boulevard; 808-591-8307, fax 808-593-2901. BUDGET TO DELUXE.

Ryan's Grill is one of Honolulu's hottest after-work hangouts for singles who want to become un-single, and the place is packed from 5 p.m. until after 1 a.m. Comfortable leather chairs and marble-topped tables create a cozy, modern atmosphere. Grilled and steamed fish and fowl, pizzas, salads and fettuccine are among the many culinary options for those who go to eat instead of drink. ~ 1200 Ala Moana Boulevard; 808-591-9132, fax 808-591-0034; e-mail ryansgrill@aol.com. MODERATE TO ULTRA-DELUXE.

There are lots of other options at Ward Warehouse next door. Dinner at **The Old Spaghetti Factory**, which many locals frequent, is like eating in a mansion where the Victorian designer got carried away. There are overstuffed chairs, a brass bed made into a table, stained-glass windows and elaborate chandeliers. And there's also spaghetti, of course, in a variety of styles, as well as other Italian treats. Each dinner comes with a salad and an individual loaf of homemade bread. This is a great place for kids. ~ 1050 Ala Moana Boulevard; 808-591-2513, fax 808-591-0524. BUDGET TO MODERATE.

Plate Lunches

There's nothing more Hawaiian than the plate lunch. It's soul food at its finest, but not for the faint at heart. Nor for those counting calories or concerned about the fat content of their food. A local culinary tradition, the plate lunch combines Japanese, Chinese, Korean, Hawaiian, American and Filipino fare into a meal that is not only delicious but more food for the price than you're likely to find anywhere.

The plate lunch tradition began in the sugar plantation days when women would deliver plates of food to family plantation workers. These plates would usually consist of two scoops of white rice, a scoop of potato or macaroni salad and a variety of meat and fish, including teriyaki pork, beef, chicken or fish; pork or chicken *luau*; or *kalua* pig. Some entrepreneurial villagers started up businesses selling lunches to field workers without families.

Little-changed today, the plate lunch still consists of two scoops of white rice and possibly a third scoop of macaroni or potato salad, as well as the main selections, which could be just about anything. A local favorite is *loco moco*, a hamburger steak topped with fried egg and gravy. There are also *kalbi* (Korean beef ribs), teriyaki beef, chicken and pork *katsu*, and stir-fried shrimp.

Plate lunches are served in simple restaurants, usually a drive-in or coffee shop. They also can be found at any of the lunch trucks parked at places around Honolulu, near the University of Hawaii or on the North Shore. Although there are probably as many opinions on the best plate lunches as there are people in Oahu, here are a few favorites.

Like Like Drive Inn is one of the oldest and most well-established plate lunch eateries in Honolulu and very popular with the locals. This comfy coffee shop has the feel of the '50s and serves up some good home-style comfort food. ~ 745 Keeaumoku Street; 808-941-2515.

Grace's Inn, with several locations around Oahu, is famed for its chicken *katsu* and homemade *kim chi*. It also serves beef stew, beef curry and a variety of other dishes. Their Beretania eatery is the best known of the "chain." ~ 1296 South Beretania Street; 808-593-2202, fax 808-732-0695.

You'll never be far from an **L & L Drive-Inn**. With more than 20 restaurants around Oahu, the chain has been voted by the readers of the *Honolulu Advertiser* as serving the best plate lunches. Stir-fried shrimp and hamburger steak are among the offerings, and the breakfasts come complete with rice and a Hawaiian favorite, Spam. Visit the original diner. ~ 1711 Liliha Street; 808-533-3210.

Honolulu has numerous seafood restaurants. Some of them, fittingly enough, are located right on the water. But for an authentic seafront feel, it's nice to be where the fishing boats actually come in. **Fisherman's Wharf** provides just such an atmosphere. This family restaurant serves seafood dishes as well as pasta and steaks. ~ 1009 Ala Moana Boulevard; 808-538-3808. DELUXE TO ULTRA-DELUXE.

Fresh *ono*, mahimahi, *opakapaka* and ahi highlight the vast seafood menu at **John Dominis**. A sprawling establishment midway between Waikiki and Downtown Honolulu, it features huge pools filled with live fish. The wood-paneled dining room overlooks the water and the chefs know as much about preparing seafood as the original Polynesians. For landlubbers, steak and veal are also on the menu. No lunch. ~ 43 Ahui Street; 808-523-0955, fax 808-526-3758; e-mail jdominis@lava.net. ULTRA-DELUXE.

The menu at **Ba-Le Sandwich Shop** specializes in the delicious concept of "gourmet Vietnamese sandwiches": loaves of French bread layered with various meats and marinated vegetables. Request it spicy; you can cool off your mouth after the meal with a choice from the long list of soothing puddings. No dinner on Saturday. Closed Sunday. ~ 1154 Fort Street Mall; phone/fax 808-521-4117. BUDGET.

Auntie Pasto's is a popular Italian restaurant with oilcloth on the tables and a map of the mother country tacked to the wall. Pasta is served with any of a dozen different sauces—meat sauce, clams and broccoli, creamy pesto, carbonara and seafood. There are salads aplenty plus an assortment of entrées that includes veal marsala, chicken cacciatore and calamari piccata. No lunch

AUTHOR FAVORITE

Located in the ultracontemporary Restaurant Row shopping mall, **Sunset Grill** is a minimalist's delight. Track lights, exposed pipes, raw wood and poured concrete establish a kind of early-21st-century motif. The only area devoted to excess is the kitchen, which serves up a lavish array of *kiawe*-grilled dishes, such as smoke-infused marinated salmon. It's hard to go wrong here. No lunch Saturday or Sunday. ~ 500 Ala Moana Boulevard, #1-A; 808-521-4409, fax 808-523-5190; www.sunsetgrill.biz, e-mail stu@sunsetgrill.biz. MODERATE TO DELUXE.

on weekends. ~ 1099 South Beretania Street; 808-523-8855, fax 808-524-6267; www.auntiepastos.com. BUDGET TO MODERATE.

Just down the street, **Wisteria Restaurant** has been pleasing local Japanese Hawaiians for years. This is where they come to celebrate birthdays, anniversaries and other milestones. The setting is padded booths—coffeeshop style. The food is Japanese home-style cooking, just like *obachan* (grandma) used to make. The sukiyaki and teriyaki are particularly tasty. ~ 1206 South King Street; 808-591-9276, fax 808-596-0976. MODERATE.

For a taste of Southeast Asian cuisine, try the **Pae Thai**. At this café you can savor *tom yum* (spicy lemongrass soup), chicken satay or a tasty garlic shrimp dish. Closed Sunday. ~ 1246 South King Street; phone/fax 808-596-8106. BUDGET TO DELUXE.

Up on the second level of the Aloha Tower Marketplace, toward the back overlooking the water, there's the **Kau Kau Corner Food Lanai**. This cluster of food stands ranges from Villa Pizza to Belinda's Aloha Kitchen to Yokozuna and beyond. There is comfortable seating in an attractive setting, all at economical prices. ~ Aloha Tower Marketplace, Pier 8; 808-528-5700, fax 808-524-8334. BUDGET.

Satisfying your senses is easy at **Chai's Island Bistro**. Ample portions of distinctive dishes such as seafood risotto with Big Island heart of palm or Asian-style osso buco with kabocha squash sate the taste buds, while the presentation pleases the eyes. The service is friendly and evening brings the sounds of Hawaii's contemporary musicians to touch your heart. ~ Aloha Tower Marketplace, 1 Aloha Tower Drive; 808-585-0011, fax 808-585-0012; www.chaisislandbistro.com. ULTRA-DELUXE.

Near the city's financial center there's a modest restaurant that I particularly like. **People's Café** is owned by an Okinawan family, but the food is primarily Polynesian: this is a good spot to order poi, *lomi* salmon, *kalua* pig and other island favorites. *Ono, ono!* Closed Sunday. ~ 1310 Pali Highway; phone/fax 808-536-5789. BUDGET TO MODERATE.

There is nothing else in Honolulu quite like **LaMariana Sailing Club**. Located on the shores of the Keehi Lagoon and reached through the industrial port area off Sand Island Access Road, LaMariana Sailing Club plays host to an assortment of old salts who dance the hula, sing, party and provide more local color than you'll find just about anywhere else in town. What's more,

◀ HIDDEN

the food, with a focus on fresh fish, seafood, prime rib and steaks, is good and the service friendly. ~ 50 Sand Island Access Road; 808-848-2800, fax 808-841-2173. MODERATE TO DELUXE.

HIDDEN ►   **Itochan Sushi** serves sushi-bar quality sushi at economical prices in a tiny four-table-and-counter hole in the wall in The Arcade, a minimall of shops and restaurants in the heart of downtown. ~ 212 Merchant Street; 808-545-7848. BUDGET.

HIDDEN ►   For Chinese food hereabouts, try **Yong Sing Restaurant**. This high-ceilinged establishment, catering to local businesspeople, has some delicious dishes. I thought the oyster-sauce chicken particularly tasty. With its daily lunch specials, Yong Sing is a perfect stopoff when you're shopping or sightseeing downtown. ~ 1055 Alakea Street; 808-531-1367. BUDGET TO MODERATE.

But for the true flavor of China, head over to Chinatown, just a few blocks from the financial district. Amid the tumbledown buildings and jumble of shops, you'll happen upon **Double Eight Restaurant**. Although the service is forgettable and the decor nonexistent, they do know how to cook up Hong Kong–style delicacies. One fortuitous sign of quality is that few of the employees speak any English. Good luck and *bon appetit!* ~ 1113 Maunakea Street; 808-526-3887. BUDGET.

HIDDEN ►   There's **A Little Bit of Saigon** right in the heart of Chinatown. Small it may be, but this café represents a triple threat to the competition—attractive decor, good prices and excellent food. Little wonder it has gained such a strong reputation among the local gentry. The menu covers the spectrum of Vietnamese dishes, with a smattering of Italian and vegetarian fare, and the interior, lined with tropical paintings, is easy on the eyes. ~ 1160 Maunakea Street; phone/fax 808-528-3663. BUDGET TO MODERATE.

And there's a little bit of every other ethnic cuisine at the food stalls in **Maunakea Marketplace**. Here you'll find vendors dispensing steaming plates of Thai, Chinese, Japanese, Hawaiian, Filipino, Korean, Vietnamese and Italian food. Italian? Small tables are provided. ~ Hotel and Maunakea streets. BUDGET.

By way of Filipino food, **Mabuhay Cafe** comes recommended by several readers. It's a plainly adorned place on the edge of Chinatown that serves a largely local clientele. The menu is extensive, covering all types of Filipino dishes. ~ 1049 River Street; 808-545-1956. BUDGET.

Eating at **Duc's Bistro** is like entering a French salon. This quiet oasis may be on the edge of Chinatown, but it seems a world away. White tablecloths and vases full of flowers adorn the tables and gallery-quality paintings decorate the walls. Light jazz provides a soothing atmosphere to enjoy the French-Vietnamese cuisine that has gained this restaurant a loyal following among locals. Fresh fish, prawns, duck and chicken are prepared French fashion with a touch of Vietnam. No lunch on Saturday or Sunday. ~ 1188 Maunakea Street; 808-531-6325; www.ducsbistro.com. MODERATE TO ULTRA-DELUXE.

Indigo is one of Chinatown's treats. This Eurasian dining room casts an aura of the Orient with its dark wicker chairs, ornamental gong and intaglio-carved furnishings. You can expect more than a dozen dim sum dishes plus "Peking pizzettas." The soups and salads include tomato-garlic crab soup and goat cheese wontons. Among the entrées, they offer miso-marinated seared salmon and Mongolian lamb chops with mint-tangerine sauce. What an adventure! No lunch Saturday. Closed Sunday and Monday. ~ 1121 Nuuanu Avenue; 808-521-2900, fax 808-537-4164; www.indigo-hawaii.com. MODERATE TO DELUXE.

The decor belies the food at the **Zaffron Restaurant**. Fairly uninteresting red booths and stiff backed chairs lining long picnic-like tables do not an exotic experience make. But the North Indian food itself will transport you and the prices will keep you there. Try the chick pea curry, and order as much *naan* bread as you can stuff in. No lunch Sunday through Tuesday. ~ 69 North King Street; 808-533-6635; www.zaffronhawaii.com, e-mail zaffron hawaii@zaffronhawaii.com. BUDGET TO MODERATE.

Legend Seafood Restaurant in the Chinese Cultural Plaza will leave you impressed—first by the sheer scope of the menu, second

THE MERRY MONARCH

The king who commissioned the Iolani Palace, David Kalakaua, was a world traveler with a taste for the good life. Known as the Merry Monarch, he planned for his coronation the greatest party Hawaii had ever seen. He liked to spend money with abandon and managed to amass in his lifetime a remarkable collection of material goods, not the least of which was his palace.

by the excellent food. Obviously, seafood is the specialty, but the options include tempting vegetarian and meat dishes as well. If you stop by for lunch, you'll be very happy with the dim sum, a varied selection of savory bite-sized morsels. ~ 100 North Beretania Street; 808-532-1868, fax 808-532-3832. MODERATE.

For anyone who thinks a meal without meat isn't a meal, a visit to **Legend's Buddhist Vegetarian Restaurant** might make a health-food nut out of you. Yes, it's vegan (i.e., no animal products)—but the dim sum is darn good. Run by the same people as Legend Seafood Restaurant, this eatery is located in the same building. No dinner. Closed Wednesday. ~ 100 North Beretania Street; 808-532-8218. BUDGET TO MODERATE.

A giant red neon sign announces that you've arrived at **Sam Choy's Breakfast, Lunch & Crab**, a noisy, bustling restaurant with marine decor accentuated by a dry-docked fishing boat. Chef Sam Choy, a local boy who has helped Hawaii Regional cuisine establish an international reputation, serves crab (Dungeness, Maryland Blue, Florida Gold, Alaskan King) fresh from the open kitchen. There's also lobster, shrimp, fish and, for those unclear on the concept, chicken and beef dishes. ~ 580 North Nimitz Highway; 808-545-7979, fax 808-545-7997; www.sam choy.com, e-mail samchoy@lava.net. MODERATE TO ULTRA-DELUXE.

GROCERIES Midway between Waikiki and Downtown Honolulu there's a **Safeway** store. ~ 1121 South Beretania Street; 808-592-6499. There's another **Safeway** in Downtown Honolulu. ~ 1360 Pali Highway; 808-538-3953.

Also look for **The Carrot Patch**, with its health and diet products and sandwiches. ~ 700 Bishop Street; 808-531-4037.

HEART OF A NEIGHBORHOOD

Some of Chinatown's woodframe buildings still suggest the old days and traditions. Wander down side streets like Maunakea Street and you will encounter import stores, Chinese groceries and noodle factories. You might also pop into one of the medicinal herb shops, which feature unique potions and healing powders. There are chop suey joints, acupuncturists and outdoor markets galore, all lending a priceless flavor of the Orient.

R. Field Wine Co. specializes in fine wines and gourmet groceries. ~ 1460 South Beretania Street; 808-596-9463.

You might want to browse around the mom-and-pop grocery stores spotted throughout Chinatown. They're marvelous places to pick up Chinese foodstuffs and to capture the local color.

Don't miss the **Open Market** in Chinatown. It's a great place to shop for fresh foods. There are numerous stands selling fish, produce, poultry, meat, baked goods and island fruits, all at low-overhead prices. ~ Along North King Street between River and Kekaulike streets.

◄ *HIDDEN*

One of Honolulu's sleeker shopping malls is **Ward Centre** on Ala Moana Boulevard. Streamlined and stylized, it's an elite enclave filled with designer shops, spiffy restaurants, boutiques and children's shops. Adorned with blond-wood facades, brick walkways and brass-rail restaurants, the shopping complex provides a touch of Beverly Hills. ~ 1200 Ala Moana Boulevard.

SHOPPING

Anchoring Ward Centre at the far end is **Borders Books & Music** (808-591-8995), a superstore that is chockablock with everything for your reading and listening pleasure. They have two floors of paperbacks, hardbacks, audiotapes and CDs.

Just down the walkway in Ward Centre, you can home in on **Sedona**, the self-proclaimed "unique place to find yourself." It stocks aromatherapy oils, visionary music, inspirational gifts—and personal psychic readings. ~ 808-591-8010.

Black Pearl Gallery features lustrous Tahitian black pearls that highlight its jewelry collection. ~ 808-597-1477.

In the same complex, there's an excellent selection of women's clothing and accessories at **The Ultimate You**. This designer consignment store offers great bargains. ~ 808-591-8388.

Ala Moana Center may be the biggest, but the smaller **Ward Warehouse,** on Ala Moana Boulevard between Waikiki and Downtown Honolulu, is another very interesting shopping center. It features stores such as **Mamo Howell** (808-592-0616), which stocks original Hawaiian wear—aloha shirts and dressy muumuus. **Nohea Gallery** (808-596-0074) displays quilts, jewelry, pottery, glassware, lamps and wooden bureaus—all made in Hawaii by local artists. At **Flags Flying** (808-591-8999) the flags of more than 150 countries decorate T-shirts, shorts, stickers and even soccer balls. ~ 1020 Ala Moana Boulevard.

A California-style affair complete with white stucco walls and curved tile roof, **Aloha Tower Marketplace** is located on the waterfront overlooking Honolulu Harbor. With its flagstone walkways and open-air courtyards, it's worth visiting even if buying something is the last thing on your mind. Among the over 70 shops are about 25 devoted to apparel, a handful of galleries and perhaps three dozen specialty shops. Among them are **Hula Prints** (808-528-0395), which sells Hawaiian tourist poster prints of the 1920s and other art. **Martin & MacArthur** (808-524-6066) specializes in Hawaiian crafts, such as quality *koa* wood items. Betty Boop meets Mickey Mouse and Winnie the Pooh at **Animation Magic** (808-545-8666), a shop where customers of all ages can celebrate cartoons. There are also several full-service restaurants. Tucked between the Hawaii Maritime Museum and Aloha Tower, it's set near one of the busiest parts of the harbor. ~ Pier 8; 808-528-5700.

If you're seeking Oriental items, then Chinatown is the place. Spotted throughout this neighborhood are small shops selling statuettes, pottery and other curios. It's also worthwhile wandering through the **Cultural Plaza**. This mall is filled with Asian jewelers, bookstores and knickknack shops. ~ Corner of Beretania and Maunakea streets; 808-521-4934.

If you love those claustrophobic antique stores that have keepsakes stacked to the rafters and spilling into the aisles, then the 900 block of Maunakea Street is calling. Here **Aloha Antique & Collectibles** extends for seven storefronts with everything imaginable in the priceless-to-worthless range. ~ 920 Maunakea Street; 808-536-6187.

Also abundant on Maunakea are lei shops. Perhaps more than anything else, leis are symbolic of the beauty and generosity of Hawaii. Originally designed as a token of esteem for gods, family and oneself, they're still given on all types of occasions. You'll have no trouble tracking down a lei in Chinatown, but to narrow down your search, give **Maunakea Street Florist** a try. They're fairly inexpensive and are open late. You can also ship your purchases home. ~ 1189 Maunakea Street at Beretania Street; 808-537-2373; www.flowerleis.net.

While you're in Chinatown, pick up some crackseed for a taste of authentic Hawaii. Crackseed encompasses a range of dried fruits and nuts, which are preserved using a plum-based flavoring called *le hing mui*. The extreme taste may not be to everyone's liking—the sweetness of the fruit combined with the sourness/saltiness of the powder is intense—but you might surprise yourself.

At the edge of Chinatown along Nuuanu Avenue are several galleries and shops worthy of a visit. The **Pegge Hopper Gallery** is here, displaying acrylic paintings and the female portraits for which she is renowned. Closed Sunday and Monday. ~ 1164 Nuuanu Avenue; 808-524-1160.

NIGHTLIFE

A harbor view and Hawaiian contemporary music played on Thursday, Friday and Saturday by acoustic guitarists and bands make **Kincaid's** a good choice for a relaxing evening. This lounge is part of a popular Honolulu restaurant in Ward Warehouse. ~ 1050 Ala Moana Boulevard; 808-591-2005.

Near downtown, the ultracontemporary Restaurant Row offers several nightspots including a restaurant called **The Ocean Club**. This upscale club features nightly deejay dance music. Dress code. Cover. ~ 500 Ala Moana Boulevard; 808-526-9888.

Chai's Island Bistro in the Aloha Tower Marketplace often hosts Hawaiian entertainers. It's a fairly intimate setting, especially if you get there early and have dinner. You can get up-close and personal. Call and check who will be there—you're apt to find Jerry Santos or the Brothers Cazimero. ~ Aloha Tower Marketplace, 1 Aloha Tower Drive; 808-585-0011, fax 808-585-0012; www.chaisislandbistro.com.

Indigo, an attractive Asian restaurant with a patio, has hip-hop dancing and contemporary music Tuesday through Saturday. On several nights the sound is live; other nights it's deejay driven. Closed Sunday and Monday. Cover. ~ 1121 Nuuanu Avenue; 808-521-2900.

AUTHOR FAVORITE

There's nothing quite like a Friday or Saturday evening at **LaMariana Sailing Club**. A festive group of locals takes over the floor to entertain you with their song and dance. If you're lucky, it will be someone of note who dropped by to talk story or strum his or her uke. There's live piano music Wednesday through Saturday evenings. ~ 50 Sand Island Access Road; 808-848-2800, fax 808-841-2173.

There's deejay dancing, theme nights and billiards at the **World Cafe**, which also regularly books national acts. ~ 1130 North Nimitz Highway, B-100; 808-599-4450.

For something more refined and classical, consider **Chamber Music Hawaii**, which presents a series of concerts annually at several different locations around the city. They also perform on the windward side of the island. ~ 808-543-0935.

The **Hawaii Theatre** offers the best in Broadway performances, dance troupes, classical music and much more. The Hawaii International Film Festival is held here every November. ~ 1130 Bethel Street; 808-791-1305, 808-528-0506 (tickets).

The **Honolulu Symphony**, with a season that runs from September to May, provides a delightful schedule of programs. ~ 650 Ewalei Road; 808-524-0815, box office 808-524-0815.

At the **Hawaii Opera Theater,** you can see works like Saint-Saens' *Samson and Delilah*, Puccini's *Madame Butterfly* and *Die Fledermaus* by Strauss. This regional company features stars from the international opera scene. ~ 987 Waimanu Street; 808-596-7372, box office 808-596-7858.

A variety of youth- and family-oriented productions are performed by the **Honolulu Theater for Youth**, at a number of venues throughout Oahu. The company also tours the neighbor islands twice a year. Make reservations two weeks in advance. ~ 2846 Ualena Street; 808-839-9885.

At the other end of the cultural spectrum (and at the other end of town), the Honolulu red-light scene centers around Hotel Street in Chinatown. This partially refurbished, partially run-down strip is lined with hostess bars and adult bookstores. Prostitutes, straight and gay, walk the street regularly.

BEACHES & PARKS

HIDDEN ►

KAKAAKO WATERFRONT PARK Located near downtown Honolulu and popular with local picnickers, this rock-fringed park has a promenade with a view spanning from Diamond Head to the harbor. There are picnic tables, pavilions, showers, restrooms and large grassy plots. There's a surfing break offshore but no swimming. ~ End of Cooke Street off Ala Moana Boulevard.

HIDDEN ►

SAND ISLAND STATE RECREATION AREA This 140-acre park wraps around the south and east shores of Sand Island, with sections fronting both Honolulu Harbor and the open sea. Despite the name, there's only a small sandy beach here, and jet traffic from nearby Honolulu International might disturb your snoozing. But there is a great view of Honolulu. While the swimming and snorkeling are poor here, there are good surf breaks in summer and fishing is usually rewarding. *Papio* and *moano* are the prime catches. Facilities include restrooms and a picnic area. ~ From Waikiki, take Ala Moana Boulevard and Nimitz Highway several miles west to Sand Island Access Road.

▲ State permit required for tent camping in the grassy area facing the ocean.

SIX

Greater Honolulu

Framed by the Waianae Range in the west and the Koolau Range to the east, Honolulu is a nonstop drama presented within a natural amphitheater. Honolulu Harbor sets the stage to the south; at the center lie Waikiki and Downtown Honolulu. Wrapped around these tourist and business centers is a rainbow-shaped congeries of sights and places that, for lack of a better name, constitutes "Greater Honolulu."

Greater Honolulu is where most of the people of Honolulu live. It extends from navy-gray Pearl Harbor to the turquoise waters of the prestigious Kahala district and holds in its ambit some of the city's prettiest territory. Here are the neighborhoods, which, as the city grew, stretched farther east, west and north. Here are working-class enclaves with neat, even rows of houses and wonderful ethnic restaurants. Here, too, is the realm of the well-to-do with their neighborhoods by the waterfront and homes perched on the hillsides overlooking the city.

Each part of greater Honolulu is defined not only by its geographic characteristics but also by the type of people who settled there. Manoa Valley, for example, became home to the descendants of the early missionaries, who built New England saltbox–style homes quite different than those in other areas. Portuguese immigrants, many of whose families had come to work on the sugar plantations, put down roots on the slopes of Punchbowl and named their streets after Lisbon, the Azores, Madeira and other places that reminded them of home.

The sights of Greater Honolulu are dotted all across the city and require a bit of planning to see. You'll need to ride buses or taxis or rent a car, but it is well worth the extra effort. You'll be away from the crowds of tourists and get a chance to meet the locals and get a singular perspective on island life and culture.

Many of the points of interest below are frequented more by local residents than tourists. Others contain an interesting mix of local folk and out-of-towners. In any case, be sure to take the time to explore some of these outlying spots.

KALIHI–NUUANU AVENUE AREA The first district is actually within walking distance of Downtown Honolulu, but it's a relatively long walk, so transportation is generally advised. Nuuanu Avenue begins downtown and travels uphill in a northeasterly direction past several noteworthy points. First stop is **Soto Mission of Hawaii,** home of a meditative Zen sect. Modeled after a temple in India where the Buddha gave his first sermon, this building is marked by dramatic towers, and beautiful Japanese bonsai plants decorate the landscape. ~ 1708 Nuuanu Avenue.

Here and at nearby **Honolulu Myohoji Temple** the city seems like a distant memory. The latter building, placidly situated along a small stream, is capped by a peace tower. ~ 2003 Nuuanu Avenue.

Uphill from these shrines lies **Honolulu Memorial Park.** There is an ancestral monument here, bordered on three sides by a pond of flashing carp and a striking three-tiered pagoda. ~ 22 Craigside Place. This entire area is a center of simple yet beautiful Asian places of worship. For instance, **Tenrikyo Mission** is a wood-frame temple that was moved here all the way from Japan. One intriguing fact about this fragile structure is that large sections were built without nails. ~ 2236 Nuuanu Avenue.

The Hawaiian people also have an important center here. The **Royal Mausoleum** is situated across the street from the Tenrikyo Mission. This was the final resting place for two of Hawaii's royal families, the Kamehameha and Kalakaua clans. Together they ruled 19th-century Hawaii. Today the area is landscaped with palms, ginger, plumeria and other beautiful plants and flowers. ~ 2261 Nuuanu Avenue.

◄ HIDDEN

PUNCHBOWL AND TANTALUS It is a few miles from Downtown Honolulu to **Punchbowl,** the circular center of an extinct volcano. You'll find it northeast of town, at the end of Ward Avenue and just off Prospect Drive, which circles the crater. A youngster in geologic terms, the volcano is a mere 150,000 years old. From the lip of the crater, there is a marvelous vista sweeping down to Diamond Head, across Honolulu and all the way out to the Waianae Range.

The most important feature here, however, is the **National Memorial Cemetery**, located in the extinct volcano known as *Puowaina*, Hawaiian for "hill of sacrifice." Over 42,000 war dead have been interred, including victims of both World Wars, as well as the Korean, Spanish-American and Vietnam wars. There is also an impressive monument to the "Courts of the Missing," which lists the names of soldiers missing in action. The top of the monument is anchored by the "Court of Honor,"an area with a memorial chapel featuring several map galleries. These galleries depict engagements in the Pacific Theater during World War II and the Korean War. The 30-foot statue of Columbia, a female figure holding a laurel branch, is most impressive. Ironically, of all the people buried here, the most famous was not a soldier but a journalist—Ernie Pyle, whose World War II stories about the average GI were eagerly followed by an entire nation. Near his grave you will also find the burial site of Hawaii's first astronaut, Ellison Onizuka, who died in the *Challenger* space shuttle disaster. Guided walking tours are offered by the American Legion. Fee. ~ 808-946-6383, fax 808-947-3957; e-mail aldepthi@rr.com.

HIDDEN ► Near Punchbowl, on Prospect Street, you might want to drop by the **Tennent Art Foundation Gallery**, which displays works (drawings, paintings and large three-dimensional female Polynesian figures) by Madge Tennent, a.k.a. "Hawaii's Gauguin," and one of the state's best-known painters. Closed Monday; call ahead for hours. ~ 203 Prospect Street; 808-531-1987.

HIDDEN ► You can explore the heights by following Tantalus Drive as it winds up the side of **Tantalus**, a 2013-foot mountain. Together with Round Top Drive, Tantalus Drive forms a loop that circles through the residential areas hidden within this rainforest. There are spectacular views all along the route, as well as hiking trails that lead from the road into verdant hilltop regions. Here you'll encounter guava, banana, eucalyptus and ginger trees as well as wildflowers and an occasional wild pig.

One of the best views of all is found at **Puu Ualakaa Park**, a lovely retreat located along the drive. The vista here extends from Diamond Head west to Pearl Harbor, encompassing in its course a giant swath of Honolulu and the Pacific.

En route stop by the **Contemporary Museum**. In addition to changing exhibitions of contemporary art, the museum features the works of several well-known artists in its sculpture garden

Greater Honolulu

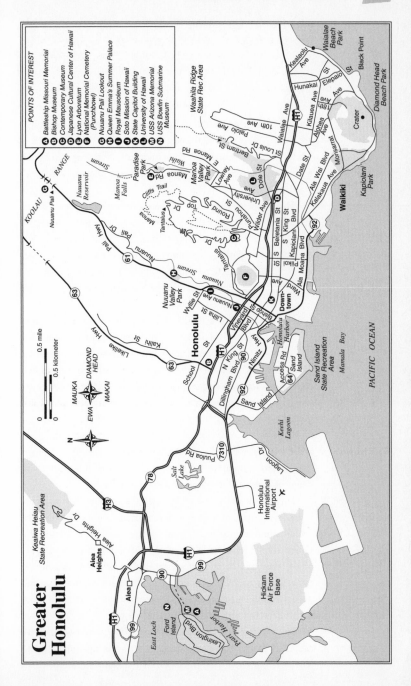

POINTS OF INTEREST

- **(A)** Battleship Missouri Memorial
- **(B)** Bishop Museum
- **(C)** Contemporary Museum
- **(D)** Japanese Cultural Center of Hawaii
- **(E)** Lyon Arboretum
- **(F)** National Memorial Cemetery (Punchbowl)
- **(G)** Nuuanu Pali Lookout
- **(H)** Queen Emma's Summer Palace
- **(I)** Royal Mausoleum
- **(J)** Soto Mission of Hawaii
- **(K)** State Capitol Building
- **(L)** University of Hawaii
- **(M)** USS Arizona Memorial
- **(N)** USS Bowfin Submarine Museum

KOOLAU RANGE

Nuuanu Reservoir

Manoa Falls

Paradise Park

Manoa Valley Park

Nuuanu Pali Lookout

Nuuanu Stream

Manoa Stream

Cliffs Trail

Tantalus Dr

Round Top Dr

Manoa Rd

E Manoa Rd

Waahila Ridge State Rec Area

Nuuanu Valley Park

Wyllie St

Lilha St

Vineyard Blvd

Pali Hwy

Likelike Hwy

School St

Kalihi St

Dillingham Blvd

N King St

Nimitz Hwy

Sand Island Access Rd

Puuloa Rd

Honolulu Harbor

Sand Island State Recreation Area

Keehi Lagoon

Salt Lake

Honolulu International Airport

Hickam Air Force Base

Ford Island

East Loch

Pearl Harbor

Lexington Blvd

Aiea

Aiea Heights

Keaiwa Heiau State Recreation Area

Aiea Heights Dr

MAUKA

DIAMOND HEAD

EWA

MAKAI

0   0.5 mile
0   0.5 kilometer

Honolulu

Downtown

Waikiki

Kapiolani Park

Diamond Head Beach Park

Waialae Beach Park

Black Point

Crater

Monsarrat Ave

Kalakaua Ave

Ala Wai Blvd

Kapiolani Blvd

S King St

S Beretania St

University Ave

Dole St

Wilder Ave

Punahou St

Ward Ave

Ala Moana Blvd

Iwilei

Waialae Ave

Kilauea Ave

10th Ave

Alohea Ave

St Louis Dr

Bertram St

Palolo Ave

Kealaolu Ave

Hunakai

Elepaio St

Kealaolu Ave

Wahi St

Lowrey Ave

PACIFIC OCEAN

Mamala Bay

61 **63** **63** **92** **H1** **H2** **H3** **78** **90** **99** **7310** **64** **92**

and galleries, including David Hockney, Robert Arneson, Charles Arnoldi and Tom Wesselman. Boasting five galleries, an inspired gift shop and a gourmet café, the museum is nevertheless up-staged by its magnificently landscaped grounds. Closed Monday. Admission. ~ 2411 Makiki Heights Drive; 808-526-1322, fax 808-536-5973; www.tcmhi.org, e-mail info@tcmhi.org.

CROSS-ISLAND EXPRESS   Along the outskirts of Honolulu, there are several more points of interest. The best way to tour them is while traveling along the two highways that cut across the Koolaus, connecting Honolulu directly with the island's Windward Coast.

The Likelike Highway, Route 63, can be reached from Route H-1, the superhighway that serves Honolulu. Before heading up into the mountains, you will encounter the **Bishop Museum** near the intersection of Routes 63 and H-1. Built around the turn of the 20th century, it houses an excellent collection of Hawaiian and Pacific artifacts.

If you were a fan of *Blue Hawaii*, you might recall the view from Puu Uala-kaa Park. It's where Elvis decides he wants to become a tour guide.

Here you'll also find outrigger canoes, thrones, primitive artworks and fascinating natural-history exhibits. There are plaited mats woven from pandanus, drums made with shark skin, 19th-century surfboards, and helmets decorated with dog teeth and pearl shells. The 19th-century whaling trade is represented with menacing harpoons and yellowing photographs of the oil-laden ships. Of all the exhibits, the most spectacular are cloaks worn by Hawaiian kings and fashioned from tens of thousands of tiny feathers. There are displays capturing the Japanese, Chinese and Filipino heritage in Hawaii and a hall devoted to other cultures of the Pacific.

HIDDEN ►

The Bishop also offers a **"behind the scenes" tour**, which covers territory the general public doesn't get to see. Following a 25-minute dramatic presentation on the reign of King Kalakaua and Queen Kapiolani, a small group is ushered into the storage areas of the museum. Here they are treated to artifacts focusing on Hawaii's monarchy period: personal effects of Hawaii's kings and queens including royal jewels and garments and a series of other royal relics and treasures. Additional fee for the tour.

The museum also houses a planetarium, various children's activities, and classes in quilting, hula dancing, lei-making and weaving. The Bishop is truly one of the finest museums of its kind in the world. Admission. ~ 1525 Bernice Street; 808-847-3511, fax 808-842-4703; www.bishopmuseum.org, e-mail info@ bishopmuseum.org.

The other, more scenic road across the mountains is the Pali Highway, Route 61. As it ascends, it passes **Queen Emma's Summer Palace.** Constructed in 1848, the palace was originally used as a mountain home by King Kamehameha IV and his wife, Queen Emma. Today the gracious white-pillared house is a museum. Here you can view the Queen's personal artifacts, as well as various other period pieces. The Palace's gardens are especially beautiful; you can almost see the Queen entertaining her guests by the lily pond. The gift shop has a nice selection of local crafts and books. Admission. ~ 808-595-3167, fax 808-595-4395; www.daughters ofhawaii.org, e-mail doh@pixi.com.

You can also walk the tree-shaded grounds of **Nuuanu Pali Drive** and follow until it rejoins the highway. This residential boulevard, with its natural canopy and park-like atmosphere, is one of Honolulu's many idyllic hideaways. ◄ HIDDEN

Farther along Pali Highway, there is a turnoff to **Nuuanu Pali Lookout.** It is a point that must not be missed, and is without doubt Oahu's finest view. Gaze down the sheer, rugged face of the Koolau cliffs as they drop 3000 feet to a softly rolling coastal shelf. Your view will extend from Makapuu Point to the distant reaches of Kaneohe Bay, and from the lip of the cliff far out to sea. It was from these heights, according to legend, that a vanquished army was forced to plunge when Kamehameha I captured Oahu in 1795.

For a quiet stroll or picnic, drive out to **Moanalua Gardens,** part of a large private estate open to the public and maintained by the Damon family. The park is often deserted, perhaps due to the lack of facilities, so you'll be assured plenty of solitude for wandering among the native plants and meandering stream. Kamehameha V's summer home is here as well. The trees, especially the centuries-old monkey pods, are the most outstanding feature of the park. ~ Entrance and parking lot are along the Puuloa Road off-ramp from westbound Moanalua Freeway; 808-833-1944.

PEARL HARBOR Many people consider a trip to Pearl Harbor a pilgrimage. It was here on a sleepy Sunday morning, December 7, 1941, that the Japanese launched a sneak attack on the United

States naval fleet anchored in the port, immediately plunging the nation into World War II. As Japanese planes bombed the harbor, over 2400 Americans lost their lives. Eighteen ships sank that day in the country's greatest military disaster.

The battleship USS *Arizona* was hit so savagely by aerial bombs and torpedoes that it plunged to the bottom, entombing over 1100 sailors within its hulk; today they remain in that watery grave. A special **USS Arizona Memorial** was built to honor them; it's constructed directly above the ship, right in the middle of Pearl Harbor. The memorial includes a shrine with the name of each sailor who died aboard the ship carved in marble. Gazing at this too, too long list of names, and peering over the side at the shadowy hull of the ship, it's hard not to be overcome by the tragic history of the place. Daily from 7:30 a.m. to 3 p.m., the United States Navy sponsors free boat tours out to this fascinating memorial. Before boarding, be sure to remember, no bathing suits or bare feet are permitted. Pearl Harbor, several miles northwest of Downtown Honolulu, can be reached by car or bus. ~ 808-422-2771, fax 808-483-8608; www.nps.gov/usar.

For another perspective on World War II, visit the **Battleship Missouri Memorial**. Launched in 1944, the *Missouri*, or Mighty Mo as it is usually called, was the last U.S. battleship ever built. It was aboard this 887-foot vessel on September 2, 1945, that General Douglas MacArthur accepted the surrender of the Japanese forces, thus ending World War II. The decommissioned battleship is now docked in Pearl Harbor, off Ford Island, within

AUTHOR FAVORITE

Founded in 1889 by Charles Reed Bishop in honor of his late wife, Princess Bernice Pauahi Bishop, the last descendant of the royal Kamehameha family, the **Bishop Museum** now includes over two million artifacts, documents and photographs about Hawaii as well as other Pacific island cultures. Built on the original site of the Kamehameha Schools for Boys, a school established to educate Hawaiian children, the museum was created to augment their education and instill a greater pride in their Hawaiian heritage. The one remaining building from the school, which was relocated in the '60s, is Bishop Hall. The museum is a must-see for anyone interested in Hawaiiana. See page 156 for more information.

sight of the USS *Arizona* Memorial. Tours depart from the ticket office of the *Bowfin* submarine. Guided tours are available, or you can tour the Mighty Mo on your own, getting a first-hand glimpse of its massive armaments, the surrender deck and the commanding bridge. Plan to spend an hour on the self-guided tour. Reservations recommended. Admission. ~ 808-423-2263, 888-877-6477; www.ussmissouri.com, e-mail bigmo@ussmissouri.org.

Anchored nearby the *Arizona* visitors center is the **USS Bowfin Submarine Museum**. This World War II–era submarine is a window into life beneath the waves. It provides an excellent opportunity to tour the claustrophobic quarters in which 80 men spent months at a time. The accompanying museum, filled with submarine-related artifacts, will help provide an even fuller perspective. Admission. ~ 808-423-1341, fax 808-422-5201; www.bowfin.org.

Atlantis Adventures offers a 90-minute deluxe package that includes transfers from Waikiki, tours of sunken ships and airplanes, and lunch, with an optional dive stop. Transfers to the ship itself are by open-air trolley via the Ford Island Bridge. Steep admission. ~ 808-973-9800, 888-732-5782, fax 808-973-9840.

ALA MOANA–MOILIILI–KAPAHULU–KAIMUKI AREA   Bordering the *ewa* direction of Waikiki, just Diamond Head–side of Downtown Honolulu, is Ala Moana (which means "pathway to the sea"). Its claim to fame is a very large family-oriented park that extends from the Ala Wai Yacht Harbor along the ocean to Kewalo Basin. **Ala Moana Beach Park** is where Honolulu residents flock to on the weekends to hold family reunions or company picnics, or to play volleyball, softball or tennis with their friends. The sandy beach that lines the park is a safe place for swimmers, especially near **Magic Island** (Ala Moana Regional Park), the peninsula on the east side of the park. Long-distance swimmers practice swimming the length of the park, while joggers run alongside the shore to get into shape. Watching the sun set from this spot is the sport of choice for many locals and tourists alike.

Across the street, **Ala Moana Center** is the shop-'til-you-drop capital of the islands (and almost anywhere else in the U.S.). In addition to over 200 shops, Ala Moana Center is the main transfer point for most island buses, so if you ride TheBus, you'll likely end up here at some point. ~ www.alamoana.com.

Just *mauka* (toward the mountains) of Ala Moana are several working-class communities—Moiliili, Kapahulu and Kaimuki. They skirt the University on one side and Waikiki on the other. What's best about these neighborhoods is the handful of restaurants that are far enough away from the madding crowd of Waikiki to make eating out a pleasure. Restaurants in every budget category can be found in these enclaves, and best of all, you'll more than likely be dining with a local crowd.

HIDDEN ►   In Moiliili, the **Japanese Cultural Center of Hawaii** sponsors a permanent exhibit focusing on Hawaiian-Japanese culture. In addition to the gallery, there's a little gift shop. The Resource Center contains an extensive collection of books, pamphlets, periodicals and oral histories of the Japanese in Hawaii. It also hosts festivals marking traditional Japanese holidays; call ahead for details. Closed Sunday and Monday. Admission. ~ 2454 South Beretania Street; 808-945-7633, fax 808-944-1123; www.jcch. com, e-mail jcch@lava.net.

MANOA VALLEY   Residents of a different sort are found in the city's beautiful Manoa Valley, a couple of miles northeast of Waikiki. Among the elegant homes decorating the region are some owned by the New England families that settled in Hawaii in the 19th century.

The **University of Hawaii** has its main campus here; almost 20,000 students and 2000 faculty members attend classes and teach on these grounds, which are set amid rolling lawns and backdropped by the Koolau Mountains. ~ 2444 Dole Street; 808-956-8111; www.hawaii.edu.

Don't miss the opportunity to visit the **University of Hawaii Art Gallery**. The gallery, employing modular and movable walls, constantly reinvents itself to the configurations of visiting exhibits. Recent exhibits include intricately patterned Japanese fishermen's coats and contemporary Korean art. My favorite is the ever-popular triennial International Shoebox Sculpture Exhibitions, which challenge artists to create small-scale works with big impact. Artists from all over the world have used a range of materials that included desiccated vegetables, computer chips and human hair. You never know what the gallery will offer up. Closed Saturday. ~ Art Building, University of Hawaii at Manoa; 808-956-6888; www. hawaii.edu/artgallery, e-mail gallery@hawaii.edu.

The
Neighborhoods

The neighborhoods of Honolulu stretch along the flatlands that spread out from downtown and snake their way up the valleys and over the hills that surround the city. They provide a social history of this Polynesian metropolis, as its population grew and its economy expanded.

One of the oldest neighborhoods, **Kalihi**, still thrives as a working-class enclave west of downtown. As Honolulu grew, wealthy and middle-class people moved farther eastward and northward to the outer reaches of the city. The poorer Hawaiian residents of Kalihi were joined by immigrants and people leaving the plantations for an urban lifestyle. In Kalihi, they were close to factory jobs and small farms still scattered through the area. They opened clubs and restaurants and established schools and churches, many of which still exist today.

Manoa, the valley neighborhood that serves as home to the University of Hawaii, served as a popular retreat of Hawaiian royalty in the early 19th century. It was later settled by descendants of missionaries, who built homes reminiscent of their New England origins. The estate of the Cooke family, who founded Castle & Cooke, one of the Big Five companies that controlled the state, can be found here.

The neighborhood was also settled by Chinese, who favored Manoa for its excellent *feng shui*. Because the mountains on both sides act as protection and funnel energy through the valley, the Chinese people believed living there would bring good luck. Manoa owes its natural heritage partly to the founder of the Lyons Arboretum, who at the turn of the 20th century planted trees from around the world in what was to become a verdant valley.

The **Kahala District**, which stretches out along the coast east of Diamond Head became one of the realms of the rich, with their beautiful homes lined along the beach. This neighborhood remains quiet and peaceful, blessed by the breezes that blow in from its shores and unsullied by the kind of development that has commercialized other urban beach areas. Although the beach is shaded by coconut palms, local residents don't have to worry about falling coconuts. They're all picked by local Tongan tree climbers, hired to prevent the dropping fruit from bonking heads.

HIDDEN ▶

On a hot day, the **John Young Museum of Art** on campus may be just the place to take refuge. The museum centers around Asian art, including ancient Chinese tomb figures, modern Japanese pottery, Korean Buddha figurines and works from many other Asian nations. There's also tribal art and a variety of works from other parts of the world. After wandering around the exhibition area, take time to walk the grounds as well; there's a quiet courtyard with sculptures, a water garden and a reflecting pool. Closed Monday, Wednesday, Thursday and Saturday. ~ Krauss Hall, 2500 Dole Street; 808-956-3634; www.outreach.hawaii.edu/jymuseum.

HIDDEN ▶

Also on campus is the **East-West Center**, a private research facility. Designed by noted architect I. M. Pei, the center is devoted to the study of Asian and American cultures. The center also contains a number of priceless Asian artworks, well worth viewing. ~ John Burns Hall, 1601 East-West Road; 808-944-7111; www.ewc.hawaii.edu, e-mail ewcinfo@eastwestcenter.org.

From campus you can head deeper into Manoa Valley along Oahu Avenue and Manoa Road. You'll pass the **Waioli Tea Room** (808-988-5800), a cozy dining room tucked into a garden setting where you can enjoy breakfast or high tea, a bakery and a gift shop. Here also is the **Little Grass Shack** that was once occupied by novelist Robert Louis Stevenson (or so the story goes), and a small chapel replete with stained-glass windows. ~ 2950 Manoa Road.

Farther down Manoa Road is **Lyon Arboretum**, a magnificent 194-acre garden with over 8000 plant species, research greenhouses, hiking trails and perhaps the world's largest collection of palm trees. The arboretum also offers one-day classes on topics such as horticulture and lei-making. Closed Sunday. ~ 3860 Manoa Road; 808-988-0456; www.hawaii.edu/lyonarboretum.

KAHALA AREA Diamond Head Beach Park, a twisting ribbon of white sand, nestles directly below the famous crater. Whenever the wind and waves are good, you'll see windsurfers and surfers galore sweeping in toward the shoreline. The coral reef here makes for good skindiving, too. It's a pretty beach, backdropped by the Kuilei cliffs and watched over by the **Diamond Head Lighthouse**.

From Diamond Head, continue east along Diamond Head Road and Kahala Avenue. These will lead through the Kahala District, home to the island's elite. Bordered by the ocean and the exclusive Waialae Country Club is a golden string of spectacular oceanfront homes with carefully manicured lawns.

Tobacco heiress Doris Duke, a socialite celebrity of the mid-20th century, built a fantasy home on a five-acre site on the lava rock headland called Black Point, just to the east of Diamond Head. Duke, who died in 1993, created a museum of the house, which she'd romantically named **Shangri La**, after the legendary Himalayan valley where peace and good health prevailed. Intrigued by Islamic art, Duke designed the home with Islamic architectural features, furnishings and artworks. The museum, in Kahala, is open to a limited number of visitors daily, with departures from the Honolulu Academy of Arts. Advance bookings are required for the docent-led tour. ~ For details and tour options contact the Honolulu Academy of Arts; 808-532-8701.

LODGING

If you're arriving via Honolulu International Airport, you can't get much more convenient than the **Best Western Plaza Hotel**. The 274 guest rooms are basic and comfortable; all have refrigerators. Amenities include a pool and a restaurant. There's free shuttle service 24 hours a day to and from the airport. ~ 3253 North Nimitz Highway; 808-836-3636, 800-800-4683, fax 808-834-7406; www.bestwesternhonolulu.com, e-mail info@bestwestern honolulu.com. MODERATE TO DELUXE.

Pacific Marina Inn bills itself as a "little oasis near the Honolulu airport." That may be hyperbolic, but it *is* convenient and comfortable: the suites have refrigerators, there's free shuttle

AUTHOR FAVORITE

Hawaii's foremost bed-and-breakfast inn rests in a magnificent old mansion near the University of Hawaii campus. Set in the lush Manoa Valley, the **Manoa Valley Inn** is a 1915 cream-colored Victorian featuring seven guest rooms and an adjacent cottage. Decorated with patterned wallpaper and old-style artworks, the rooms are furnished in plump antique armchairs. Guests enjoy a spacious veranda and lawn. For luxury and privacy, this historic jewel is one of the island's finest spots. Continental breakfast is included. ~ 2001 Vancouver Drive; 808-947-6019, 800-634-5115, fax 808-946-6168; www.aloha.net/~wery, e-mail manoavalleyinn@aloha.net. MODERATE TO ULTRA-DELUXE.

service to the airport, a swimming pool, a restaurant and laundry facilities, as well as karaoke in the bar. In addition, the hotel is adjacent to the Keehi Lagoon Park, where there are tennis courts. ~ 2628 Waiwai Loop; 808-836-1131, 800-548-8040, fax 808-833-0851; www.castleresorts.com/pmi. MODERATE.

The **Nuuanu** YMCA has inexpensive accommodations for men. Complete athletic facilities are available. ~ 1441 Pali Highway; 808-536-3556, fax 808-521-1181; e-mail nuuanu-ymca@hotmail.com. BUDGET.

The **Pagoda Hotel** is sufficiently removed from the crowds but still only a ten-minute drive from the beach. Spacious studio and one-bedroom units put the accent on rattan furniture. The carpeted rooms feature views of the hotel garden or distant mountains. Two-bedroom units in the adjoining Pagoda Terrace offer kitchens. ~ 1525 Rycroft Street; 808-941-6611, 800-367-2373, fax 808-955-5067; www.pagodahotel.com, e-mail reservation@hthcorp.com. MODERATE.

The **Ala Moana Hotel** provides a nice balance of luxury and Hawaiian culture. The 1152-plus comfortable guest rooms range from standard (with a refrigerator, air conditioning and other basic amenities) to "superior" (with views of the city, the Koolau Mountains or the ocean). Hawaiians from other islands often stay here: you can walk to Ala Moana Shopping Center and Ala Moana Regional Park. The Hawaii Convention Center is just across the street, and Polynesian music and fire dance is performed nightly. ~ 410 Atkinson Drive; 808-955-4811, 800-367-6025, fax 808-944-2974; www.alamoanahotel.com, e-mail reservations@alamoanahotel.com. MODERATE TO DELUXE.

Also in Manoa Valley, the **Fernhurst** YWCA is an appealing three-story lowrise that provides a residence for women. Rooms are single or double occupancy with shared baths. Among the facilities are microwaves, refrigerators, laundry, dining room, swimming pool and lounge. Rates include breakfast and dinner Monday through Friday. ~ 1566 Wilder Avenue; 808-941-2231, fax 808-949-0266; www.fernywcaoahu.org. BUDGET.

The **Atherton** YMCA is a coed facility with accommodations for men and women. Across the street from the University of Hawaii campus, it's open year-round to full-time students (of any institution, but you have to show registration and student ID) and during the summer to the general public. There's a nonrefundable application fee and a refundable deposit. Facilities include laundry, lounge and a full kitchen. Reservations must be booked at least two weeks in advance and the facility is closed weekends and holidays, so plan accordingly. ~ 1810 University Avenue; 808-946-0253, fax 808-941-7802; e-mail ymca@hawaii.edu. BUDGET.

Hostelling International—Honolulu is a dormitory-style crash pad with separate living quarters for men and women, although there are a few studios available. Shared kitchen facilities, television lounge, garden patio and laundry are available. Visitors can book island tours through the hostel. ~ 2323-A Sea View Avenue; 808-946-0591, fax 808-946-5904; www.hostelsaloha.com, e-mail hihostel@lava.net. BUDGET.

For a real splurge you might want to check into **Kahala Mandarin Oriental Resort**. Located right on a secluded beach, this exclusive hostelry offers myriad activities (all complimentary, naturally) for adults and kids. There's a natural-looking lagoon where you can get up close and personal (read: swim) with the resident dolphins. Or you can attend some of the fitness and cultural (lei-making, ukulele-playing) classes. ~ 5000 Kahala Avenue; 808-739-8888, 800-367-2525, fax 808-739-8800; www.mandarin oriental.com, e-mail sales@mohg.com. ULTRA-DELUXE.

DINING

Liliha Seafood Restaurant, a neighborhood café out past Downtown Honolulu, comes highly recommended by local folks. This could very well be the only Hawaiian dining spot that offers sweet-and-sour sea bass, squid with sour mustard cabbage and fried squid with *ong choy*. In addition to two dozen seafood dishes, they have a host of chicken, pork, vegetable and noodle selections. ~ 1408 Liliha Street; 808-536-2663. BUDGET TO MODERATE.

◄ HIDDEN

AUTHOR FAVORITE

One of my favorite Japanese eateries is **Irifune**, a warm and friendly place frequented by a local crowd. In fact, around dinnertime, you will likely find yourself in line. The decor gives off a fun, casual air: fishing nets, Kabuki masks and other assorted wallhangings. On the menu are tasty curry, sushi, teriyaki and tempura dishes, plus several other Asian delectables. Closed Sunday and Monday. ~ 563 Kapahulu Avenue; 808-737-1141. BUDGET TO MODERATE.

HIDDEN ► Quietly hidden away in a tiny storefront in the Kalihi district, **Helena's Hawaiian Foods** has been dishing up *kalua* pig, *lomi* salmon and *pipikaula* for more than 50 years. The food is served in tiny dishes, so you can sample a selection. The luau chicken cooked with taro leaves and coconut milk is a knockout. The place only has 13 tables, which means there's often a wait. But it's worth it. Closed Saturday through Monday. ~ 1240 North School Street; 808-845-8044. BUDGET.

Sari Sari is a Kalihi culinary treasure. This '50s-style coffee shop with a counter, booths and paneled and mirrored walls specializes in such Filipino favorites as pork *adobo*, *pansit*, *bangus sinigang*, beef *asada* and *lumpia*. Though it claims to be the "home of the finest Filipino food in Kalihi," some say it's the finest in all of Honolulu. ~ 2153 North King Street; 808-845-0340. BUDGET.

In Kalihi, **Meg's Drive-In** is a small eatery serving breakfast, local-style plate lunches and daily specials such as fried noodles with teriyaki beef. You can take your meal to go or dine on the adjoining lanai. No dinner Saturday. Closed Sunday. ~ 743 Waiakamilo Road; 808-845-3943. BUDGET.

For prime rib, Alaskan snow crab legs, shrimp and vegetable tempura, try the **Pagoda Floating Restaurant**. This restaurant-in-the-round sits above a pond populated with gaily colored tropical saltwater fish. Several cascades and a fountain feed the pond. The surrounding grounds have been carefully landscaped. This dining room offers lunch and dinner buffets with themes such as prime rib night. ~ 1525 Rycroft Street; 808-941-6611, fax 808-946-6596. DELUXE.

To go where the local gentry dine, head to **Alan Wong's Restaurant**. "Appeteasers" in the form of quarter-sized burgers made from an ahi tuna combination hint at bigger and better things to come. Alan Wong himself will concoct a meal for you, surprising you with the Chef's Tasting Menu; or you can select from a menu filled with locally caught fish, home-grown produce and a wealth of meat and poultry dishes. One of the *in* places to dine on Hawaiian Regional cuisine, so reservations are suggested. ~ 1857 South King Street; 808-949-2526, fax 808-951-9520; www.alanwongs.com. DELUXE.

HIDDEN ► The decor at **Jimbo's Restaurant** is simple but the noodles are superb. Jimbo's serves Japanese *udon*—thick, white and perfectly cooked—in a broth so delicious your taste buds will rejoice. This is Japanese soul food at its finest and no doubt the best *udon* this side of Tokyo. No wonder there's always a line outside. ~ 1936 South King Street; 808-947-2211, fax 808-951-9554. BUDGET.

A rising star on the Honolulu culinary scene is **Chef Mavro's.** Chef George Mavrothalassitis, formerly of the Four Seasons Resort in Wailea, now presides over his own corner in Honolulu. The unassuming building on South King Street does not hint at what awaits inside—an elegant yet understated dining room adorned with local artwork. The French-inspired cuisine arrives at the table in an equally sublime presentation. The dishes are five-star and the service impeccable. One claim to fame of Chef Mavro is the perfect pairing of the wine with every item on the menu. A place for that special night. Dinner only. Closed Monday. ~ 1969 South King Street; 808-944-4714; www.chef mavro.com, e-mail mavro@gte.net. ULTRA-DELUXE.

For crafts, sushi, fresh produce and even feng shui advice, visit the Honolulu Street Market. Open Saturday from 8 a.m. to 2 p.m. ~ 90 Pohukaina Street; 808-221-6042.

McCully Chop Suey, one of Honolulu's best budget-priced Chinese restaurants, is rather bland but offers a menu that contains everything imaginable. There are over 160 items to choose from—two dozen poultry dishes, eight different sizzling platters, and a host of beef, noodle and seafood dishes. ~ 2005 South King Street; 808-946-4069. BUDGET.

Right next to Waikiki, in Ala Moana Center, there are numerous ethnic takeout restaurants that share a large dining pavilion called **Makai Market.** Best of all is **Patti's Chinese Kitchen** (808-946-5002, fax 808-943-4355), a crowded and noisy gathering place. At Patti's you can choose from over 20 entrées plus a side order of fried rice or *chow fun*. The courses include dim sum, orange chicken, beef and broccoli, tofu, beef tomato, sweet-and-sour ribs, barbecued pork and shrimp with vegetables. There's also the **Poi Bowl** (808-949-8444), a takeout stand serving traditional Hawaiian dishes. **Tsuruya Noodle Shop** (808-946-7214) features bowls of Japanese soba and udon noodles. ~ BUDGET.

◄ HIDDEN

Or you can ride the escalator to the upper level of Ala Moana Center. Here **Shirokiya,** a massive Asian department store, features an informal Japanese à la carte–style buffet. ~ 808-973-9111. MODERATE.

HIDDEN ▶

A few blocks away at Daiei, a grocery and department store filled with an amazing variety of Asian and Hawaiian foods and goods features the **Daiei Food Court,** an incredibly popular spot with local shoppers. Choose from places like **Sushi Robot,** which serves pre-made bento lunch boxes and made-to-order sushi. **Harpos** turns out pizza and spaghetti, and **Manapua** creates such Chinese favorites as roast duck and pork and noodles. ~ 801 Kaheka Street; 808-973-4800. BUDGET.

Hawaiian regional cuisine accented by island fruits is featured at the **Prince Court.** The Hawaii Prince Hotel's harborside restaurant, this dining room is known for dishes like sea scallops and lobster. An extensive wine list is another plus at this Polynesian-style dining room appointed with floral bouquets. ~ 100 Holomoana Street; 808-956-1111. DELUXE TO ULTRA-DELUXE.

Near the University of Hawaii campus, there are pizzas, sub sandwiches and chicken dinners at **Magoo's.** Open for lunch on weekends and dinner daily, it's a great place to snack or stop for a cold beer. ~ Puck's Alley, 1015 University Avenue; 808-949-5381. BUDGET TO MODERATE.

Or you can check out **Anna Bannana's,** a combination bar and restaurant that draws a swinging crowd. Located a half-mile from campus, this dim eatery serves calamari, buffalo wings and other savory favorites. Decorated in slapdash fashion with propellers, antlers, surfboards, boxing gloves and trophies, Anna's is the local center for slumming. ~ 2440 South Beretania Street; 808-946-5190. BUDGET.

Fiery Szechuan-style cooking is done with competence and style at the tastefully elegant **King Tsin Restaurant,** a popular Chinese eatery. The locale is well away from Waikiki's hustle and bustle, although still easily reached. The extensive menu offers

SWAP 'EM, BRAH

For a variety of secondhand items, try the **Kam Super Swap Meet.** It's a great place to barter for bargains, meet local folks and find items you'll never see in stores. It's open on Wednesday, Saturday, Sunday and some holidays. ~ 98-850 Moanalua Road; 808-483-5933, 808-483-5535 legendary potstickers, honey-glazed spareribs, garlic eggplant and other spicy treats. Most items are hot, but there are a few mild dishes for the more timid. ~ 2140 Beretania Street; 808-946-3273. MODERATE.

With a conveyor belt that propels the meandering sushi bar, **Genki Sushi** is one of Honolulu's most enjoyable and best-priced sushi restaurants. Be prepared for a 15- to 20-minute wait for a table, then dig in. ~ 885 Kapahulu Avenue; 808-735-7700, fax 808-735-7708. BUDGET TO MODERATE.

Quantity and quality don't usually come together, particularly where gourmet restaurants are concerned. But at **Sam Choy** you can count on platter-size portions of macadamia-crusted *ono*, Oriental lamb chops or oven-roasted duck. Considered one of the top Hawaiian cuisine restaurants on the island, it sits with unassuming grace on the second floor of a strip mall. Eat heartily (and well)! Dinner and Sunday brunch. ~ 449 Kapahulu Avenue, Suite 201; 808-732-8645, fax 808-732-8683; www.samchoy.com. DE-LUXE TO ULTRA-DELUXE.

For local-style plate lunches, cruise in to **Rainbow Drive-In**.   ◄ HIDDEN
Popular with *kamaainas* and tourists alike, the menu includes hamburger steak, beef curry, breaded and grilled mahimahi, chili and fried chicken served with two scoops of rice and macaroni salad. ~ 3308 Kanaina Avenue; 808-737-0177. BUDGET.

Ono Hawaiian Foods is a must for all true Hawaii lovers. It's a hole-in-da-wall eatery on a busy street. But if you're lucky enough to get one of the few tables, you can feast on *laulau*, *kalua* pig, *pipikaula*, poi and *haupia*. The walls are papered with signed photographs of local notables and the place is packed with locals, notable and otherwise. Closed Sunday. ~ 726 Kapahulu Avenue; 808-737-2275. BUDGET TO MODERATE.

Waialae Avenue, a neighborhood strip several miles outside Waikiki, has developed into a gourmet ghetto. **Azteca Mexican Restaurant** is a vinyl-booth-and-plastic-panel eatery that serves a delicious array of Mexican food. ~ 3617 Waialae Avenue; 808-735-2492. BUDGET TO MODERATE.

Award-winning **3660 On the Rise** is a local favorite, blending Asian influences with a definite touch of California cuisine. Try their signature ahi katsu: deep-fried ahi wrapped in nori with a wasabi-ginger sauce. Finish off the meal with Harlequin crème brûlée, which is difficult to describe without salivating but basically involves vanilla-bean custard and chocolate mousse glazed with caramel. Dinner only. Closed Monday. ~ 3660 Waialae Avenue; 808-737-1177, fax 808-735-6105; www.3660.com, e-mail 3660@flex.com. ULTRA-DELUXE.

HIDDEN ►

For spicy and delicious Asian dishes, it is hard to find a more appealing place than **Hale Vietnam**. A family restaurant that draws a local crowd, it has traditional Vietnamese soup and a host of excellent entrées. ~ 1140 12th Avenue; 808-735-7581. MODERATE.

After shopping at the upscale Kahala Mall, slip over to the **Olive Tree Cafe** for some delightful Greek and Middle Eastern food served in a no-nonsense atmosphere. Classics like falafel, souvlakis, *babaghanouj* and hummus are excellent, and the salads, lamb, fish and chicken dishes are also good. The tasty cuisine makes up for the spartan dining room. You can also bring your own beer and wine, and there's no corkage fee. ~ 4614 Kilauea Avenue; 808-737-0303. BUDGET TO MODERATE.

GROCERIES In Kalihi, you can find a **Times Supermarket** (open 6 a.m. to 11 p.m.) at 1290 South Beretania Street, 808-532-5400; or in Kaimuki (open 7 a.m. to 10 p.m.) at 3221 Waialae Avenue, 808-733-5050. In Moiliili near the University, **Star Market** is open 5 a.m. to 2 a.m. ~ 2470 South King Street; 808-973-1666. In Kahala, there's a **Star Market** in the Kahala Mall that's open 6 a.m. to 12 a.m. ~ 808-733-1366.

The best place in Honolulu to buy health foods is at **Down To Earth Natural Foods**. ~ 2525 South King Street; 808-947-7678. **Kokua Market** is another excellent choice. ~ 2643 South King Street; 808-941-1922.

SHOPPING Scattered around town are several shops that I recommend you check out. At **Lanakila Crafts** most of the goods are made by the disabled, and the craftsmanship is superb. There are shell necklaces, woven handbags, monkeypod bowls and homemade dolls. You'll probably see these items in other stores around the islands, with much higher price tags than here at the "factory." ~ 1809 Bachelot Street; 808-531-0555.

Out at the Bishop Museum be sure to stop by **Shop Pacifica**, which offers a fine selection of Hawaiiana. There are books on island history and geography, an assortment of instruments that include nose flutes and gourds, plus cards, souvenirs and wooden bowls. ~ 1525 Bernice Street, near the intersection of Routes 63 and H-1; 808-848-4158.

Ala Moana Center, on the outskirts of Waikiki, is the state's largest shopping center. This multitiered complex has practically everything. Ala Moana features three department stores: **Sears** (808-947-0252), **Macy's** (808-941-2345) and a Japanese emporium called **Shirokiya** (808-973-9111). You'll also find an assortment of stores selling liquor, tennis and golf supplies, stationery, leather goods, cameras, shoes, tobacco, etc. You name it, they have it. The designer shops, appropriately, are located on the upper levels. ~ 1450 Ala Moana Boulevard; 808-955-9517; www.alamoana center.com, e-mail info@alamoanacenter.com.

> The Longs Drug Store at Ala Moana Center is a good place to buy inexpensive Hawaiian curios. ~ 808-941-4433.

For a variety of secondhand items, try the **Kam Super Swap Meet**. It's a great place to barter for bargains, meet local folks and find items you'll never see in stores. It's open on Wednesday, Saturday, Sunday and some holidays. ~ 98-850 Moanalua Road; 808-483-5933, 808-483-5535.

One of Honolulu's more upscale shopping centers is **Kahala Mall**, where you'll find designer shops galore. This attractive complex also hosts almost 100 moderately priced stores. **Barnes & Noble** (808-737-3323) has a superstore here. In addition to a comprehensive line of books, they sell tapes and CDs and feature a café on the premises. ~ 4211 Waialae Avenue; 808-732-7736.

Outside Honolulu there are usually a couple of spots to hear Hawaiian music. Pick up a copy of *Spotlight's Oahu Gold* or *This Week Oahu* magazine to see what's going on.

NIGHTLIFE

At **Rumours**, theme nights are the spice of life. Salsa, retro, hip-hop and Top 40 are all featured, along with "Big Chill" night on Friday featuring '60s music. Located in the Ala Moana Hotel, this club is decorated with artwork and neon fixtures. Cover. ~ 410 Atkinson Drive; 808-955-4811; www.alamoanahotel.com.

Located east of Waikiki, the **Hard Rock Cafe** is always a kick. Decorated with tons of rock-and-roll memorabilia, this restaurant/bar is a popular nightspot for those who like loud music and a big crowd. Live bands play on Friday night. ~ 1837 Kapiolani Boulevard; 808-955-7383; www.hardrock.com.

Over by the University of Hawaii's Manoa campus, there's **Anna Bannana's**. A popular hangout for years, this wildly decorated spot has all types of live music on Thursday, Friday and Saturday nights. Cover for live shows. ~ 2440 South Beretania Street; 808-946-5190.

BEACHES & PARKS

HIDDEN ▶

KEAIWA HEIAU STATE RECREATION AREA 🏃 Amazing as it sounds, this is a wooded retreat within easy driving distance of Honolulu. Situated in the Koolau foothills overlooking Pearl Harbor, it contains the remains of a *heiau*, a temple once used by Hawaiian healers. There's a forest extending to the far reaches of the mountains and a loop hiking trail. Facilities include picnic area, showers and restrooms. ~ Located in Aiea Heights. To get there from Honolulu, take Route 90 west to Aiea, then follow Aiea Heights Drive to the park.

▲ Tents only. State permit required.

HIDDEN ▶

ALA MOANA REGIONAL PARK 🏊 🎣 🏄 🍴 This 119-acre park is a favorite with Hawaii residents. On weekends every type of outdoor enthusiast imaginable turns out to swim, snorkel, fish (common catches are *papio*, bonefish, goatfish and *moano*), jog, sail model boats and so on. It's also a good place to surf; there are three separate breaks here: "Concessions," "Tennis Courts" and "Baby Haleiwa" all have summer waves. There's a curving length of beach, a grassy park area, a helluva lot of local color and facilities that include a picnic area, restrooms, showers, concession stands, tennis courts, a recreation building, a bowling green and lifeguards. Fun fact: in the opening credits of "Gilligan's Island," the ship set sail out of the harbor near here. ~ On Ala Moana Boulevard at the west end of Waikiki, across from Ala Moana Center.

HIDDEN ▶

DIAMOND HEAD BEACH PARK 🏊 🎣 🏄 🍴 A heaven to windsurfers, this twisting ribbon of white sand sits directly below the crater. It's close enough to Waikiki for convenient access but far enough to shake most of the crowds. The Kuilei cliffs, covered with scrub growth, loom behind the beach. Snorkeling is good as a coral reef extends offshore through this area. There's also a good year-round surf break called "Lighthouse." And for the anglers, your chances are good to reel in *ulua*, *papio* or *mamao*. A shower is the sole facility. ~ Located just beyond Waikiki along Diamond Head Road at the foot of Diamond Head; watch for parked cars.

KUILEI CLIFFS BEACH PARK AND KAALAWAI BEACH 🏊

🛶 ⚓ ⛴ 🎣 Extending east from Diamond Head Beach Park, these sandy corridors are also flanked by sharp sea cliffs. Together they extend from Diamond Head Lighthouse to Black Point. The aquatic attractions are the same as at Diamond Head Beach Park and both beaches can be reached from it (or from cliff trails leading down from Diamond Head Road). A protecting reef makes for good swimming at Kaalawai Beach (which can also be reached via a public accessway off Kulumanu Place).

WAIALAE BEACH PARK 🏊 🛶 🎣 Smack in the middle of Honolulu's prestigious Kahala district, where a million dollars buys a modest house, sits this tidy beach. Its white sand neatly groomed, its spacious lawn shaded by palms, Waialae is a true find. It has good swimming and fishing. There are bathhouse facilities, beachside picnic tables and a footbridge arching across the stream that divides the property. To the west of the park lies **Kahala Beach**, a long, thin swath of sand that extends all the way to Black Point. There's good snorkeling near the Kahala Mandarin Oriental Hotel. ~ Located on the 4900 block of Kahala Avenue in Kahala.

SEVEN

Southeast Oahu

Out past Honolulu, beyond the glitter of Waikiki and the gilded neighborhoods of Kahala, the pace slows down, the vistas open up and Oahu begins to look more like a tropical island. The road—Route 72, the Kalanianaole Highway—leads out of Honolulu and hugs the rugged coastline as it climbs up and down and back and forth along the edge of a series of volcanic ridges. The jagged, jade-colored peaks of the Koolau Mountains on one side and the sparkling blue sea on the other provide some of the most striking scenery the state has to offer.

Fortunately, there are lots of places to stop and admire it along the way. Some of Hawaii's best snorkeling is at Hanauma Bay, a marine nature preserve. Koko Head and Koko Crater have hiking trails, and a swim is an option at any of a number of pocket beaches that dot the shore. For those who long for more "traditional" amusements, there is also Sea Life Park, a marine theme park, about midway along the Southeast Coast.

Eventually the road drops down and continues alongside fields to Waimanalo, the center of a farming region that once long ago was a sugar plantation but now supplies much of the fruit and flowers that appear in Honolulu's markets. The town preserves a bit of the Hawaiian Wild West, with people parading through town in pickups and a yearly spring rodeo that attracts *paniolos* (cowboys) from around Oahu and the Neighbor Islands. Waimanalo, and the surrounding rural lands, are another side of the multifaceted island of Oahu, and one that warrants a closer look.

The highway streams through Hawaii Kai and other residential areas, then ascends the slopes of an extinct volcano, 642-foot **Koko Head**. Here Madame Pele is reputed to have dug a hole for the last time in search of fiery volcanic matter.

Koko Crater, the second hump on the horizon, rises to over 1200 feet. This fire-pit, according to Hawaiian legend, is the vagina of Pele's sister. It seems that Pele, goddess of volcanoes, was being pursued by a handsome demigod. Her sister, trying to distract the hot suitor from Pele, spread her legs across the landscape.

From the top of Koko Head, a well-marked road and sidewalk lead down to **Hanauma Bay**, one of the prettiest beaches in all Hawaii. The word *hanauma* means "the curved bay," and you will clearly see that Hanauma Bay was once a circular volcano, one wall of which was breached by the sea. This breathtaking place is a marine preserve filled with multicolored coral and teeming with underwater life. Little wonder that Hollywood chose this spot as the prime location for Elvis Presley's movie, *Blue Hawaii*. Elvis' grass shack was right here, and the strand was also a setting in the classic film *From Here to Eternity*.

The swimming and snorkeling are unmatched anywhere and the mazework of coral formations along the bottom adds to the snorkeling adventure. Or you can stroll along the rock ledges that fringe the bay and explore **Toilet Bowl**, a tidepool that "flushes" as the waves wash through it. The best time to come is early morning before other swimmers stir up the waters. Hanauma Bay is an extremely popular picnic spot among local folks, so it is also advisable to visit on a weekday rather than face bucking the crowds on Saturday and Sunday. Because of its popularity, the preserve cuts off entrance to the park when the parking lot is full (another good reason to arrive early). Closed Tuesday. ~ Located on Kalanianaole Highway about 12 miles east of Waikiki; 808-396-4229.

From Hanauma Bay the highway corkscrews along the coast. Among the remarkable scenes you'll enjoy en route are views of Lanai and Molokai, two of Oahu's sister islands. On a clear, clear day you can also see Maui, an island that requires no introduction.

At an overlook you will encounter **Halona Blowhole**, a lava tube through which geysers of seawater blast. During high tide and when the sea is turbulent, these gushers reach dramatic heights. *Halona* means "peering place," and that is exactly what everyone seems to do here. You can't miss the spot, since the roadside parking lot is inevitably crowded with tourists. Between December and April this vista is also a prime whale-watching spot.

Just beyond spreads **Sandy Beach,** one of Hawaii's most renowned bodysurfing spots. It's a long, wide beach piled with fluffy sand and complete with picnic areas and showers. Inexperienced bodysurfers are better off enjoying the excellent sunbathing here, since the dramatic shorebreak that makes the beach so popular among bodysurfers is dangerous for beginners.

HIDDEN ▶

Across from the beach a side road leads up to **Koko Crater Botanical Gardens,** a 60-acre collection of cacti, plumeria and other water-thrifty plants. ~ Kealahou Street, off of Kalanianaole Highway; 808-522-7060.

Route 72 rounds Oahu's southeastern corner and sets a course along the eastern shoreline. It also climbs to a scenic point from which you can take your first view of the Windward Coast. You will be standing on **Makapuu Point.** Above you rise sharp lava cliffs, while below are rolling sand dunes and open ocean. The slope-faced islet just offshore is Rabbit Island. The distant headland is Makapuu Peninsula, toward which you are bound.

Ihiihilauakea Preserve is a 30-acre site above Hanuama Bay protected by the Nature Conservancy. A dry dusty crater in summer, the rare *Marsilea villosa* fern lies dormant until the wet weather.

From this perfect perch you can also spy a complex of buildings. That's **Sea Life Park,** a marine-world attraction comparable to those in California and Florida. Among the many features at this park is the "Hawaiian Reef," a 300,000-gallon oceanarium inhabited by about 4000 sea creatures. To see it you wind through a spiral viewing area that descends three fathoms along the tank's glass perimeter. At times a scuba diver will be hand-feeding the fish. Swimming about this underwater world are sharks, stingrays and a variety of lesser-known species. The park also features a turtle lagoon, penguin habitat and the only known *wholphin* (half whale, half dolphin) living in captivity. Admission. ~ Makapuu Point; 808-259-7933, fax 808-259-7373.

Across the road from Sea Life Park spreads **Makapuu Beach Park,** another fabled but daunting bodysurfing spot that is set in a particularly pretty location. Nearby black lava cliffs are topped by a white lighthouse and **Rabbit Island** is anchored just offshore. Rabbit Island, located off Makapuu Point, resembles a bunny's head, but was actually named for a former rabbit-raising farm there. Makapuu Beach itself is a short, wide rectangle of white sand. It's an ideal place to picnic, but when the surf is up, beware of the waves.

The road continues along the shoreline between soft sand beaches and rugged mountain peaks. For the next 30 miles your attention will be drawn back continually to those rocky crags. They are part of the **Koolau Range**, a wall of precipitous mountains that vault up from Oahu's placid interior. Their spires, minarets and fluted towers are softened here and there by lush, green valleys, but never enough to detract from the sheer beauty and magnitude of the heights. Light and shade play games along their moss-covered surfaces, while rainbows hang suspended between the peaks. If

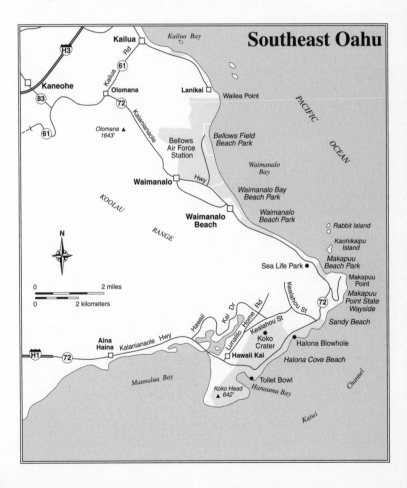

Southeast Oahu

wind and weather permit, you will see hang gliders dusting the cliffs as they sail from the mountains down to the distant beach.

The road continues through **Waimanalo**, an old ranching area that today has been turned to fruit and flower cultivation. Outside town you will see **Olomana Peak**. Favored by rock climbers, it is a double-barreled peak that seems to belong in the Swiss Alps.

LODGING   If you want to follow the footsteps of James Michener and hang out at Waimanalo Beach, you might consider tucking yourself into **Kom A'ona Inn Bed & Breakfast**. Here you'll find eight bedrooms (each with a queen-size bed and ceiling fan) and a full bath, plus barbecue facilities, a billiard room, and use of a kitchen. ~ 41-926 Laumilo Street, Waimanalo; 808-259-8180; e-mail innkeep@aloha.net. MODERATE TO DELUXE.

Nalo Winds Bed & Breakfast offers "a home away from home." There are three accommodations, each with private bath, queen-size beds, fresh flowers and ceiling fans; one suite sleeps up to six people. Ideal for families. Boogieboards, snorkeling gear, beach chairs and a barbecue round out the amenities. Fresh papaya grow on the trees, and for a lazy afternoon in the sun, sink into the hammock with a good book. For those who can't get away from it all, there's even a modem hookup. ~ Hihimanu Street, Waimanalo; 808-224-6213, 866-625-6946, fax 808-524-0999; www.nalowinds.com, e-mail beachhousehawaii@aol.com. MODERATE.

DINING   Spotted along Oahu's southeastern shore are a couple of moderately priced restaurants (and an expensive but worthy one) that may prove handy if you're beachcombing or camping. All are located on or near Route 72 (Kalanianaole Highway).

You're bound to feel Eurocentric at the **Swiss Haus**, where the menu includes wienerschnitzel, bratwurst and, for non-meat lovers, vegetarian pasta. On the dessert menu you'll find Swiss chocolate mousse, peach melba and fresh fruit tarts. The wood-paneled Old World look features pictures of villages that make you yearn for the Matterhorn. Closed Monday and Tuesday. ~ Niu Valley Shopping Center, 5730 Kalanianaole Highway; 808-377-5447, fax 808-377-1151. MODERATE TO DELUXE.

Assaggio Hawaii Kai is an excellent neighborhood-style Italian restaurant with an extensive menu. You'll find dishes like

TheBus

There is perhaps no greater Hawaiian bargain than TheBus. Although you can rent a car to explore Oahu, you can also do it by the island's remarkable public transportation system, known quite simply as TheBus.

TheBus is a great way to sightsee at a leisurely pace—and peoplewatch at the same time. Hop aboard the #19 (or another downtown-bound bus) from Waikiki and you'll pass Ala Moana Center, the fishing boats of Kewalo Boat Basin and the historic Mission Houses before entering Chinatown. There tiny wizened *obachans* (grandmas) speaking a patois of Japanese-English climb patiently aboard, while mothers with a child in one arm and a shopping bag in the other negotiate the steep steps.

Or take the #52 Circle Island route and get the grand tour of the island. You'll pass through sleepy villages and alongside strands of sandy beaches while getting an upclose view of local life. Twice hourly buses give ample opportunity to stop and check out the sights along the way.

TheBus covers 90 percent of the 60-square-mile island. The fleet of 525 buses that are on the road travel a combined total of 60,000 miles every day, carrying 260,000 passengers daily—between 30,000 and 35,000 of them are visitors.

Buses generally operate between 5 a.m. and 10 p.m. (The last Waikiki-bound bus, however, leaves the airport at 11:45 p.m. and arrives in Waikiki by 12:30 a.m.) Unless you have to be somewhere during rush hour, the best times to travel are between 9 a.m. and 3 p.m. or after 6 p.m. Some 60 percent of all buses operate with wheelchair lifts, making them accessible to physically disabled riders.

Because so many local residents rely on public transportation, service is reliable and buses run frequently, even outside of Honolulu. With each ticket, riders can request a transfer that must be used to transfer to a different route within one and a half hours. The transfer can't be used for another ride on the same bus route. There's also a four-day Oahu Discovery Passport with unlimited rides that is sold at all ABC stores.

TheBus operates a 24-hour recorded information line (808-296-1818) that lists which buses to take to various attractions and destinations from Waikiki. There's also a bus information service (808-848-5555), with operators giving directions between the hours of 5:30 a.m. and 10 p.m. Those with Internet access can print out directions and time tables by contacting www.thebus.org.

butter-steamed Manila clams, linguine chicken and osso buco, as well as a fresh catch-of-the-day and seafood. There are four other locations in Mililani, Ala Moana, Manoa and Kailua, though I like this one for its yacht-club ambience and marina-side seating. No lunch on Sunday. ~ Koko Marina Shopping Center, 7192 Kalanianaole Highway, Hawaii Kai; 808-396-0756, fax 808-396-0757. MODERATE TO DELUXE.

HIDDEN ▶   **Thai Valley Cuisine** is tucked away in a tiny shopping center in Kalama Village, a suburban residential neighborhood built in the center of Koko Head Crater. The restaurant serves a variety of Thai appetizers, curries, noodles and such entrées as basil eggplant, fresh mushrooms in garlic sauté, stuffed chicken wings and deep-fried snapper. No lunch. ~ 501 Kealahou Street, Kalama Village; 808-395-9746. BUDGET TO MODERATE.

Dave's Ice Cream scoops up gourmet ice cream in flavors like azuki bean, cotton candy and *poha*, made from gooseberries grown on the Big Island. It also serves guava and passion fruit sherbet, among many other selections. ~ 41-1537 Kalanianaole Highway, Waimanalo; 808-259-0356. BUDGET.

Keneke's has breakfasts, plate lunches and sandwiches at greasy-spoon prices. No gourmet's delight, this tiny eatery is well placed for people enjoying Waimanalo's beaches. ~ 41-857 Kalanianaole Highway, Waimanalo; 808-259-5266. BUDGET.

GROCERIES   A convenient place to shop in Oahu's southeast corner is at the Koko Marina Shopping Center's **Foodland**. ~ 7192 Kalanianaole Highway, Hawaii Kai; 808-395-3131. Proceeding north along the coast, there's **Mel's Market**, a small store in Waimanalo. Its crowded

AUTHOR FAVORITE

Tucked away in unassuming fashion in a business park is one of my favorite dining spots. You'll have to travel all the way to Hawaii Kai, several miles east of Waikiki, to find **Roy's Restaurant**. It is, to say the least, ultracontemporary, from the magazine clips framed on the walls to the cylindrical fish tank near the door. One of the most innovative of Hawaii's Pacific Rim cuisine dining rooms, it specializes in fresh local ingredients. Wildly popular, so reserve in advance. Dinner only. ~ 6600 Kalanianaole Highway, Hawaii Kai; 808-396-7697, fax 808-396-8706; www.roysrestaurant.com, e-mail honolulu@roysrestaurant.com. DELUXE TO ULTRA-DELUXE.

aisles contain a cornucopia of Hawaii's culinary ingredients, from *kim chi* and cream cheese to ahi tuna and tempura mix. ~ 41-1029 Kalanianaole Highway, Waimanalo; 808-259-7550.

There aren't many places on Oahu more Hawaiian than Waima-   **SHOPPING**
nalo, so **Naturally Hawaiian** fits the landscape nicely. Featuring fine art and homemade gifts, the shop sells *puka*-shell necklaces, *koa* wood pieces, prints and paintings, and Hawaiian commemorative stamps. ~ 41-1025 Kalanianaole Highway, Waimanalo; 808-259-5354.

HANAUMA BAY NATURE PRESERVE 🏊 🤿 One of Oahu's   **BEACHES**
prettiest and most popular beaches, this curving swath of white   **& PARKS**
sand extends for almost a half-mile. The bottom of the bay is a maze of coral reef, and the entire area has been designated a marine preserve; fishing is strictly prohibited. As a result, the skin-diving is unmatched and the fish are tame enough to eat from your hand. (Just beware of "Witch's Brew," a turbulent area on the bay's right side, and the "Molokai Express," a wicked current sweeping across the mouth of the bay.) You can also hike along rock ledges fringing the bay and explore some mind-boggling tide-pools. Crowded though it is, this is one strand that should not be bypassed. Get here early—the beach closes at 6 p.m. (it opens at 6 a.m.), and once the parking lot fills up, entrance to the park is cut off. Facilities include a picnic area, restrooms, showers, a snack bar, snorkeling equipment rentals and lifeguards. Closed Tuesday. Parking fee, $1; nonresident day-use fee, $3 per person. ~ Located about nine miles east of Waikiki. Take Kalanianaole Highway (Route 72) to Koko Head, then turn onto the side road near the top of the promontory. This leads to a parking lot; leave your vehicle and walk the several hundred yards down the path to the beach. ~ 808-396-4229.

HALONA COVE BEACH 🏊 🤿 ⛱ This is the closest you'll   ◄ *HIDDEN*
find to a hidden beach near Honolulu. It's a patch of white sand wedged between Halona Point and the Halona Blowhole lookout. Located directly below Kalanianaole Highway (Route 72), this is not exactly a wilderness area. But you can still escape the crowds massed on the nearby beaches. Swimming and snorkeling are good when the sea is gentle but extremely dangerous if it's rough. Prime catches are *ulua*, *papio* and *mamao*. There are no

facilities. ~ Stop at the Halona Blowhole parking lot on Kalani-anaole Highway (Route 72), about ten miles east of Waikiki. Follow the path from the right side of the lot down to the beach.

SANDY BEACH 🏖 🏄 This long, wide beach is a favorite among Oahu's youth. The shorebreak makes it one of the finest, and most dangerous, bodysurfing beaches in the islands. Surfing is good and very popular but beware of rip currents. Lifeguards are on duty. It's a pleasant place to sunbathe, but if you go swimming, plan to negotiate a pounding shoreline. Anglers try for *ulua*, *papio* and *mamao*. There are picnic areas, restrooms and showers. Should you want to avoid the crowds, head over to **Wawamalu Beach Park** next door to the east. ~ Head out on Kalani-anaole Highway (Route 72) about 12 miles east of Waikiki.

MAKAPUU POINT STATE WAYSIDE 🏃 This state park encompasses Makapuu Beach, lookout and the lighthouse that overlooks the east Oahu coast. The mile-long asphalted trail leading to the lighthouse has become a popular family excursion; you can take the trail's uphill segments at a leisurely pace. The heat can be draining by midday, so a morning or afternoon hike is recommended, particularly on weekends when crowds abound. Panoramic views are the reward, with brisk tradewinds likely. ~ Off Kalanianaole Highway between Sandy Beach and Makapuu Lookout.

The two islands offshore near Makapuu Beach are bird sanctuaries. The large one is known as Rabbit Island. The Hawaiians call it Manana Island, which means to stretch out or protrude.

MAKAPUU BEACH PARK 🏖 Makapuu is set in a very pretty spot with lava cliffs in the background and Rabbit Island just offshore. This short, wide rectangle of white sand is Hawaii's most famous bodysurfing beach. With no protecting reef and a precipitous shoreline, Makapuu is inundated by awesome swells that send wave riders crashing onto shore. Necks and backs are broken with frightening regularity here, so if the waves are large and you're inexperienced—play the spectator. If you take the plunge, prepare for a battering! Snorkeling is usually poor and surfing is not permitted here. Common catches are *ulua*, *papio* and *mamao*. The only facilities are restrooms and a lifeguard. ~ Located on Kalani-anaole Highway (Route 72) about 13 miles east of Waikiki.

WAIMANALO BEACH PARK AND WAIMANALO BAY BEACH PARK 🏖 Located at the southeast end of Waimanalo's three-

and-a-half-mile-long beach is a spacious 38-acre park. It's studded with ironwood trees and equipped with numerous recreation facilities including a playground, a basketball court and a baseball field. Waimanalo Beach Park and Waimanalo Bay Beach Park, a mile farther north, are both excellent spots for picnicking, swimming, snorkeling, bodysurfing and sunbathing. The latter is farther removed from the highway in a grove of ironwood trees known to local residents as "Sherwood Forest." Waimanalo is a good place to fish for *papio*, bonefish, milkfish and goatfish. There are picnic areas, restrooms and showers at both. ~ Waimanalo Beach Park is located at 41-741 Kalanianaole Highway (Route 72) about 15 miles east of Waikiki. Waimanalo Bay Beach Park is on Aloiloi Street a mile farther north.

▲ A county permit required at both of the parks for tent and trailer camping.

BELLOWS FIELD BEACH PARK 🐟 🏄 🚶 🛶 One of Oahu's ◄ *HIDDEN* prettiest parks, there's a broad white-sand beach bordered by ironwood trees and a marvelous view of the Koolau mountains. It's a great place for swimming and snorkeling and it's also a good surf spot for beginners; fishing usually rewards with *papio*, bonefish and goatfish. Sounds great, huh? The catch is that Bellows Park is situated on a military base and is open to visitors only from Friday noon until 8 a.m. Monday. Facilities include a picnic area, showers, a restroom and a lifeguard. ~ Turn off Kalanianaole Highway (Route 72) toward Bellows Air Force Station. The park is located near Waimanalo, about 17 miles east of Waikiki.

▲ County permit required.

EIGHT

Windward Coast

 Named for the trade winds that blow with soothing predictability from the northeast, this sand-rimmed shoreline lies on the far side of the *pali* from Honolulu. Between these fluted emerald cliffs and the turquoise ocean are the bedroom communities of Lanikai, Kailua and Kaneohe and the agricultural regions of the Waiahole and Waikane valleys. As suburbs give way to small farms, this florid region provides a relaxing transition between the busy boulevards of Honolulu and the wild surf of the North Shore.

Kailua, which was previously a quiet suburb, has become a windsurfing mecca, attracting beginning and intermediate sailors from around the world to its shores. A protective reef, a lack of breakers and on-shore trade winds create near perfect conditions for the sport, and the residents of Kailua haven't overlooked the opportunities. Scores of families operate bed and breakfasts in residential neighborhoods, and windsurfers have become a part of the community. It's the kind of low-key place where even the likes of Robin Williams, who reportedly vacations there, can find an escape.

Moving north, the highway hugs the coast, revealing a steady succession of beaches, and passes through sleepy rural communities, where life seems little changed by the procession of tourists in rental cars and buses that pass by daily. In Laie, the Mormons set about creating a religious community that draws students from throughout the South Pacific to a branch of Brigham Young University and tourists to the Polynesian Cultural Center, which the students operate as the most popular tourist attraction on Oahu.

Leaving Laie, one returns to the sleepy ways of rural Oahu, arriving in Kahuku, where the former sugar mill has been turned into a tiny shopping mall. Tourism has replaced sugar as an economic endeavor, just as it has in most other places on Oahu.

From the southeastern corner of the island, the Kalanianaole Highway flows into **Kailua**, where it intersects with Route 61, or Kailua Road. If you go right for a quarter of a mile along this road you will encounter **Ulupo Heiau** (it's behind the YMCA). ◄ *HIDDEN* According to Hawaiian legend, this temple (which stands 30 feet high and measures 150 feet in length) was built by *Menehunes*, who passed the building stones across a six-mile-long bucket brigade in a one-night construction project.

A slight detour down Route 61 toward the Pacific will bring you to one of Oahu's premier neighborhoods—**Lanikai**—and one of its most beautiful beaches—**Lanikai Beach**. Actually, Lanikai has one of the world's best beaches. The sand is powder-fine; palm trees sway in the wind, providing enough shade to make for ideal sunbathing; and the water, protected by an offshore reef, is the color of Indian turquoise.

Offshore are two small islands, **Moku Iki** and **Moku Nui**, bird sanctuaries known as the **Mokuluas**. You can kayak (or swim) out to these dry, barren islands from Lanikai Beach. On Moku Nui you'll find a fine-sand beach, where hundreds of birds will probably be your only company. The strand where you disembark from your kayak has a unique feature—the waves come from both sides of the island and create an enormous clashing sound. Around the back of the island is a little cove where people often swim, though the currents can be dangerous and the surf quite high, so be cautious.

Heading back to the main highway, you will find that Route 72 immediately merges into Route 61, which then continues for two miles to Route 83, the Kamehameha Highway. Above this thoroughfare, spreading across 400 acres at the foot of the *pali* is **Hoomaluhia Botanical Garden**, a relaxing nature conservancy. ◄ *HIDDEN* With sheer cliffs rising on one side and a panoramic ocean view opening in the distance, it is a special place indeed. There is a 32-acre lake (no swimming) as well as a visitors center and hiking trails. Camping is available on weekends (permit required—get one at the garden office, which is closed Sunday). The fruits, flowers and trees include hundreds of species native to Hawaii as well as tropical regions around the world. ~ Off Route 83 at the end of Luluku Road, Kaneohe; 808-233-7323, fax 808-233-7326; www.co.honolulu.hi.us/parks/hbg.

The Kahekili Highway will also carry you to the graceful **Haiku Gardens**, located just outside Kailua. Formerly a private estate, the gardens rest in a lovely spot with a lofty rockface backdrop. Within this preserve are acres of exotic plant life, including an enchanting lily pond as well as numerous species of flowers. Hawaii specializes in beautiful gardens; the frequent rains and lush terrain make for luxuriant growing conditions. This happens to be one of the prettiest gardens of all. ~ 46-336 Haiku Road, Kaneohe; 808-247-6671, fax 808-247-5886; www.haikugardens weddings.com.

An alternate route through Kailua and Kaneohe will carry you near the water, though the only really pretty views of Kaneohe Bay come near the end. Simply follow North Kalaheo Avenue through Kailua, then pick up Kaneohe Bay Drive, and turn right on Route 836, which curves for miles before linking with Route 83. At Heeia Kea Boat Harbor on Route 836, you can take an hour-long glass-bottom boat ride aboard the **Coral Queen**. Closed Sunday. ~ 808-235-2192, fax 808-236-0722.

Kaneohe Bay is renowned for its coral formations and schools of tropical fish that are as brilliantly colored as the coral. This expansive body of water possesses the only barrier reef in Hawaii. Along its shores are **ancient Hawaiian fishponds**, rock-bound enclosures constructed by the early Polynesians to raise fresh seafood. Though they once lined the shores of Oahu, today only a quarter (about 100) remain in usable condition. Several rest along this Windward Coast. One of the largest is located near Heeia State Park. It's an impressive engineering feat that measures 500 feet in length and once contained an 88-acre fish farm. The stone walls in places are 12 feet thick. ~ Located along Kamehameha Highway (Route 836), a few hundred yards before it merges with Route 83.

Continuing along Route 836 you'll come to **Heeia State Park**, a small greensward located on Kealohi Point, anchored by a lighthouse. Kealohi Point was a significant spot for ancient Hawaiians: it was thought to be a jumping-off point of the soul into the spirit world. This park is a perfect spot for a picnic with lovely views of the bay and the ancient fishpond. Offshore you'll see **Coconut Island**, made famous in the opening of TV's "Gilligan's Island." Adjacent to the park is **Heeia Kai Boat Harbor**.

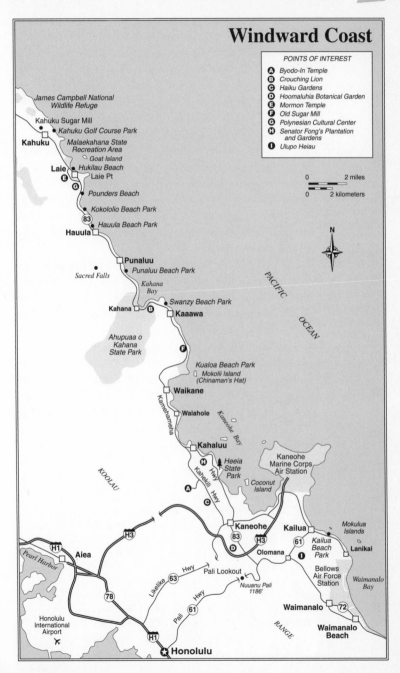

Windward Coast

POINTS OF INTEREST

A Byodo-In Temple
B Crouching Lion
C Haiku Gardens
D Hoomaluhia Botanical Garden
E Mormon Temple
F Old Sugar Mill
G Polynesian Cultural Center
H Senator Fong's Plantation and Gardens
I Ulupo Heiau

0   2 miles
0   2 kilometers

N

James Campbell National Wildlife Refuge
Kahuku Sugar Mill
Kahuku Golf Course Park
Kahuku
Malaekahana State Recreation Area
Goat Island
Laie
Hukilau Beach
Laie Pt
Pounders Beach
Kokololio Beach Park
Hauula Beach Park
Hauula
Punaluu
Punaluu Beach Park
Sacred Falls
Kahana Bay
Swanzy Beach Park
Kahana
Kaaawa
Ahupuaa o Kahana State Park
Kualoa Beach Park
Mokolii Island (Chinaman's Hat)
Waikane
Waiahole
Kamehameha
Kaneohe Bay
Kahaluu
Heeia State Park
Kaneohe Marine Corps Air Station
Kahekili Hwy
Coconut Island
KOOLAU
Kaneohe
Kailua
Mokulua Islands
Aiea
Kailua Beach Park
Lanikai
Pearl Harbor
Olomana
Bellows Air Force Station
Waimanalo Bay
Likelike Hwy
Pali Lookout
Nuuanu Pali 1186'
Pali Hwy
Waimanalo
Honolulu International Airport
Waimanalo Beach
RANGE
Honolulu

PACIFIC OCEAN

High above Kaneohe, gazing down upon the bay, is **Senator Fong's Plantation and Gardens**. Here you can take a narrated tram tour of 725 acres of gardens and orchards. This luxurious preserve was donated by one of Hawaii's most famous U.S. senators, so be prepared to venture from Eisenhower Valley to Kennedy Valley (sugar cane) to the Johnson Plateau (fruit orchards) to Nixon Valley (gardens) to the Ford Plateau (pine trees). Admission. ~ 47-285 Pulama Road, Kaneohe; 808-239-6775.

Route 83 soon becomes known as the Kamehameha Highway as it courses past lazy fishing boats then enters **Waiahole Valley** and **Waikane Valley**, some of the last places on the island where Hawaiian farmers grow crops in the traditional way. Fruit stands line the highway. The roads off the highway lead to small Hawaiian enclaves, where you'll see taro patches and papaya trees in the backyards.

As you round the bend you'll come to one of the loveliest regional parks on the island. Worthy of a stop-off just to see the setting is **Kualoa Beach Park** (see "Beaches & Parks" below); Kualoa in Hawaiian means "long back," and this area is rich in ancient and sacred history.

That cone-shaped island offshore is **Chinaman's Hat**. It was named for its resemblance to a coolie cap, though the Hawaiians had another name for it long before the Chinese arrived in the islands. They called it Mokolii Island, or "little dragon," and claimed it represented the tail of a beast that resided under the

AUTHOR FAVORITE

The **Valley of the Temples** is a verdant chasm folded between the mountains and the sea. Part of the valley has been consecrated as a cemetery honoring the Japanese. Highlighting the region is the **Byodo-In Temple**. Rimmed by 2000-foot cliffs, this Buddhist shrine is a replica of a 900-year-old temple in Kyoto, Japan. It was constructed in 1968 in memory of the first Japanese immigrants to settle in Hawaii. The simple architecture is enhanced by a bronze bell weighing seven tons that visitors are permitted to ring. A statue of Buddha dominates the site. Walk along the placid reflecting pool with its swans, ducks and multihued carp and you will be drawn a million miles away from the bustle of Honolulu. Admission. ~ 47-200 Kahekili Highway, Kaneohe; 808-239-8811, fax 808-239-8997.

water. Watch for frigate birds and delicate white-tailed tropical birds flying overhead.

Right past the entrance to the regional park on the *mauka* side of the highway is **Kualoa Ranch,** one of the settings for *Jurassic Park* and *Godzilla*. Unfortunately, you're only likely to see horses grazing in the pasture with white herons on their back. Today the ranch offers visitors a variety of sporting activities, including snorkeling, scuba, horseback riding and ATV four-wheelers. The ranch is also the site of **Molii Fishpond,** one of the ancient fishponds used by Hawaiians. ~ Kualoa Ranch and Activity Club, Kaaawa; 808-237-7321; www.kualoa.com.

Just down the road, the **Old Sugar Mill,** Oahu's first, lies in ruin along the side of the road. Built during the 1860s, it fell into disuse soon after completion and has since served only as a local curiosity.

Continuing along you'll pass the community of **Kaaawa** and **Swanzy Beach Park** (see "Beaches & Parks" section below). A few miles later be on the lookout for the Hawaii Visitors Bureau marker noting **"Crouching Lion"** (there's also a restaurant by the same name just below the mountain). To the ancient Hawaiians, who had never experienced the king of the jungle, the stone face was, in fact, that of Kauhi, a demigod from the island of Tahiti who was turned into stone during a struggle between Pele and her sister Hiiaka.

Next is the coral-studded **Kahana Bay.** Once the sight of a burgeoning Hawaiian fishing village, Kahana Bay is now a tranquil spot for a picnic or swim in the sea. Be sure to look out for the ruins of **Huilua Fishpond,** the oldest of Oahu's many fishponds. Across the highway is **Ahupuaa o Kahana State Park.** If you like to hike there's a trail up the valley through lush foliage that weaves past old farmsteads.

Then the highway, still crowding the coastline, traverses the roadside community of **Punaluu,** legendary home of the demigod Kamapuaa, one of Pele's lovers. There's a long, narrow strand of sand and ocean at **Punaluu Beach Park,** which offers pleasant swimming opportunities because of an offshore reef. (However, use caution when the weather is stormy.) The roadway continues up to the small town of **Hauula** with its old **Hauula Door of Faith Church,** a small chapel of clapboard design surrounded by palms. Not far from here is another aging woodframe sanctuary, **Hauula**

Congregational Christian Church, built of wood and coral back in 1862.

The nearby town of **Laie**, once thought to have been an ancient place of refuge for Hawaiians, is now a stronghold for Mormons. The Hawaii campus of **Brigham Young University** is located here, as well as the **Mormon Temple**. The Mormons settled here back in 1864; today there are about 55,000 in Hawaii. The courtyards and grounds of the temple are open to the public, but only Mormons are permitted to enter the temple sanctuary.

The Mormons also own Oahu's most popular tourist attraction, the **Polynesian Cultural Center**. Set right on Kamehameha Highway in Laie, it represents one of the foremost theme parks in the entire Pacific, a 42-acre attempt to re-create ancient Polynesia. As you wander about the grounds you'll encounter ersatz villages portraying life in the Marquesas, Tahiti, Fiji, Tonga, New Zealand and old Hawaii. Step over to the Tahitian hamlet and you will experience the rocking *tamure* dance. Or wander onto the islands of Samoa, where the local inhabitants demonstrate how to climb coconut trees. In Tonga a native will be beating tapa cloth from mulberry bark, while the Fijians are pounding rhythms with poles of bamboo. These mock villages are linked by waterways and can be visited in canoes. The boats will carry you past craftsmen preparing poi by mashing taro roots, and others husking coconuts.

The most popular shows are the "Pageant of the Long Canoes," in which the boats head up a lagoon amid a flurry of singing and dancing, and "Horizons." The latter is an evening show similar to Waikiki's Polynesian revues, though generally considered more elaborate. Most of the entertainers and other employees at this Hawaiian-style Disneyland are Mormon students attending the

MYTHICAL MAKERS

The *Menehunes*, in case you haven't been introduced, were tiny Hobbit-like creatures who inhabited Hawaii even before the Polynesians arrived. They were reputed to be superhumanly strong and would work all night to build dams, temples and other structures. Several mysterious manmade objects in the islands that archaeologists have trouble placing chronologically are claimed by mythmakers to be *Menehune* creations.

local university. Closed Sunday. Admission. 53-370 ~ Kamehameha Highway, Laie; 808-293-3000, fax 808-293-3339; www.
polynesia.com.

Be sure to take in the town's natural wonder, **Laie Point**. This
headland provides extraordinary ocean views sweeping for miles
along the shoreline. Since the breezes and surf are wilder here than
elsewhere on the Windward Coast, you'll often encounter waves
lashing at the two offshore islets with amazing force. The island
with the hole in it is **Kukihoolua** or, as the locals call it, Puka Rock.
~ Head toward the ocean on Anemoku Street, off Kamehameha
Highway, then turn right on Naupaka Street.

Along the oceanside, a few miles outside of Laie, hidden behind
the vines hugging the road is **Malaekahana State Recreation Area**   ◀ **HIDDEN**
(see "Beaches & Parks" for added description). This gem of a
park offers a long strand of white sand lined with ironwood trees.
Offshore is **Goat Island**, or Mokuauia, a bird sanctuary you can
actually wade over to when the tide is right (be sure to wear reef
slippers or some such foot covering and be careful of the currents).

Out in the suburban town of Kailua, where trim houses front a   **LODGING**
beautiful white-sand beach, you'll discover **Pat's Kailua Beach
Properties**. Overlooking Kailua Beach Park and about 100 yards
from the beach sits a cluster of woodframe cottages. Each is
equipped with a full kitchen, cable television and a telephone.
Some of the furniture is nicked, but these duplex units are clean
and cozy. They sit in a yard shaded with monkeypod, coconut
and breadfruit trees and provide an excellent value. ~ 204 South
Kalaheo Avenue, Kailua; 808-262-4128, 808-261-1653, fax 808-
261-0893; www.patskailua.com, e-mail pats.kailua@verizon.net.
MODERATE.

Carol Naish of **Naish Hawaii**, the oldest windsurfing business in Hawaii, operates a bed-and-breakfast referral service for
windsurfers and others who would prefer to stay in a quiet community rather than busy Waikiki. She represents 40 homes and
attempts to carefully match guests with hosts so that all will have
a good time. ~ 155-A Hamakua Drive, Kailua; 808-261-3539,
fax 808-263-9723; www.naish.com. BUDGET TO ULTRA-DELUXE.

Located in a quiet canal-side neighborhood two blocks from
Kailua Beach, **Sharon's Serenity** is a popular bed and breakfast
with two rooms and a suite. Guests have use of the swimming

pool and access to a comfortable spacious living room. Host Sharon Price serves an expanded continental breakfast and offers up plenty of advice to those who want it. This B&B can be booked directly; there is a three-night minimum stay. ~ 127 Kakahiaka Street, Kailua; 808-263-3634, 800-914-2271; www.sharonsserenity.com, e-mail sharon@sharonsserenity.com. MODERATE.

> Hawaiians use a variety of plants in herbal healing (*laau lapau*). One of the most important plants is the popolo plant (Black Nightshade), used to combat fevers and respiratory infections or strengthen the body

I don't recommend **Hawaii's Hidden Hideaway** just because of its name. It really is a lovely bed and breakfast, with lots of privacy. There are a suite and two studios available; the suite has an outdoor spa with an ocean view. All three have private entrances, parking and decks, and kitchenettes stocked with breakfast goodies. You're quite close to the beaches of Lanikai and Kailua, and a 30-minute or so drive to Waikiki. Three-night minimum stay—not that that will be difficult. ~ 1369 Mokolea Drive, Kailua; 808-2626-6560, fax 808-262-6561; www.ahawaiibnb.com, e-mail hhhhideaway @yahoo.com. MODERATE TO DELUXE.

HIDDEN ▶

You can't get much closer to the water than **Schrader's Windward Country Inn**. With about 50 units for rent, this unusual resting place consists of several woodframe buildings right on the edge of Kaneohe Bay. There are picnic tables, barbecue grills and a pool on the two-acre property, as well as a tour boat that can take you snorkeling, kayaking or sightseeing on the bay. The guest rooms are cottage style with kitchenettes; many have lanais and bay views. Prices include continental breakfast. ~ 47-039 Lihikai Drive, Kaneohe; 808-239-5711, 800-735-5711, fax 808-239-6658; www.hawaiiscene.com/schrader, e-mail schrader@lava.net. MODERATE.

The **Ali'i Bluffs Bed & Breakfast** offers two rooms with private baths. The Victorian room features antiques and vintage paintings, while the Circus room has large circus posters, many of them originals, from around the world. This contemporary Hawaiian home has a shake roof and is furnished in antiques and Persian rugs. A full breakfast is served poolside every morning. ~ 46-251 Ikiiki Street, Kaneohe; 808-235-1124, 800-235-1151, fax 808-236-4877; www.hawaiiscene.com/aliibluffs, e-mail donm@lava.net. BUDGET TO MODERATE.

Windsurfing

There's no better place to learn windsurfing than on Oahu. The water is warm and the conditions are near perfect. Although not a particularly easy sport to learn, in a week or two you could be holding your own as you glide over the waves.

Windsurfing, also known as boardsailing, is a technique sport rather than a muscle sport, no doubt one of the reasons women can learn to do it faster than men. At the beginning you will use a 12-foot board, known as a learner board, or in sailboard slang, an aircraft carrier. These have a dagger board for stabilization and a small soft sail that flutters in the wind as you move slowly across the water. Most people spend just a few days learning on one of these boards, before progressing to a shorter or "fun board."

The shorter the board, the more wind you need. For an eight-and-a-half-foot board, 15 to 20 knots of wind are required. Because these boards don't usually have a dagger board, sailors use the wind to steer by tipping their board in the direction they want to go.

In order to sail, you have to be balanced. And in order to be balanced, you have to position yourself properly on the board. The faster you go, the more the board is out of the water. Your feet should be in the center of the "wetted" surface, the part of the board that's in the water. Advanced sailors wear a harness around their waists. The harness has a hook that fits into loops hanging from the boom. It helps sailors hold the sail without effort.

If you would like to learn how to windsurf, there's no place better than Kailua, a bedroom community on Oahu. It is the state's best spot for those who are at beginning and intermediate levels in the sport. A protective reef and no breakers mean the waters aren't too rough, and the local community has established scores of low-key B&Bs to cater to the windsurfing crowd.

If you don't mind funky living, check out the **Countryside Cabins** in Punaluu, run by the Naii family since the '50s. The rustic clapboard cabins are set in beautiful garden surroundings across the street from the ocean; they were formerly used as army barracks in World War II. Depending on your taste, you'll find the one-room cottages either claustrophobic and untidy or quaint. But no one will find fault with the low prices on these units and the two-bedroom cottages. ~ 53-224 Kamehameha Highway, Punaluu; phone/fax 808-237-1203; www.hawaii-cabins.com, e-mail info@hawaii-cabins.com. BUDGET.

The **Laie Inn** is a low-slung motel with two floors of rooms surrounding a swimming pool. This is a standard Coke-machine-in-the-courtyard facility located next to the Polynesian Cultural Center. ~ 55-109 Laniloa Street, Laie; 808-293-9282, 800-526-4562, fax 808-293-8115; www.laieinn.com, e-mail laieinn@ha waii.rr.com. MODERATE.

DINING

Kailua has a collection of eating establishments spread throughout the town. Among them is **Buzz's Original Steak House**, right across the street from the beach. The place is popular not only with windsurfers, but with Honolulu residents who drive out on the weekends to enjoy the surf and a meal at this upscale beach shack, which has been in business since 1962. Burgers, steaks and seafood are the specialties here, and all entrées include a trip to the salad bar at dinnertime. ~ 413 Kawailoa Road, Kailua; 808-261-4661. MODERATE TO ULTRA-DELUXE.

Assaggio Ristorante Italiano in the downtown Kailua Business Center is another restaurant that attracts crowds with its pasta, chicken, eggplant parmigiana and veal scallopine. No lunch on Saturday and Sunday. ~ 354 Uluniu Street, Kailua; 808-261-2772. MODERATE TO DELUXE.

You can try **Times Coffee Shop** for fried rice, hamburger steaks or sandwiches. ~ 43-3 Oneawa Street, Kailua, 808-262-7122; 153 Hamakua Street, Kailua, 808-262-0300. BUDGET.

Saeng's Thai Cuisine is a freshly decorated ethnic restaurant with a hardwood bar and potted plants all around. Located in a strip mall, it nevertheless conveys a sense of elegance. The menu focuses on vegetarian, seafood and curry dishes. No lunch on weekends. ~ 315 Kailua Road, Kailua; 808-263-9727. BUDGET TO MODERATE.

One of Hawaii's great Mexican restaurants is **Bueno Nalo**,   ◀ *HIDDEN*
which may be short on looks, but it's definitely long on taste. ~
20 Kainehe Street, Kailua; 808-263-1999. BUDGET TO MODERATE.

Known for years as a prime breakfast and lunch place, **Cin-**   ◀ *HIDDEN*
namon's Restaurant draws a local crowd, which sits beneath the
dining room gazebo or out on the patio. The menu is best described as Continental cuisine with local flavors. Try the chicken
cashew sandwich or the carrot pancakes—all made from scratch!
No dinner Sunday through Wednesday. ~ Kailua Square Shopping Center, 315 Uluniu Street, Kailua; 808-261-8724, fax 808-
262-9910. MODERATE TO DELUXE.

Kailua residents will tell you the pastas at **Baci Bistro** are all
homemade and beautifully prepared at this small dining room
with greenhouse windows and romantic ambience. There are veal
and fish entrées, risotto dishes and an array of antipasti. No lunch
on Saturday and Sunday. ~ 30 Aulike Street, Kailua; 808-262-
7555, fax 808-261-2857. MODERATE TO DELUXE.

Cisco's Cantina is a neighborhood-style Mexican restaurant
with all the expected menu options; the *chile relleno* is particularly good. Whatever you order, healthy portions are the rule. ~
131 Hekili Street #103, Kailua; 808-262-7337, fax 808-230-2266.
BUDGET TO MODERATE.

In Kaneohe you might like **Koa Omelette House**. It's a tastefully appointed restaurant with a breakfast bill of fare that includes pancakes and crêpes suzette and a lunch menu with salads,
sandwiches, teriyaki chicken and seafood. No lunch on Sunday.
~ 46-126 Kahuhipa Street, Kaneohe; 808-235-5772. BUDGET.

AUTHOR FAVORITE

I found the staff so friendly at **Ahi's Restaurant** that dining in
this family-run restaurant was kind of like eating in the home of a friend. The
restaurant, in fact, was previously in the owner's house in Kahuku until it
burned down and he relocated to Punaluu. The green woodframe building
with stucco interior and screened-in porch catches the island breezes
and provides a comfortable environment in which to dine. Although
Ahi's serves a variety of meats, fish and chicken, the specialty is shrimp
cooked in four different ways—scampi, cocktail, tempura and deep
fried. There aren't too many places quite like this one. ~ 53-146
Kamehameha Highway, Punaluu; 808-293-5650. BUDGET TO MODERATE.

What sets **Haleiwa Joe's Seafood Grill** apart is its idyllic setting. A terraced dining area overlooks sharp cliffs and peaceful flower beds, making this a choice stop for dinner. Though the atmosphere varies from the average Chart House, the menu is quite similar: steak, seafood and prime rib, but with a Pan-Asian influence. ~ 46-336 Haiku Road, Kaneohe; 808-247-6671, fax 808-247-5886; www.haleiwajoes.com. MODERATE TO DELUXE.

The "Twin Islands," tiny bird sanctuaries, rest off the shore of Lanikai Beach.

The **Crouching Lion Inn**, set in a vintage 1927 wood-shingle house, serves sandwiches and hamburgers, rotisserie chicken, mahimahi and teriyaki steak for lunch. At dinner there's a surf-and-turf menu. Enjoying a beautiful ocean view, this attractive complex is popular with tour buses, so try to arrive at an off-hour. ~ 51-666 Kamehameha Highway, Kaaawa; 808-237-8511, fax 808-237-7061; www.honolulurestaurantguide.com/crouchinglion. DELUXE TO ULTRA-DELUXE.

GROCERIES   In Kailua and Kaneohe, you'll encounter large supermarkets. In the Kailua Shopping Center there's **Times Supermarket**. ~ Kailua Road, Kailua; 808-262-2366. **Foodland** is in the Windward City Shopping Center. ~ At Kamehameha Highway and Kaneohe Bay Drive, Kaneohe; 808-247-3357.

Between these major shopping complexes there are smaller facilities such as the **7-11**. ~ 51-484 Kamehameha Highway, Kaaawa; 808-237-8810.

You can get fresh fish at **Masa and Joyce Fish Market** in the Temple Valley Shopping Center. ~ Kahekili Highway (Route 83), just north of Kaneohe; 808-239-6966.

There's a large **Foodland** grocery store in the Laie Village Shopping Center. Closed Sunday. ~ Kamehameha Highway, Laie; 808-293-4443.

SHOPPING   **Kailua Shopping Center** offers a wide range of services at 20 stores. ~ Kailua Road and Hahani Street, Kailua.

Island Treasures Art Gallery offers an exceptional collection of pottery, wooden boxes, jewelry, paintings, handcrafted wooden furniture, shell candles and etched glass with island designs, all created by artists living in Hawaii. ~ 629 Kailua Road, Suite 103, Kailua; 808-261-8131.

Kaneohe Shopping Center serves the region with eight stores. ~ 45-934 Kamehameha Highway, Kaneohe; 808-847-2345.

Another similar store in Kaneohe chockfull of treasures by local artists is **Jeff Chang Pottery & Fine Crafts**. Among the items are ceramics, glass clocks, jewelry, mobiles, wood bowls and figurines. ~ 45-781-B Kamehameha Highway, Kaneohe; 808-235-2808.

The **Livingston Galleries** at the Crouching Lion Inn sells original paintings and prints by local and international artists, as well as estate jewelry, sculpture and handcrafted gift items. ~ 51-666 Kamehameha Highway, Kaaawa; 808-237-7165.

The nearby **Lance Fairly Gallery** has original paintings by local artists, limited-edition prints and enameled tropical fish. ~ 53-839 Kamehameha Highway, Punaluu; 808-293-9009.

NIGHTLIFE

Nights on the Windward Coast are quiet and peaceful, and most people like it that way. For those who prefer a bit of action, however, head to Kailua, where you can catch live entertainment every Thursday, Friday and Saturday at **Jaron's Restaurant**. On Thursday, it's contemporary Hawaiian music and on the weekends dance tunes from reggae to rock. Occasional cover on Friday and Saturday. ~ 201 Hamakua Drive #A, Kailua; 808-261-4600.

BEACHES & PARKS

KAILUA BEACH Stretching for two miles with white sand all the way and tiny islands offshore, this is one of the prettiest beaches around. It's in the suburban town of Kailua, so you'll trade seclusion for excellent beach facilities. The center of activity is **Kailua Beach Park**, at the end of Kailua Road near the south end of the beach. This 30-acre facility has a grassy expanse shaded by ironwood and coconut trees and perfect for picnicking. There are restrooms and a pavilion with a snack bar. **Kalama Beach County Park**, a small park with restrooms in the middle of Kailua Beach, is less crowded. Swimming, surfing and bodysurfing are good all along the strand and windsurfing is excellent, but exercise caution. ~ You can access Kailua Beach via side streets off Kalaheo Avenue; Kalama Beach County Park is located at 250 North Kalaheo Avenue.

LANIKAI BEACH Everyone's dream house is on the beach at Lanikai. This sandy stretch, varying from 20 to 100 feet in width, extends for over a mile. The entire beach in this residential community is lined with those houses everybody wants. The water is the color of cobalt and the protecting reef offshore makes the entire beach safe for swimming. Lanikai has also become a windsurfing favorite. No facilities; the nearest facilities are at Kailua Beach. ~ The strand parallels Mokulua Drive in Lanikai, which in turn is reached by driving south along the beachfront roads in Kailua.

HEEIA STATE PARK 🏃 This small pocket park located off of Kamehameha Highway at Kealohi Point is an ideal spot to picnic when traveling around the island. The views of Kaneohe Bay and the ancient Hawaiian fishpond are noteworthy. Numerous indigenous plants thrive here and there are educational programs offered by Friends of Heeia State Park. In addition, there's a pavilion, picnic tables and restrooms. ~ Route 836 (Kamehameha Highway) just outside of Kaneohe.

KUALOA BEACH PARK 🏊 🐟 🚿 You could search the entire Pacific for a setting as lovely as this one. Just 500 yards offshore lies the islet of Mokolii, better known as Chinaman's Hat. Behind the beach the *pali* creates a startling background of fluted cliffs and tropical forest. The beach is a long and narrow strip of sand paralleled by a wide swath of grass parkland. Little wonder this is one of the Windward Coast's most popular picnic areas. It's also a favorite for swimming, snorkeling and fishing (common catches are *papio*, bonefish, milkfish and goatfish). Facilities include picnic areas, restrooms and showers. ~ 49-479 Kamehameha Highway (Route 83) about ten miles north of Kaneohe.

▲ Tent camping permitted. County permit required.

SWANZY BEACH PARK, PUNALUU BEACH PARK AND HAUULA BEACH PARK 🏊 🐟 🏕 🚿 These three county facilities lie along Kamehameha Highway (Route 83) within seven miles of each other. Swimming is generally good at each. Along this coast the most abundant fish is *papio*, followed by bonefish, milkfish and goatfish. Camping is allowed at all except Punaluu, but none compare aesthetically with other beaches to the north and south. Swanzy (open weekends only) is located on the highway but lacks a sandy beach. However, it has the best diving. Its surf break, "Crouching Lion," is for experts only; Punaluu, though possessing a pretty palm-fringed beach, is cramped; and Hauula, a spacious park with a beach and a winter surf break for beginners, is visited periodically by tour buses. So put these beach parks near the bottom of your list, and bring them up only if the other beaches are too crowded. All three beaches have picnic areas and restrooms. ~ These parks are all located along Kamehameha Highway (Route 83). Swanzy lies about 12 miles north of Kaneohe, Punaluu is about four miles north of Swanzy, and Hauula is about three miles beyond that.

▲ Tent and trailer camping allowed at Hauula Beach Park, as well as at Swanzy Beach Park on weekends. A county permit is required.

AHUPUAA O KAHANA STATE PARK 🏃 ⛵ 🚣 This 5228-acre paradise, set on a white-sand beach, offers something for every adventurer. You can pick fruit in a lush forest, picnic in a coconut grove and sightsee an ancient fishpond. You can also fish for *papio*, bonefish, milkfish and goatfish. Swimming is generally good. Surfing is a possibility but is mediocre at best. There are picnic areas and restrooms. ~ 52-222 Kamehameha Highway (Route 83) about 14 miles north of Kaneohe.

> Check out the orientation center at Ahupuaa O Kahana State Park. Besides its many natural features, cultural resources within the park include Huilua Fishpond and an ancient fishing shrine and lookout.

▲ There's tent camping on the beach; $5 per night. State permit required; 808-587-0300, fax 808-587-0311.

KOKOLOLIO BEACH PARK ⛵ 🏄 🚣 Here's one of the prettiest beaches on the Windward Coast. With trees and a lawn that extends toward the white-sand beach, it's a highly recommended spot for day-tripping. It's also a good beach for swimming and bodysurfing and in winter there are breaks up to six feet, with right and left slide. Common catches include *papio*, bonefish, goatfish and milkfish. There are picnic areas and restrooms. ~ 55-017 Kamehameha Highway (Route 83) in Laie about 20 miles north of Kaneohe.

▲ Camping allowed with county permit.

POUNDERS BEACH ⛵ 🚣 Named for the crushing shorebreak that makes it a popular bodysurfing beach, this quarter-mile-long strand features a corridor of white sand and a sandy bottom. Swimming is good near the old landing at the western end of the beach. Be careful of currents when swimming anywhere along the beach. Anglers try for *ono*, *moi* and *papio*. There are no facilities here. ~ Located along Kamehameha Highway north of Kakela Beach.

HUKILAU BEACH This privately owned facility fronts a beautiful white-sand beach that winds for more than a mile. Part of the beach is lined with homes, but much of it is undeveloped. Several small islands lie offshore, and the park contains a lovely stand of ironwood trees. All in all this enchanting beach is one of the finest on this side of the island. Swimming is good; bodysurfing is also recommended. Snorkeling is usually fair and there are small surfable waves with left and right slides. The principal catch is *papio*; milkfish, bonefish and goatfish are also caught. There are no facilities here. ~ Located on Kamehameha Highway (Route 83) in Laie about 22 miles north of Kaneohe.

HIDDEN ►

MALAEKAHANA STATE RECREATION AREA AND GOAT ISLAND This is a rare combination. The Malaekahana facility is one of the island's prettiest parks. It's a tropical wonderland filled with palm, *hala* and ironwood trees, and graced with a curving, white-sand beach. Goat Island lies just offshore. When the tide is right you can wade out to it. Other times, grab a boogie board or surf board and paddle out with a picnic lunch. It's a small, low-lying island covered with scrub growth and scattered ironwood trees. On the windward side is a coral beach; to leeward lies a crescent-shaped white-sand beach. It's a good place to swim because it is shallow and well-protected. There are also good places for snorkeling and, in winter, you can paddle out to a break with a left slide. Feel like fishing? You may well reel in *papio*, the most abundant fish along here; goatfish, milkfish and bonefish are also caught. Goat Island is now a state bird refuge, so you might see wedge-tailed shearwaters nesting. Whatever activity you choose, make sure you don't disturb the birds. Goat Island will return the favor—there'll be nothing here to disturb you either. Facilities include showers, bathrooms and barbecue pits. ~ Located on Kamehameha Highway (Route 83) in Laie about 23 miles north of Kaneohe.

▲ There are two sections to the park. The Laie section includes Goat Island and is administered by the state. The Kahuku section (Puuhonua o Malaekahana, or Place of Refuge) is operated by the Friends of Malaekahana, the first native Hawaiian group to operate a park in the islands.

Laie Section: Tent camping allowed. State permit required.

Kahuku Section: There are rustic cabins available here. These beachfront units include 40 campsites and 7 beach cabins—6 beach houses with two or three bedrooms, private baths and kitchens ($80 per night on weekends)—and a six-room cabin with a game room and a commercial kitchen ($250 per night). There are also pop-up trailers ($30 per night) and a thatched hut near the beach ($30 per night). Tent sites are $5 per person, per night. Cabins are equipped with beds, kitchen facilities and bathrooms. Bring your own bedding and cooking gear and be prepared for rustic accommodations. For information or reservations, call 808-293-1736, fax 808-293-2066.

KAHUKU GOLF COURSE PARK Other than Goat Island, this is about the closest you'll come to a hidden beach on the Windward Coast. Granted, there's a golf course paralleling the strand, but sand dunes hide you from the duffers. The beach is long, wide and sandy white. Swimming is fair, but exercise caution. In winter, surfers work the "Seventh Hole" breaks, which reach up to eight feet and have a right and left slide. *Papio*, bonefish, goatfish and milkfish are common catches. There are restrooms at the golf course. ~ In Kahuku, about 25 miles north of Kaneohe, turn off Kamehameha Highway (Route 83) toward the ocean. Park at the golf course, then walk the gated road to the beach.

NINE

North Shore

Wide, wide beaches heaped with white, white sand roll for miles along the North Shore, which curves from Kahuku Point in the east to Kaena Point in the west. Although they can compete with the most beautiful beaches anywhere, it's not the sand or their size that is the main attraction here. Rather it is the winter waves, and these waves have made Oahu's North Shore legendary. Surfers come from around the world to try their skill at one of the world's best spots for the sport.

If you have ever owned a surfboard, or even a Beach Boys album, you know Waimea Bay and Sunset Beach. The names are synonymous with surfing. They number among the most challenging and dangerous surf spots anywhere. During the winter, 15- to 20-foot waves are as common as blond hair and beach buggies. The infamous "Banzai Pipeline," where surfers risk limb and longevity as thunderous waves pass over a shallow reef, is here as well.

The surf is not only superb. The setting is stunning. Oahu's two mountain ranges form the backdrop, while 4025-foot Mt. Kaala, the island's highest peak, towers above all. Small ranches and farms checkerboard the tableland between the mountains and the sea. The old-time farmers, the surfers and the counterculture types who live in the area all come to Haleiwa for shopping, dining and socializing. Haleiwa, a restored plantation town with old clapboard buildings and wooden sidewalks, preserves the spirit of a rural way of life that is rapidly disappearing.

The plantations that established Oahu's economic base have all closed. In fact, the last sugar mill on the island, located in the North Shore town of Waialua, shut down in 1996, marking the end of a major chapter in Oahu's history. Although the Waialua Sugar Company now no longer processes cane, this low-key village west of Haleiwa still has the feel of a sugar town. The mill, which stands at its center, and the Sugar Bar, a bar and pizza place in the old Bank of Hawaii building, serve as reminders of a past that just yesterday was the present.

As the hub of sugar production has shifted to other areas of the world, the farmers of Oahu have filled the vacuum. Coffee experienced a bum crop when it was first planted here in the early 1800s. Locals gave it a more successful try in 1825, however, and it's now experiencing a production boom. The soil and climate of this island lend themselves to excellent crops of the beans, which thrive in moist soil rich in the organic matter of volcanic rock and leaf mold. The land near Waialua, the sleepy little sugar plantation town, is ideal for coffee production: the absorbent soil is loose enough to drain excess water, and the temperature and elevation further the perfect conditions. The sorghum and wiliwili trees of the North Shore currently protect the crop; ultimately, the recently planted Norfolk pines will become the primary guardian against wind damage to the coffee trees.

The main road along the North Shore begins with the small town of **Kahuku**. This is where many residents call home. For a taste of the rural Hawaii of old, take a detour into this little village. Kahuku is also the home of the **Kahuku Sugar Mill**, a turn-of-the-20th-century plant. In an effort to refurbish the old mill several years ago, gears and crushers were painted tropical hues and the entire complex was turned into an entertaining museum-cum-shopping mall. The place has been struggling for years, and the shops never quite made it, but you will find a restaurant there.

Facilitating the recovery of four endangered bird species—the black-necked Hawaiian stilt, Hawaiian moorhen, Hawaiian coot and Hawaiian duck—is the **James Campbell National Wildlife Refuge** in Kahuku. Two units comprise this 142-acre reserve: the Punamaoo Pond is a spring-fed marsh; the Kii Unit is made up of former sugar cane waste–settling basins. Free guided tours of the wetlands are offered August to mid-February. Reservations required. ~ 66-590 Kamehameha Highway, Haleiwa, HI 96712; 808-637-6330.

◄ HIDDEN

As you continue along the highway you will skirt **Kaihalulu Beach**, which continues out to **Kahuku Point**, the northernmost point on Oahu. The current here is strong and the rocky bottom makes swimming difficult, but it is a wonderful spot to spend the afternoon beachcombing. The road then makes a bend past **Kuilima Cove**, the windswept white-sand strand fronting the Turtle Bay Resort.

Roadside vendors at locations along the way sell sweet corn, watermelon, papaya, mango and tropical flowers from local farms and gardens, fresh-caught fish and shrimp from the area's aquaculture ponds. You'll get a warm welcome and a chance to "talk story" with the locals as well as the opportunity to enjoy some of Hawaii's natural treasures.

Stretching for two miles and averaging 200 feet in width, **Sunset Beach** (Kamehameha Highway) is one of Hawaii's largest strands. While Sunset Beach is actually only a single surfing spot, the name has become synonymous with a two-mile-long corridor that includes Banzai Beach and the adjacent Pipeline. When the surf is up you can watch world-class athletes shoot the curl. When it's not, Sunset becomes a great place to swim. The best place to go is **Ehukai Beach Park**, just off Kamehameha Highway about seven miles northeast of Haleiwa. Just 100 yards to the west sits the **Banzai Pipeline** (Ke Nui Road), where a shallow coral shelf creates tubular waves so powerful and perfect they resemble pipes. First surfed in 1957, it lays claim to cracked skulls, lacerated legs and some of the sport's greatest feats.

On a plateau between Sunset Beach and Waimea Bay is **Puu o Mahuka Heiau**, Oahu's oldest temple. A split-level structure built of stone, it once was used for human sacrifices. Today you will encounter nothing more menacing than a spectacular view and perhaps a gentle breeze from the ocean. To get there from Kamehameha Highway, turn left near the Sunset Beach Fire Station onto Pupukea Road, then follow the Hawaii Visitors & Convention Bureau signs.

An altogether different religious site is **St. Peter & Paul**, a Catholic church. Built on a former rock-crushing plant, this quaint church, with its steeple constructed from the remaining rocks of the plant, seems to stand watch over Waimea Bay.

At **Waimea Falls Park** you can wander through a tropical preserve and cultural park stretching across 1800 acres. Once a Hawaiian village, it is crisscrossed with hiking trails and archaeological ruins. A tram carries visitors to **Waimea Falls**, where you can picnic, swim and watch a cliff-diving exhibition. There are also an arboretum featuring tropical and subtropical trees from

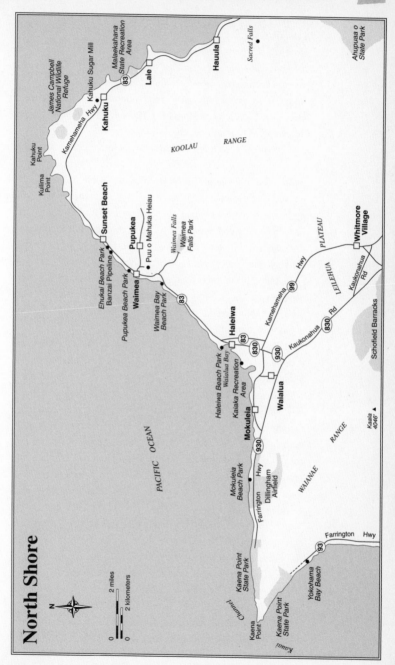

North Shore

N

0   2 miles
0   2 kilometers

PACIFIC OCEAN

James Campbell National Wildlife Refuge

Kahuku Point

Kuilima Point

Kahuku Sugar Mill

Kamehameha Hwy

Kahuku

Malaekahana State Recreation Area

(83)

Laie

Hauula

Sacred Falls

Ahupuaa o State Park

KOOLAU   RANGE

Sunset Beach

Ehukai Beach Park
Banzai Pipeline

Pupukea

Puu o Mahuka Heiau

Waimea Falls
Waimea Falls Park

Pupukea Beach Park

Waimea

Waimea Bay Beach Park

(83)

Haleiwa

(83)
(830)
(930)

PLATEAU

Whitmore Village

Kamehameha Hwy

(99)

LEILEHUA

Kaukonahua Rd

(830) Rd

Schofield Barracks

Kaukonahua

Haleiwa Beach Park
Waialua Bay

Kaiaka Recreation Area

Mokuleia

Waialua

(930)

Kaala
4046'

WAIANAE   RANGE

Mokuleia Beach Park

Farrington Hwy

Dillingham Airfield

Kaena Point State Park

Farrington   Hwy

(93)

Yokohama Bay Beach

Kaena Point

Kaena Point State Park

Oahu

Kauai

around the world, beautiful botanical gardens including one local Hawaiian species, and a playground for children. Then there are the birds that populate the complex; since this nature park serves as a bird sanctuary, it attracts a varied assortment. Activities for visitors include horseback riding, kayaking, mountain biking, hiking tours and a hula show. Steep admission. ~ Kamehameha Highway, five miles northeast of Haleiwa; 808-638-8511, fax 808-638-7900; e-mail waimeafalls@aol.com.

Across the road looms **Waimea Bay**, another fabled place that sports the largest surfable waves in the world. When surf's up in winter, the monster waves that roll in are so big they make the ground tremble when they break. Salt spray reaches as far as the highway. Thirty-foot waves are not uncommon. Fifty-foot giants have been recorded; though unsurfable, these are not tidal waves, just swells rising along the incredible North Shore. In December, the Hawaiian Triple Crown—basically the Super Bowl of surfing—takes place. In summer, Waimea is a pretty blue bay with a white-sand beach. The water is placid and the area perfect for picnicking and sunbathing. So when you visit Waimea, remember: swim in summer, sunbathe in winter.

Next, the Kamehameha Highway crosses Anahula River and a double rainbow–shaped bridge en route to **Haleiwa**, an old plantation town with a new facelift. Fortunately, the designers who performed the surgery on this village had an eye for antiquity. They planned it so the modern shopping centers and other facilities blend comfortably into the rural landscape. The community that has grown up around the new town reflects a rare combination of past and future. The old Japanese, Filipinos and Hawaiians have been joined by blond-mopped surfers and laid-back counterculturalists. As a result, this clapboard town with wooden sidewalks has established itself as the "in" spot on the North Shore. Its stylish nonchalance has also proved popular among canny travelers. Despite the hint of gentrification, Haleiwa holds on to its relaxed ambience with a dose of authenticity. The surf scene still adds a definite style to Haleiwa.

The little church in town is named for the queen who used to summer on the shores of the nearby Anahulu River, Queen Liliuokalani. **Liliuokalani Protestant Church** dates back to the early 1800s, though the current building was constructed in the mid-1900s. If you have a chance to enter the church, take a look at the clock that was donated by the queen—it shows the phases of the moon as well as the hour, day, month and year.

A scenic detour takes you to the town of **Waialua**, a former sugar plantation town, via Haleiwa Road. There's not much to see here except the old **Waialua Sugar Mill**, which is now headquarters for a coffee-growing concern. The mill closed its sugar operation in the mid-'90s and the cane fields around this area are being replanted with Waialua coffee. Plantation houses line the streets and it's an interesting area to look around.

If you want to take the faster route toward Kaena Point, pick up Farrington Highway (Route 930). This country road parallels miles of unpopulated beachfront, past wind-battered Mokuleia Beach and arrives at Dillingham Airfield, where you can take **The Original Glider Ride** along the Waianae Mountains. With nearly 30 years of experience, Mr. Bill knows the ins and outs of the countryside. He'll also provide you with a video of your ride. Reservations recommended. ~ 808-677-3404, fax 808-676-8520.

Beyond this landing strip, the road continues for several miles between a wild ocean and scrub brush–covered mountains before turning into a very rugged dirt track. Along this unpaved portion of roadway you can hike out about ten miles to **Kaena Point** on Oahu's northwest corner (see the "Hiking" section in Chapter Two). This is the legendary point of departure for Hawaiian souls.

sights

AUTHOR FAVORITE

I'm a surfing enthusiast so I recommend checking out **North Shore Surf and Cultural Museum**. This surfing nook displays related artifacts, boards and old photographs of the local community, and has a mini-theater showing videos of the sport. It also temporarily houses items from an 1824 shipwreck, providing a safe haven for the items while the wreck is being excavated. The museum's other claim to fame is its possession of the last two boards used by famed surfer Mark Foo before he was killed in a surfing accident in 1994. ~ North Shore Marketplace, 66-250 Kamehameha Highway, Haleiwa; 808-637-8888; www.surfmuseum.net.

LODGING

For a resort experience in a rustic setting, consider the **Turtle Bay Resort**. This rural retreat sprawls across 880 acres on a dramatic peninsula. With a broad beach at the doorstep and mountains out back, it's an overwhelming spot. Add to that riding paths, two golf courses, tennis courts and a pair of swimming pools. Every guest room features an ocean view. ~ 57-091 Kamehameha Highway, Kahuku; 808-293-8811, 800-203-3650, fax 808-293-9147; www.turtlebayresort.com. ULTRA-DELUXE.

At Mokuleia, watch for skydivers, who often use the shoreline for their beach landings.

Located on the grounds of the Turtle Bay Resort but independently operated, **The Estates at Turtle Bay** offers studio, as well as one-, two- and three-bedroom resort condominiums, each with stove, refrigerator, dishwasher, microwave, washer/dryer and cable television. There are five swimming pools and four tennis courts on the property, and guests can arrange golf and horseback riding through the resort. Closed Sunday. ~ 56-565 Kamehameha Highway, Kahuku; 808-293-0600, 888-200-4202, fax 808-293-0471; www.turtlebay-rentals.com, e-mail trtlbayest@aol.com. MODERATE TO DELUXE.

Turtle Bay Condos has one-, two- and three-bedroom units with kitchen facilities and private lanais that overlook a nine-hole golf course. In high season, studios are $90; one-bedrooms units with a loft sleeping up to four guests are $140; two-bedroom units are $160; and three-bedroom units are $175. ~ 56-565 Kamehameha Highway, Kahuku; 808-293-2800, fax 808-293-2169; www.turtlebaycondos.com.

Surfers, scuba divers and budget-minded travelers will find **Backpacker's Vacation Inn** along Oahu's vaunted North Shore. The central building provides hostel-style rooms and features a TV lounge and kitchen. There's also a back house with private rooms that share a kitchen and bath. Like a hostel, it's budget-priced. Across the street, and directly on the beach, there's a house with private apartments that include their own kitchen and bathroom and are moderately priced. In addition, there are nine restored plantation houses with shared kitchens and baths set on a landscaped acre. The Vacation Inn has guest laundry facilities and barbecue areas, which provide excellent opportunities for meeting other travelers. ~ 59-788 Kamehameha Highway, Haleiwa; 808-638-7838, fax 808-638-7515; www.backpackers-hawaii.com, e-mail bpacker@maui.net. BUDGET TO DELUXE.

Offering houses right on the beach, **Ke Iki Beach Bungalows** are located between the Banzai Pipeline and Waimea Bay. You'll find moderate- and deluxe-priced duplexes and an ultra-deluxe-priced cottage on an acre-and-a-half of palm-shaded property. They are basic woodframe buildings with bamboo and rattan furnishings; all units have full kitchens. The complex includes barbecue facilities, hammocks, a volleyball court and a wide beach. Accommodations are great for families. ~ 59-579 Ke Iki Road, Haleiwa; phone/fax 808-638-8229; www.keikibeach.com, e-mail keikibeach bungalows@hawaii.rr.com. MODERATE TO ULTRA-DELUXE.

If you need a break from the sterile comforts of commercial hotels, try the **Surfhouse**. There's camping available on the grounds and a "hostel cabin" with bunk beds (linens are provided). The private cabins are clean and comfortable, and as cheap as you'll find. The owners rely mainly on word of mouth for advertising and maintain a commercial kitchen and bathrooms, keeping the prices down and the earthy factor up. ~ 62-203 Lokoea Place, Haleiwa; 808-637-7146; www.surfhouse.com, e-mail info@surf house.com. BUDGET.

DINING

Appropriately enough, you'll find the **Country Kitchen** out in the country (and not far from the old Kahuku Sugar Mill). The menu includes Hawaiian plate lunches as well as shrimp, seafood and steak dishes. Open for breakfast and lunch daily, it's plain and informal. ~ 55-565 Kamehameha Highway, Kahuku; 808-293-2110. BUDGET.

Just down the way is **Giovanni's Aloha Shrimp Truck**, serving gourmet plate lunches that the locals claim are the best on Oahu. There's a choice of scampi, grilled shrimp or hot and spicy shrimp, and, like all plate lunches, they come with two scoops of rice. Eleven picnic tables sit under an awning for this rain-or-shine outdoor eating spot. ~ Beside The Mill, Kamehameha Highway, Kahuku; 808-293-1839; www.giosauces.com, e-mail giovanni@ hawaii.rr.com. MODERATE.

The **Turtle Bay Resort** features an upscale restaurant, a family restaurant and a poolside snack shop. **The Cove**, a *koa* wood–paneled, multi-tiered, glass-walled extravaganza with sweeping ocean views, features gourmet Continental–Pacific Rim cuisine. Expect such delights as chicken in lemongrass cream sauce, pesto mahimahi and lobster-topped veal medallions. At the **Palm**

Terrace, overlooking the hotel's lovely grounds, you'll encounter moderate-priced dining in an attractive environment. The restaurant, serving three buffet meals, offers everything from burgers to *saimin* and teriyaki to linguine. Children's prices are available. At the **Orchid Snackshop**, munch on a hamburger or taco salad while lounging in the sun. ~ 57-091 Kamehameha Highway, Kahuku; 808-293-8811, fax 808-293-9147; www.turtlebayresort. com. MODERATE TO DELUXE.

HIDDEN ► **Sunset Pizza** packs local crowds into its awning-covered picnic tables, with homemade lasagna, pizzas built from scratch, salads and an array of sandwiches made with freshly baked bread. ~ 59-176 Kamehameha Highway, Haleiwa; 808-638-7660. BUDGET TO MODERATE.

For relaxed sunset dining overlooking the ocean, try **Jameson's By the Sea**. For lunch there are sandwiches, chowders and fresh fish dishes; at dinner they specialize in seafood. Breakfast on the weekend. ~ 62-540 Kamehameha Highway, Haleiwa; 808-637-4336, fax 808-637-3225. MODERATE TO DELUXE.

The seafood at **Haleiwa Joe's Seafood Grill** is not the best I've ever had, but the salads are large and refreshing, the coconut shrimp pretty good, and the atmosphere a little more chichi than most casual beachside places. Plus, the patio has a beautiful ocean view. ~ 66-011 Kamehameha Highway, Haleiwa; 808-637-8005, fax 808-637-8861. MODERATE TO ULTRA-DELUXE.

Haleiwa Beach Grill, a small café in the center of Haleiwa, is as colorful as coral. Matter of fact, the tropic-hued walls are adorned with a wide range of vintage albums from the '60s and '70s. Read the menu and you'll discover charbroiled chicken, grilled sandwiches, burritos and "islander plates." There are *kalbi*

AUTHOR FAVORITE

At **Café Haleiwa** surfers swear by the omelettes, pancakes and "the Barrel"—a blend of eggs, potatoes, green salsa and cheese wrapped in a tortilla. Sandwiches and burgers round out the menu. Located in a century-old building featuring local artwork, surfboards and surfing memorabilia, this local favorite also serves an excellent quesadilla. No dinner. ~ 66-460 Kamehameha Highway, Haleiwa; 808-637-5516, fax 808-637-5516. BUDGET.

ribs, teriyaki chicken and a mixed grill dish that includes mahi-mahi. ~ 66-079 Kamehameha Highway, Haleiwa; 808-637-3394, fax 808-626-9475. BUDGET.

For dessert, head for **Flavor Mania**, which serves homemade ice cream, served plain or with mix-ins. Take a group and try the Big Wave Special banana boat, with four scoops of ice cream and four different toppings. ~ Haleiwa Shopping Center, 66-145 Kamehameha Highway, Haleiwa; 808-637-9362. BUDGET.

Pizza Bob's has, you guessed it, pizza. It also has burgers and pastas and a wonderful outdoor covered patio for dining. ~ Haleiwa Shopping Center, 66-145 Kamehameha Highway, Haleiwa; 808-637-5095. BUDGET.

Mexican restaurants in Hawaii are different from their counterparts elsewhere in one respect—fish tacos. True to the islands, **Rosie's Cantina** offers them, rounding out a menu filled with the culinary features found in every south-of-the-border eatery. The breakfast menu features American standbys like pancakes and omelettes, while the dinner menu ranges from tacos and enchiladas to steaks and seafood. To complement the fare Rosie's stocks the largest selection of premium tequilas in Hawaii. ~ Haleiwa Shopping Plaza, 66-165 Kamehameha Highway, Haleiwa; 808-637-3538, fax 808-637-7615. BUDGET TO DELUXE.

Join the surfers who pour into **Kua Aina Sandwich**, where they order hamburgers, french fries and mahimahi sandwiches at the counter, then kick back at one of the roadside tables. Great for light meals, this place is a scene and a half. ~ 66-214 Kamehameha Highway, Haleiwa; 808-637-6067, fax 808-637-4858. BUDGET.

Steaming fish tacos smothered in spicy salsa. Salty chips that leave oil on your napkin. Cold beer topped with lime (well, you have to provide your own, but you get the idea). Mmmm. But I digress. **Cholos Homestyle Mexican Restaurant** is ideal after-beach fare. You can dine inside or out, and the gorgeous crafts on display are for sale. Open for breakfast, lunch and dinner. ~ North Shore Marketplace, 66-250 Kamehameha Highway, Haleiwa; 808-637-3059. MODERATE.

Years ago Haleiwa was home to Da Cuppa Kope, a great café and gathering place. Today it's been supplanted by an even better coffeehouse, the **Coffee Gallery**. In addition to the best cappuccino on the island, this homespun restaurant, decorated with

◄ HIDDEN

coffee sacks, serves pastries, bagels, homemade soups and a variety of sandwiches. ~ North Shore Marketplace, 66-250 Kamehameha Highway, Haleiwa; 808-637-5355; www.roastmaster.com, e-mail coffeegalleryhawaii@yahoo.com. BUDGET.

Paradise Found Café has a juice bar and vegetarian restaurant serving sandwiches, soups and salads. ~ Inside Celestial Natural Foods, 66-443 Kamehameha Highway, Haleiwa; 808-637-4540. BUDGET.

HIDDEN ►

For an unexpected crowd that includes a big contingent of bikers, drop by the **Sugar Bar & Grill** in the ex-plantation town of Waialua, just a couple of miles from Haleiwa. Housed in what was once the town bank, it's a high-energy place with an abundance of local color, perfect for a late afternoon drink and a casual dinner. ~ 67-069 Kealohanui Street, Waialua; 808-636-2220; www.sugarbarandgrill.com. BUDGET.

GROCERIES

Out by Sunset Beach you'll find a **Foodland Super Market**. ~ 59-720 Kamehameha Highway, Haleiwa; 808-638-8081. There's also **Sunset Beach Store,** which has a small stock but is home to a modest bakery; it's conveniently located near Sunset Beach. ~ 59-024 Kamehameha Highway, Haleiwa; 808-638-8207. **Haleiwa Supermarket,** one of the few large markets on the entire North Shore, is the best place to shop. ~ 66-197 Kamehameha Highway, Haleiwa; 808-637-5004.

Celestial Natural Foods has an ample supply of health foods and fresh produce. ~ 66-443 Kamehameha Highway, Haleiwa; 808-637-6729.

SHOPPING

Calling itself **The Only Show In Town** is a slight (very slight) exaggeration, but claiming to be "Kahuku's largest antique and vintage collectible shop" is definitely warranted. Some store specialties include Japanese glass fishing floats, ivory and Coca-Cola memorabilia. Fittingly, this wonderful antique store is located in the old Tanaka Plantation Store, an early-20th-century wood-frame building. ~ 56-931 Kamehameha Highway, Kahuku; 808-293-1295, fax 808-293-8585.

Trendy shoppers head for the burgeoning town of Haleiwa. During the past several years boutiques and galleries have mushroomed throughout this once somnolent town. Since Haleiwa is

How to Beat the Heat
with a Sweet Treat

Since the early days of Hawaiian royalty, people have complained
about Honolulu's shirt-sticking weather. Come summer,
temperatures rise and the trade winds stop blowing. Visitors seeking
a golden tan discover they're baking without browning. And residents
begin to think that their city, renowned as a cultural melting pot, is
actually a pressure cooker.

With the ocean all around, relief is never far away. But a lot of folks,
when not heading for the beaches, have found another way to cool
off: shave ice. Known as ice frappes among the Japanese originators
and snow cones back on the mainland, these frozen treats are
Hawaii's answer to the Good Humor man.

They're made with ice that's been shaved from a block into thin
slivers, packed into a cone-shaped cup and covered with sweet syrup.
Health-minded people eat the ice plain or with a low-calorie or
sugar-free syrup, and some folks ask for a scoop of ice cream or
sweet black beans (*azuki* beans) underneath the shavings. Most
people just order it with their favorite syrup flavors—grape, root
beer, cola, cherry, orange, lemon-lime, vanilla, fruit punch, banana,
strawberry or whatever.

Whichever you choose, you'll find it only costs about a buck at the
many stands sprinkled around town. Watch for stands up on the
North Shore, too. No doubt you'll see a long line outside Oahu's
most famous shave ice store, **Matsumoto's**. ~ 66-087 Kamehameha
Highway, Haleiwa; 808-637-4827.

As a matter of fact, anyplace where the sun blazes overhead you're
liable to find someone trying to beat the heat by slurping up a "snow
cone" before it melts into mush.

a center for surfers, it's a good place to buy sportswear and aquatic equipment.

Iwa Gallery features a unique collection of artwork by a number of local island artists. ~ 66-119 Kamehameha Highway, Haleiwa; 808-637-4865.

Oogenesis Boutique has a creative selection of women's fashions. ~ 66-249 Kamehameha Highway, Haleiwa; 808-637-4580.

The North Shore Marketplace is an eclectic collection of exceptional shops selling everything from surfing gear to handblown glass. **Polynesian Treasures** (808-637-1288) sells handicrafts from Fiji, Tonga, Samoa and Hawaii. At **Silver Moon Emporium** (808-637-7710) you'll find women's wear and jewelry. **Twelve Tribes International Imports** (808-637-7634) sells ethnic clothes, gifts, sandals, incense and sarongs. **Jungle Gems** (808-637-6609) is a gallery of gorgeous jewelry made from semiprecious gems, crystals, silver and inlaid woods. Just in case you forgot your bathing suit, women can pick one from the scores of bikinis and swim suits on display at **North Shore Swimwear** (808-637-6859) or order a custom-made creation. Glass artists fashion whales, sharks, reef fish and turtles in elegant designs while you watch at **Oceans in Glass** (808-637-3366). **Boardriders Club** (808-637-5026) has a huge selection of surfboards and gear. ~ North Shore Marketplace, 66-250 Kamehameha Highway, Haleiwa.

Strong Current stocks everything imaginable that's related to surfing. They even have a small "surfing museum," consisting of memorabilia from the sport's early days. Then there are the books, videos, posters, boards and other appurtenances, all relating to a single theme. ~ North Shore Marketplace, 66-250 Kamehameha

---

SNORKELER'S PARADISE

Some of the island's best snorkeling is at **Pupukea Beach Park**, a marine reserve on Kamehameha Highway six miles northeast of Haleiwa. This 80-acre park, fringed by rocky shoreline, divides into several sections. Foremost is "Shark's Cove," located on the north side of the fire station, which contains spectacular tidepools. Underwater caves draw divers (experienced only—there have been a number of drownings in these deep and maze-like caverns). ~ Kamehameha Highway at Papukea Road.

Highway, Haleiwa; 808-637-3406; www.strongcurrenthawaii.
com, e-mail info@strongcurrenthawaii.com.

Entertainment is a rare commodity on the North Shore, but you   **NIGHTLIFE**
will find contemporary Hawaiian music at the Turtle Bay Resort's
Bay View; on Saturday they feature disco music. ~ 57-091 Kamehameha Highway, Kahuku; 808-293-8811.

In Haleiwa, **Pizza Bob's** has occasional live entertainment on
the weekends. ~ Haleiwa Shopping Center; 808-637-5095.

To mix with the locals, head to the **Sugar Bar & Grill**, where
you'll find live rock, rhythm-and-blues or Hawaiian music Wednesday, Friday, Saturday and Sunday. ~ 67-069 Kealohanui Street,
Waialua; 808-636-2220.

SUNSET BEACH 🏊 🏖 🚻 ⚓ As far as surfing goes, this is   **BEACHES**
the place! I think the best way to do Sunset is by starting from   **& PARKS**
Ehukai Beach Park. From here you can go left to the "Banzai Pipeline," where crushing waves build along a shallow coral reef to
create tube-like formations. To the right lies "Sunset," with
equally spectacular surfing waves. Throughout the area the swimming is fair in summer; however, in winter it is extremely dangerous. From September to April, high waves and strong currents
prevail. Be careful! Game fish caught around Sunset include *papio*,
menpachi and *ulua*. Facilities at Ehukai Beach Park include picnic areas, restrooms and showers. Snorkeling here is poor but it's
excellent at **Pupukea Beach Park**, located on Kamehameha Highway six miles northeast of Haleiwa. An 80-acre marine reserve,
it has fabulous tidepools and dive sites. ~ Ehukai Beach Park is
located off Kamehameha Highway (Route 83) about seven miles
northeast of Haleiwa.

WAIMEA BAY BEACH PARK 🏊 🏖 🚻 ⚓ If Sunset is *one* of
the most famous surfing spots in the world, Waimea is *the* most
famous. The biggest surfable waves in the world (40 feet in winter!) roll into this pretty blue bay. There's a wide white-sand beach
and a pleasant park with a tree-studded lawn. It's a marvelous
place for picnicking and sunbathing. During the winter crowds
often line the beach watching top-notch surfers challenge the curl;
in summer the sea is flat and safe for swimming; you can also bodysurf in the shorebreak and snorkel when the bay is calm. *Papio*,

menpachi and *ulua* are common catches. Facilities include a picnic area, restrooms, showers and a lifeguard. ~ On Kamehameha Highway (Route 83) about five miles northeast of Haleiwa.

HALEIWA BEACH PARK This is an excellent refuge from the North Shore's pounding surf. Set in Waialua Bay, the beach is safe for swimming almost all year. You can snorkel, although it's only fair. Surfing in not possible here but "Haleiwa" breaks are located across Waialua Bay at Alii Beach Park. Facilities include a picnic area, restrooms, showers, a snack bar, a ball field, a basketball court, volleyball courts and a playground. The primary catches at Haleiwa are *papio*, *menpachi* and *ulua*. ~ On Kamehameha Highway (Route 83) in Haleiwa.

HALEIWA ALII BEACH PARK Haleiwa Alii Beach Park, across from Haleiwa Beach Park, is where you go to surf. Swells can top 20 feet here, which is why it's the site of several surfing and bodyboarding tournaments—you can watch the pros do things that seem to defy gravity. If you've come on one of the few days that surfing is not ideal, or if you're a beginner, bring your boogieboard and join the kids on the more manageable waves. If you're visiting in winter, you're in luck: lifeguards give free surfing lessons in the morning (it's a good idea to reserve a spot ahead of time; head for the lifeguard tower to sign up). Facilities include a picnic area, restrooms and year-round lifeguards. ~ On Kamehameha Highway (Route 83) in Haleiwa; 808-637-5051, fax 808-637-5052.

KAIAKA RECREATION AREA The setting at this peninsular park is beautiful. There's a secluded area with a tree-shaded lawn and a short strip of sandy beach. A rocky shoreline borders most of the park, so it's more for picnics than water sports. You *can* swim and snorkel but there's a rocky bottom. Fishing is good for *papio*, *menpachi* and *ulua*. The facilities here include a picnic area, showers and restrooms. ~ Located on Haleiwa Road just outside Haleiwa.

▲ Permitted; a county permit is required.

HIDDEN ▶ **MOKULEIA BEACH PARK AND MOKULEIA BEACH** The 12-acre park contains a sandy beach and large unshaded lawn. An exposed coral reef detracts from the swimming, but on either side of the park lie beaches with sandy ocean bottoms.

If you do swim, exercise caution, especially in the winter months; there's no lifeguard. There's good snorkeling and in winter the surf breaks up to ten feet near Dillingham Airfield. Anglers try for *papio*, *menpachi* and *ulua*. Whatever your activity of choice, you'll have to contend with the noise of small planes from nearby Dillingham Airfield. The park is also an excellent starting point for exploring the unpopulated sections of Mokuleia Beach. Facilities include picnic areas, restrooms and showers. ~ On Farrington Highway (Route 930) about seven miles west of Haleiwa. To the west of the park, this beach stretches for miles along a secluded coast. You can hike down the beach or reach its hidden realms by driving farther west along Farrington Highway (Route 930), then turning off onto any of the numerous dirt side roads.

▲ Tent and trailer camping are allowed with a county permit. Unofficial camping along the undeveloped beachfront is common.

MOKULEIA ARMY BEACH This is the widest stretch of sand   ◄ HIDDEN
along the Mokuleia shoreline, and probably the most untamed. Once maintained by the Army for the exclusive use of their personnel, it's now open to the public but has no facilities. The high surf in winter poses no challenge to natives, but surfing really isn't recommended; there have been fatalities here. The treacherous waters mean that you'll pretty much have the spot to yourself. Most visitors are locals with a strong sense of loyalty to this largely untouristed spot. ~ Route 930 near the Dillingham Airfield.

TEN

Central Oahu and Leeward Coast

Visitors often ignore Central Oahu and the Leeward Coast, which together make up the western half of Oahu. They'll buzz down Route 99, which intersects the island, on their way to or from the North Shore, and they'll avoid the Leeward Coast entirely, having been warned of potential problems with the locals. But they shouldn't. The very fact that people don't often visit these two places makes them worth going to for a glimpse of Oahu that hasn't been transformed by tourism.

The 1000-foot-high Leilehua Plateau, a bountiful agricultural region once planted with sugar and pineapple, extends from the North Shore to the southern reaches of Oahu. Spreading across the middle of the island between the Waianae and Koolau ranges, this tableland nurtured the large plantations that once formed the backbone of Oahu's agricultural infrastructure. It is now being cultivated in diversified agriculture. It has also become a vital military headquarters. Wheeler Air Force Base, Schofield Barracks and several other installations occupy large plots of land here.

Out along the west coast of Oahu, less than 30 miles from the sands of Waikiki, Hawaiian culture is making a last stand. Here on the tableland that separates the Waianae Range from the ocean, the old ways still prevail. Unlike the cool rainforests of the Windward Coast or the rain-spattered area around Honolulu, this is a region of stark beauty, resembling the American Southwest, with rocky crags and cactus-studded hills. Farther north, the spartan scenery gives way to wide vistas of massive mountains sloping gracefully to the sea.

Hawaiian and Samoan farmers tend small fields and raise chickens. Side roads off the main highway pass dusty houses and sunblasted churches before turning

218

into dirt tracks that keep climbing past truck farms and old homesteads. For entertainment, there are birthday luaus, cockfights and slack-key guitar playing.

The Leeward Coast has become the keeper of the old ways, and residents jealously guard the customs and traditions that they see slipping away in the rest of the state. Although there have been reports of outsiders being hassled by local residents, the reality, in fact, is usually the reverse. Here, far from the madding crowds of tourists and tourist businesses, the true spirit of aloha is alive and well. But who knows for how long?

"Second City," a major development already being built near the town of Ewa, will eventually add thousands of houses to the Central Oahu area. And in the southwest corner of the island the ultra-modern JW Marriott Ihilani Resort & Spa in the Ko Olina area is only the beginning of the inevitable encroachment along this side of the island. So you should consider this one of those places that needs to be seen and seen soon, before the forces of change sweep through.

Central Oahu

From Haleiwa south to Wahiawa you can take Route 803, Kaukoahuna Road, a pretty thoroughfare with excellent views of the Waianaes, or follow Route 99, the Kamehameha Highway, which passes through verdant pineapple fields.

The **Dole Pineapple Plantation**, often crowded with tourists, sells (who would have guessed) pineapple products. They offer a self-guided tour and the World's Largest Maze, a 1.7-mile labyrinth made from more than 11,000 Hawaiian plants that covers two acres. Admission for maze. ~ 64-1550 Kamehameha Highway, Wahiawa; 808-621-8408, 888-611-6747, fax 808-621-1926; www.dole-plantation.com, e-mail sales@dole-plantation.com. The **Pineapple Variety Garden** displays many different types of the fruit in a garden museum. ~ Kamehameha Highway and Kamananui Road, Wahiawa.

The east fork of Route 99 becomes **Route 80**, which passes near **Kukaniloho**, a cluster of sacred stones marking the place where Hawaiian royalty gave birth accompanied by chants, drums and offerings. Studded with eucalyptus trees, this spot has held an important place in Hawaiian mythology and religion for centuries. ~ Follow the dirt road across from Whitmore Avenue just north of Wahiawa.

◄ HIDDEN

For a scenic and historic detour from Route 80, follow Route 80 until it links with Route 99. Take Route 99 west, pull up to the sentry station at Schofield Barracks and ask directions to

Kolekole Pass. On that "day of infamy," December 7, 1941, Japanese bombers buzzed through this notch in the Waianae Range. You'll be directed through Schofield up into the Waianaes. When you reach **Kolekole Pass**, there's another sentry gate. Ask the guard to let you continue a short distance farther to the observation point. From here the Waianaes fall away precipitously to a plain that rolls gently to the sea. There's an astonishing view of Oahu's west coast. If you are denied permission to pass the sentry point, then take the footpath that begins just before the gate, leading up the hill. From near the cross at the top, you will have a partial view of both the Waianaes' western face and the central plateau region.

Retrace your steps back to **Schofield Barracks**, established in 1909 to defend the northern approach to Pearl Harbor. Since then, it's become a thriving, self-contained Army community, and the largest Army post outside the continental U.S. Not to mention the fact that it was the location for *From Here to Eternity*, starring Burt Lancaster, Deborah Kerr and Frank Sinatra. For more information about the area, visit the **Tropic Lightning Museum**. The interesting history of the barracks and the 25th Infantry is explained through exhibits and photos. Tours are available by reservation. Closed Sunday and Monday. ~ Building 361, Waianae Avenue, Schofield Barracks; 808-655-0438, fax 808-655-8301; e-mail troplight7@juno.com.

Wahiawa Botanical Gardens, spreading across 27-acres, offers a handsome retreat studded with tropical vegetation. Plants include orchids, ferns, cacti and bromeliads, as well as Heliconias, palms and gingers that thrive in a cool, moist climate. There are plants from Africa and Australia, Asian camphor trees and gum trees from New Guinea. A walk through the gardens is a feast for the senses, with fragrant flowers and spices filling the air and colors as vivid as any you've seen before. The garden specializes in introduced and native rainforest plants. Guided tours are available by appointment. ~ 1396 California Avenue, Wahiawa; 808-522-7060, fax 808-522-7050; www.co.honolulu.hi.us/parks/hbg.

Route H-2 provides the fastest means back to Honolulu; the most interesting course is along **Route 750**, Kunia Road, which skirts the Waianaes, passing sugar cane fields and stands of pine.

Along the way you can take in **Hawaii's Plantation Village**, a partially re-created and partially restored village that spreads across three acres of Waipahu Cultural Park in Waipahu. Comprised of over two dozen buildings, it includes a Japanese Shinto shrine, a company store and a Chinese Society building. Hawaii's many ethnic groups are represented in the houses, which span several architectural periods of the 19th and 20th centuries. Together they provide visitors with a window into traditional life on a plantation. Closed Sunday. Admission. ~ 94-695 Waipahu Street, Waipahu; 808-677-0110, fax 808-676-6727. From here, Honolulu is about 15 miles east along Route H-1, or you can take Route 750 south to Ewa.

Leeward Coast & Central Oahu

Leeward Coast

From Honolulu you can visit the Leeward Coast region by traveling west on Route H-1 or Route 90. If you want to tour what once was a prime sugar-growing area, take Route 90 past Pearl Harbor, then turn left on Fort Weaver Road (Route 760). This country lane leads to the plantation town of Ewa. With its old sugar mill and trim houses, Ewa is an enchanting throwback to the days when sugar was king. This town is a slow, simple place, perfect for wandering and exploring.

The transportation of late-19th- to early-20th-century Oahu centered around the railroad. You can experience the past first-hand on a ride aboard the historical **Hawaiian Railway** train, once owned by the defunct Oahu Railway and Land Company. The ride covers six miles (of the existing ten) and is fully narrated. There are historical locomotives on display, and you can picnic on the grounds. Open Sunday only. Admission. ~ 1001 Renton Road, Ewa; 808-681-5461, fax 808-681-4860; www. hawaiianrailway.com, e-mail hawaiianrailway@aol.com.

HIDDEN ►

Near Oahu's southwest corner, Routes H-1 and 90 converge to become the Farrington Highway (Route 93). From here, follow the signs to **Hawaiian Waters Adventure Park**, perfect for those who are afraid of getting a little sand in their pants but love to ride waves or splash in the water. There are inner-tube slides, a 60-foot water slide, artificial waves and much more, spread over 25 acres. Closed Tuesday and Wednesday in winter. A hefty admission. ~ 400 Farrington Highway, Kapolei; 808-674-9283; www.hawaiian waters.com, e-mail questions@hawaiianwaters.com.

The first beach you come to along the Leeward Coast is **Barber's Point**. It's not worth a detour, however, so continue along

AUTHOR FAVORITE

If I want to get away from everything I dig deep into my pockets for a short stay at the **JW Marriott Ihilani Resort & Spa**. Backed by the Waianaes and facing a curved expanse of ocean, this 387-room hideaway is part of the 640-acre Ko Olina Resort. There's a golf course, six tennis courts, four restaurants and a spa facility. More important, you'll find a string of four lagoons, each with a crescent beach and a cluster of islets that protects the mouth of the lagoon. ~ 92-1001 Olani Street, Kapolei; 808-679-0079, 800-626-4446, fax 808-679-0295; www.ihilani.com. ULTRA-DELUXE.

Route 93 to Ko Olina Resort. You might want to make a stop here and take a look at the scenery: it can be windy, but it's a beautiful and little-visited spot.

Farrington Highway continues along the coast to Kahe Point. The ugly power plant you see is a good landmark to find **Hawaiian Electric Beach Park** and a top surfing spot by the name of "Tracks." Keep going along Route 93 and you'll pass the towns of Nani-kuli, Maili and Waianae.

If you turn up Mailiilii Street in **Waianae**, you will pass placid Hawaiian homesteads and farmlands. This side road also provides sweeping views of the Waianae Range. On the northern side of town is Waianae Harbor, a small port hosting small fishing vessels as well as spiffy yachts.

Farther along is **Makaha Beach**, one of Hawaii's most famous surfing spots, and the site of an annual international surfing championship. It's also a great place for shell hunting. The **Makaha Valley**, extending from the ocean up into the Waianae Mountains, is home to the **Kaneaki Heiau**, a 15th-century temple dedicated to the god Lono. Closed Monday and when raining. ~ Take Manunaolu Street; phone/fax 808-695-8174.

The highway continues along the coastline past several mostly deserted beaches and parks. Across from Kaena Point State Park you'll come upon **Makua Cave**, a lava cavern large enough for exploring and snorkeling. Beyond that, where the paved road turns to dirt, lies **Yokohama Bay**, with its curving sand beach and inviting turquoise waters.

The road past Yokohama is partially passable by auto, but it's very rough. If you want to explore **Kaena Point** from this side of the island, you'll have to hike. It's about two miles to the northwest corner of Oahu, past tidepools teeming with marine life. On a clear day you can see Kauai from this point. (Don't leave valuables in your car in this area.)

◄ *HIDDEN*

Makaha Shores, a six-story resort condo complex, overlooks pretty Makaha Beach Park, one of Hawaii's top surfing beaches. There are studios and one- and two-bedroom units, each individually decorated by their owners. The minimum stay is one week, and the units are handled by different agents. Hawaii Hatfields (phone/fax 808-696-7121) handles most of them. ~ 84-265 Farrington Highway, Makaha. MODERATE.

LODGING

Makaha Valley Towers is a highrise set along the slopes of Makaha Valley. Units range from studios to two-bedrooms, with nightly, weekly and monthly stays available. Rates vary and accommodations are handled by local realtors. ~ End of Kili Drive, Makaha; 808-695-9568.

DINING   By way of resort restaurants, **JW Marriott Ihilani Resort & Spa** at Ko Olina has several deluxe- and ultra-deluxe-priced dining rooms. Foremost is **Azul**, where the lamb chops come with couscous, the lobster is served in *pistou* and the ideas are Mediterranean. **Ushiotei** is the ultimate in Japanese cuisine. And **Naupaka**, a poolside terrace serving cross-cultural dishes, is the Ihilani's answer to informality and easy elegance. Hours for all three vary with the season. Reservations are recommended. ~ 92-1001 Olani Street, Kapolei; 808-679-0079, fax 808-679-0295. MODERATE TO ULTRA-DELUXE.

This sparsely populated strip of shoreline has several other dining spots. All are located on Farrington Highway, the main road, and most are in the town of Waianae. **Cathay Inn Chop Suey** is a good choice for Chinese food. ~ 86-088 Farrington Highway, Waianae; 808-696-9477. BUDGET TO MODERATE.

Close by is **Hannara Restaurant** offering Korean and Hawaiian cuisines. Breakfast and lunch daily. ~ 86-078 Farrington Highway, Waianae; 808-696-6137. BUDGET TO MODERATE.

Out at the Makaha Resort Golf Club, the **19th Hole** is an open-air café overlooking the golf course, where you can pick up ready-made sandwiches or muffins, or you can sit down to *saimin*, hot dogs and blue-plate specials. ~ 84-626 Makaha Valley Road, Makaha; 808-695-7525. BUDGET.

GROCERIES   **Sack 'n Save Foods** is the prime market in this area. ~ 87-2070 Farrington Highway, Waianae; 808-668-1277.

Another popular place to shop is **The Waianae Store**, a full-service supermarket that includes a bakery and delicatessen. ~ 85-863 Farrington Highway, Waianae; 808-696-3131.

NIGHTLIFE   **Naupaka Terrace** at the Ihilani Resort features nightly live entertainment. The Ihilani is also home to the **Hokulea**, a cozy lounge perfect for a quiet rendezvous. Hours vary with season. ~ JW Marriott Ihilani Resort & Spa, 92-1001 Olani Street, Kapolei; 808-679-0079.

The Endangered Wildlife of Oahu

A way from the crowds of Waikiki and the hubbub of downtown Honolulu and high in the mountains of Leeward Oahu, a preserve operated by The Nature Conservancy is helping to save some of the island's and the world's endangered flora and fauna. The organization is trying to ensure that the land on which these threatened species exist will be cared for so that the natural history of Oahu can be perpetuated, not only for the present generation but for those to come.

The 3692-acre forest preserve stretches along the southern Waianae Mountains and down their eastern slopes. Incorporated within its boundaries are what is left of a diverse native ecosystem once common on Oahu.

The preserve harbors plant and animals species that are, or have the potential to be, endangered. Several birds, including the *pueo* (Hawaiian owl), the flycatching *elepaio*, the crimson-feathered *apapane* and the yellow-green *amakihi*, live in the Honouliuli forests. Two endangered tree snails endemic to Oahu and found nowhere else also call the preserve their home.

Animals aren't the only living things that **Honouliuli Preserve** helps to spare. Three plants found here grow nowhere else on the planet. One of these is a mint species and two are flowering lobelia species.

Because the preserve is in a remote part of the Waianae Mountains, The Nature Conservancy recommends visiting it only as part of a regularly scheduled—usually twice-monthly—guided hike or work project. For more information and to join in the organization's efforts to preserve Honouliuli, contact them at 923 Nuuanu Avenue, Honolulu, HI 96817; 808-537-4508, fax 808-545-2019; nature.org/hawaii.

BEACHES & PARKS

NANAKULI BEACH PARK 🏊 🐟 🚶 ⚓ This park is so large that a housing tract divides it into two parts. The main section features a white-sand beach, *kiawe*-studded camping area and a recreation complex. It's simply a park with everything, unfortunately including weekend crowds. Needless to say, the swimming and snorkeling are good; lifeguard on duty. There are winter breaks with right and left slides. Fishing often rewards with *papio*, *ulua*, *moano* and *menpachi*. Facilities include picnic areas, restrooms, showers, a ball field, a basketball court and a playground. ~ 89-269 Farrington Highway (Route 93) about five miles south of Waianae; 808-668-1137.

▲ Tent and trailer camping are allowed, but a county permit is required.

HAWAIIAN ELECTRIC BEACH PARK 🏊 🐟 🚶 ⚓ This once privately owned park, across the highway from a monstrous power plant, is now run by the county. There's a rolling lawn with palm and *kiawe* trees, plus a white-sand beach and coral reef. You can swim, snorkel, surf year-round and fish for *papio*, *ulua*, *moano* and *menpachi*. If you're a proficient surfer, you'll probably head for "Tracks," a top surfing break. The drawbacks are the lack of facilities (there are restrooms and a picnic area) and the park's proximity to the electric company. ~ Located on Farrington Highway (Route 93) about seven miles south of Waianae.

▲ Not allowed here; but tent and trailer camping are okay at nearby Kahe Point Beach Park, with a county permit.

MAILI BEACH PARK 🏊 🐟 🚶 ⚓ A long winding stretch of white sand is the high point of this otherwise unimpressive facility. The swimming is good in the summer; reef snorkeling is only fair. Be aware of the reef's steep dropoff. There are winter surf breaks with a right slide. The principal game fish caught here are *papio*, *ulua*, *menpachi* and *moano*. The park contains shade trees and a spotty lawn. There are restrooms and showers. ~ 87-021 Farrington Highway (Route 93) in Maili a few miles south of Waianae.

▲ Not permitted here, but tent camping, with a county permit, is allowed in the summer at nearby Lualualei Beach Park.

MAKAHA BEACH PARK 🏊 🐟 🚶 ⚓ Some of the finest surfing in the world takes place right offshore here. This is the site of international competitions, drawing championship surfers from all across the Pacific. For more relaxed sports, there's a white-sand beach to sunbathe on and some good places to skindive. Swimming and snorkeling are both good when the sea is calm; otherwise, exercise extreme caution. Check with a lifeguard about water conditions. Anglers try for *papio*, *ulua*, *moano* and *menpachi*. The precipitous Waianae Mountains loom behind the park. There are picnic tables, restrooms and showers. ~ 84-369 Farrington Highway (Route 93) in Makaha, two miles north of Waianae.

KEAAU BEACH PARK Except for the absence of a sandy beach, this is the prettiest park on the west coast. It's a long, narrow grassy plot spotted with trees and backdropped by the Waianaes. Sunsets are spectacular here, and on a clear day you can see all the way to Kauai. There's a sandy beach just west of the park. Unfortunately, a coral reef rises right to the water's edge, making entry into the water difficult. But once you're in there's great snorkeling, swimming and bodysurfing. In summer there are good surf breaks with a left slide. People fish for *papio*, *ulua*, *moano* and *menpachi*. There are picnic areas, restrooms and showers. ~ Located on Farrington Highway (Route 93) about five miles north of Waianae.

▲ Tent and trailer allowed. County permit required.

KAENA POINT STATE PARK (YOKOHAMA BAY) ◄ *HIDDEN*
This curving stretch of white sand is the last beach along Oahu's northwest coast. With the Waianae Range in the background and coral reefs offshore, it's a particularly lovely spot. Though officially a state park, the area is largely undeveloped. You can walk from Yokohama Bay past miles of tidepools to Oahu's northwest corner at Kaena Point. Keep an eye out for porpoises. Yokohama Bay is a prime region for beach lovers and explorers both. When the sea is calm the swimming is good and the snorkeling is excellent but exercise extreme caution if the surf is up. There are summer breaks up to 15 feet over a shallow reef (left slide). Fish caught in this area include *papio*, *ulua*, *moano* and *menpachi*. Restrooms and showers are the only facilities. ~ Located at the end of the paved section of Farrington Highway (Route 93), about nine miles north of the town of Waianae.

> Kaena Point, a great place to spot porpoises, is the legendary home of Nanue the Shark Man.

Index

Adventure travel, 55
Aerial tours, 30–31
Ahupuaa o Kahana State Park, 189, 199
Air travel, 26
Ala Moana Beach Park, 159
Ala Moana Center, 159; dining, 167; shopping, 171
Ala Moana neighborhood (Honolulu), 159–60
Ala Moana Regional Park, 172
Aliiolani Hale (Judiciary Building), 132
Aloha Patrol, 101
Aloha Tower, 134
Aloha Tower Marketplace, 134; dining, 143; nightlife, 149; shopping, 148
Animals, 36–41, 225
Arizona (battleship) Memorial, 158
Atlantis Adventures, 159
Atlantis XIV, 96

Banzai Pipeline, 204
Barber's Point (beach), 222–23
Battleship *Missouri* Memorial, 158–59
Bed and breakfasts, 17–18; referral services, 17–18, 191. *See also* Lodging *in area and town entries; see also Lodging Index*
Bellows Field Beach Park, 183
Biking, 60–61
Birds, 39–41, 225
Bishop Museum, 138, 156–57, 158; shopping, 170–71
Bishop Museum (Hilton Hawaiian Village), 102
Bowfin Submarine Museum, 159
Brigham Young University (Hawaii campus), 190
Bus travel, 29–30, 179
Byodo-In Temple, 188

Calendar of events, 9–13
Camping, 41–44. *See also* Camping *in area and town entries*
Canoe's Surf, 98–99
Car rentals, 28–29
Central Oahu and Leeward Coast, 8, 218–27; beaches & parks, 226–27; camping, 226, 227; dining, 224; groceries, 224; lodging, 222, 223–24; map, 221; nightlife, 224; sights, 219–23
Children, traveling with, 19–21, 108

Chinaman's Hat (island), 188–89
Chinatown (Honolulu): dining, 144–45; groceries, 147; lodging, 139; nightlife, 149; shopping, 148–49; sights, 135–38; walking tours, 137
Clothing to bring, 14, 16
Coconut Island, 186
Coconuts, 36
Condos, 15, 18, 113–14, 208, 223–24
Contemporary Museum, 154, 156
Coral Queen (boat), 186
Coral reefs, 47, 48
Coronation Pavilion, 130, 132
Crabbing, 46
Crouching Lion marker, 189
Cuisine, 86–87, 141
Cultural Plaza (shopping mall), 137
Culture, 83–93

Damien Museum, 99–100
Deep-sea fishing, 45–46. *See also* Fish and fishing
Diamond Head, 103
Diamond Head Beach Park, 162, 172–73
Diamond Head Lighthouse, 162
Dining, 18–19; price ranges used in book, 19. *See also* Dining *in area and town entries; see also Dining Index*
Disabled travelers, 24
Diving, 49–51
Dole Pineapple Plantation, 219
Dolphins, 38
Downtown Honolulu, 7, 128–51; beaches & parks, 150–51; camping, 151; dining, 140–46; driving tour, 138–39; groceries, 146–47; lodging, 139–40; map, 131; nightlife, 149–50; shopping, 147–49; sights, 129–39
Driving tours, 138–39

East-West Center, 162
Eastern Oahu. *See* Windward Coast
Ehukai Beach Park, 204, 215
Events, 9–13
Ewa: sights, 222

Falls of Clyde (ship), 134
Fauna, 36–41, 225
Fish and fishing, 38–39, 44–46; fish names, 86
Fishponds, 186, 189

Flora, 33–36, 225
Foreign travelers, 24–25
Fort DeRussy Beach, 96
Fort Street Mall, 135
Foster Botanical Garden, 137
Fruits, 35–36

Gay-friendly travel, 23; nightlife, 126–27
Geology, 33
Goat Island, 191, 200–201
Golf, 58–59
Greater Honolulu, 7, 152–73; beaches &
  parks, 172–73; camping, 172; dining,
  165–70; groceries, 170; lodging,
  163–65; map, 155; neighborhoods,
  161; nightlife, 171–72; shopping, 168,
  170–71; sights, 153–63
Ground transportation, 26–27

Haiku Gardens, 186
Haleiwa: dining, 210–12; groceries, 212;
  lodging, 208–209; nightlife, 215; shop-
  ping, 212, 214–15; sights, 203, 206–207
Haleiwa Alii Beach Park, 216
Haleiwa Beach Park, 216
Halekulani (hotel), 98; dining, 119–20;
  lodging, 107
Halona Blowhole, 175
Halona Cove Beach, 181–82
Hanauma Bay Nature Preserve, 175, 181
Hang gliding, 56–57
Hauula: sights, 189–90
Hauula Beach Park, 198–99
Hauula Congregational Christian
  Church, 189–90
Hauula Door of Faith Church, 189
Hawaii Children's Discovery Center,
  133–34
Hawaii Kai: dining, 178, 180; groceries,
  180
Hawaii Maritime Center, 135
Hawaii State Art Museum, 132
Hawaii State Public Library System, 14
Hawaii Theatre, 138
Hawaii Visitors & Convention Bureau, 13
Hawaiian cuisine, 86–87, 141
Hawaiian culture and people, 83–93
Hawaiian Electric Beach Park, 223, 226
Hawaiian language, 87–90
Hawaiian Railway, 222
Hawaiian Waters Adventure Park, 222
Hawaii's Plantation Village, 220–21
Heeia Kai Boat Harbor, 186
Heeia State Park, 139, 186, 198
Hiking, 61–64
Hilton Hawaiian Village, 96; dining, 119;
  lodging, 111; nightlife, 124; shopping,
  123
History, 65–83

Hokulea (canoe), 134
Honolulu. See Downtown Honolulu;
  Greater Honolulu; Waikiki
Honolulu Academy of Arts, 133
Honolulu Fish Market, 135
Honolulu Hale (City Hall), 130
Honolulu International Airport, 26
Honolulu Memorial Park, 153
Honolulu Myohoji Temple, 153
Honolulu Zoo, 102
Honouliuli Preserve, 225
Hoomaluhia Botanical Garden, 185
Horseback riding, 57–58
Hostels, 104–105, 165, 208
Hotels. See Lodging
Huilua Fishpond, 189
Hukilau Beach, 200
Hula, 93

Ihiihilauakea Preserve, 176
Interisland transportation, 27–28
International travelers, 24–25
Iolani Barracks, 130, 132
Iolani Palace, 130, 132, 138
Izumo Taishakyo Mission, 137

James Campbell National Wildlife
  Refuge, 203
Japanese Cultural Center of Hawaii, 160
Jeep rentals, 29
Jellyfish, 47
Jogging, 57
John Young Museum of Art, 162
Judiciary Building (Aliiolani Hale), 132

Kaaawa: dining, 196; groceries, 196;
  shopping, 197; sights, 189
Kaalawai Beach, 173
Kaena Point, 207, 223
Kaena Point State Park, 227
Kahala Beach, 173
Kahala District (Honolulu): dining, 170;
  groceries, 170; lodging, 165; shopping,
  171; sights, 161, 162–63
Kahana Bay, 189
Kahanamoku Beach, 96
Kahuku: dining, 209–10; lodging, 208;
  nightlife, 215; shopping, 212; sights,
  203
Kahuku Golf Course Park, 201
Kahuku Point, 203–204
Kahuku Sugar Mill, 203
Kaiaka Recreation Area, 216
Kaihalulu Beach, 203–204
Kailua: dining, 194–95; groceries, 196;
  lodging, 191–92; nightlife, 197; shop-
  ping, 196; sights, 185
Kailua Beach and Beach Park, 197
Kaimuki: groceries, 170; sights, 160

Kakaako Waterfront Park, 150
Kalama Beach County Park, 197
Kalama Village: dining, 180
Kalihi–Nuuanu Avenue neighborhood
  (Honolulu): dining, 166; groceries, 170;
  sights, 153, 161
Kamehameha Statue, 132
Kaneaki Heiau, 223
Kaneohe: dining, 195–96; groceries, 196;
  lodging, 192; shopping, 197; sights,
  185–86, 188
Kaneohe Bay, 186
Kapahulu: sights, 160
Kapiolani Park, 100
Kapolei: dining, 224; lodging, 222;
  nightlife, 224; sights, 222
Kawaihao Church, 129
Kayaking, 54, 56
Keaiwa Heiau State Recreation Area, 172
Keaau Beach Park, 227
Kewalo Boat Basin, 135
Kitesurfing, 53
Koko Crater, 175
Koko Crater Botanical Gardens, 176
Koko Head (volcano), 174
Kokololio Beach Park, 199
Kolekole Pass, 220
Koolau Range, 177–78
Kualoa Beach Park, 188, 198
Kualoa Ranch, 44, 189
Kuhio Beach Park, 99
Kuilei Cliffs Beach Park, 173
Kuilima Cove, 204
Kukaniloho (sacred stones), 219
Kukihoolua (island), 191
Kwan Yin Temple, 137

Laie: groceries, 196; lodging, 194; sights,
  190–91
Laie Point, 191
Language, 87–90
Lanikai Beach, 185, 197–98
Lanikai neighborhood (Windward
  Coast), 185
Leeward Coast. *See* Central Oahu and
  Leeward Coast
Leis, 22
Lesbian travelers. *See* Gay-friendly travel
Liliuokalani Protestant Church, 206–207
Little Grass Shack, 162
Lodging, 15, 16–18; price ranges used in
  book, 17. *See also* Lodging *in area and
  town entries; see also Lodging Index*
Luaus, 118
Lucoral Museum, 100
Lyon Arboretum, 162

Magic Island, 159
Mail, 25–26

Maili Beach Park, 226
Makaha: dining, 224; lodging, 223–24
Makaha Beach and Beach Park, 223,
  226–27
Makaha Valley, 223
Makapuu Beach Park, 176–77, 182
Makapuu Point, 176
Makapuu Point State Wayside, 182
Makua Cave, 223
Malaekahana State Recreation Area, 191,
  200–201
Manoa Valley neighborhood (Honolulu):
  dining, 167–69; lodging, 163, 164–65;
  nightlife, 171, 172; sights, 160, 161,
  162
Maunakea Marketplace, 136–37
Menehunes, 190
Merchant Street neighborhood
  (Honolulu): sights, 135
Mission Houses Museum, 129
Mission Memorial Building, 129–30
Missouri (battleship) Memorial, 158–59
Moana Banyan tree, 98
Moanalua Gardens, 157
Moilili: groceries, 170; sights, 160
Moku Iki (island), 185
Moku Nui (island), 185
Mokuauia (Goat Island), 191, 200–201
Mokuleia Army Beach, 217
Mokuleia Beach and Beach Park, 216–17
Mokuluas (islands), 185
Molii Fishpond, 189
Moped rentals, 29
Mormon Temple, 190
Music, 90–92

Nanakuli Beach Park, 226
Natatorium, 103
National Memorial Cemetery, 154
North Shore, 7–8, 202–17; beaches &
  parks, 215–17; camping, 216, 217;
  dining, 209–12; groceries, 212; lodging,
  208–209; map, 205; nightlife, 215;
  shopping, 212, 214–15; sights,
  203–207
North Shore Surf and Cultural Museum,
  207
Nuuanu Avenue (Honolulu). *See*
  Kalihi–Nuuanu Avenue neighborhood
Nuuanu Pali Drive and Lookout, 139,
  157

Oahu (overview): 1–93; animals, 36–41;
  areas, 6–8; culture, 83–93; dining,
  18–19; events, 9–13; geology, 33; history, 65–83; itinerary, suggested, 4–5;
  lodging, 15, 16–18; map, 3; outdoor
  adventures, 41–64; plants, 33–36;
  transportation, 26–31; visitor informa-

tion, 13–14; weather, 8–9. *See also specific areas and towns*
Ocean safety, 47, 51
Old Sugar Mill, 189
Older travelers, 23–24
Olomana Peak, 178
Original Glider Ride, 207
Outdoor adventures, 41–64
Outrigger canoes, 104
Outrigger Reef on the Beach (hotel), 98; nightlife, 124

Package tours, 14
Packing, 14, 16
Parasailing, 56
Pearl Harbor, 157–59
People, 85–86
Pidgin language, 87–90
Pineapple Variety Garden, 219
Plants, 33–36, 225
Plate lunches, 141
Polynesian Cultural Center, 190–91
Portuguese man-of-wars, 47
Pounders Beach, 199–200
Price ranges used in book: dining, 19; lodging, 17
Public transit, 29–30
Puka Rock (Kukihoolua), 191
Punaluu: dining, 195; lodging, 194; shopping, 197; sights, 189
Punaluu Beach Park, 189, 198–99
Punchbowl, 153–54
Pupukea Beach Park, 214, 215
Puu o Mahuka Heiau, 204
Puu Ualakaa Park, 154

Queen Emma's Summer Palace, 138–39, 157
Queen Kapiolani Hibiscus Garden, 100, 102
Queen's Surf (beach), 100

Rabbit Island, 176
Restaurants. *See* Dining
Riding stables, 57–58
Roadside vendors (North Shore), 204
Royal Hawaiian Hotel, 98; lodging, 112
Royal Mausoleum, 138, 153
Royal-Moana Beach, 98

Sailing, 54
St. Andrews Cathedral, 133
St. Peter & Paul Catholic Church, 204
Sand Island State Recreation Area, 150–51
Sandy Beach, 176, 182
Sans Souci Beach, 102
Schofield Barracks: sights, 219–20
Sea Life Park, 176

Sea urchins, 47
Seasons, 8–9
Seaweed gathering, 49
Senator Fong's Plantation and Gardens, 188
Senior travelers, 23–24
Shangri La, 163
Sharks, 38–39, 47
Shave ice, 213
Shellfish gathering, 48
Sheraton Moana Surfrider Resort, 98–99; dining, 116; lodging, 111–12
Sheraton Waikiki, 98; dining, 115; nightlife, 124
Signature Theater, 138–39
Skydiving, 56–57
Snorkeling. *See* Diving
Snuba, 51
Soto Mission of Hawaii, 153
Southeast Oahu, 7, 174–83; beaches & parks, 181–83; camping, 183; dining, 178, 180; groceries, 180–81; lodging, 178; map, 177; shopping, 181; sights, 174–78
Spearfishing, 46
Squidding, 46, 48
State Capitol Building, 132
Sunset Beach, 204, 215
Surfing, 51–52
Swanzy Beach Park, 189, 198–99

Tantalus (mountain), 154
Tea ceremonies, 112
Tennent Art Foundation Gallery, 154
Tennis, 59–60
Tenrikyo Mission, 153
TheBus (public transit system), 29–30, 179
Toilet Bowl (tidepool), 175
Torchfishing, 46
Tours: aerial, 30–31; driving, 138–39; package, 14; walking, 30, 31, 137
Transportation, 26–31
Tree frogs, 40
Tropic Lightning Museum, 220
Turtles, 37, 39

Ulupo Heiau, 139, 185
University of Hawaii, 160. *See also* Manoa Valley neighborhood
University of Hawaii Art Gallery, 160
U.S. Army Museum of Hawaii, 96, 98
USS *Arizona* Memorial, 158
USS *Bowfin* Submarine Museum, 159
USS *Missouri* Memorial, 158–59

Vacation rental companies, 15
Valley of the Temples, 188
Vegetables, 35–36

Visitor information, 13–14

Wahiawa: sights, 219, 220
Wahiawa Botanical Gardens, 220
Waiahole Valley, 188
Waialae Beach Park, 173
Waialua: dining, 212; nightlife, 215; sights, 207
Waialua Sugar Mill, 207
Waianae: dining, 224; groceries, 224; sights, 223
Waikane Valley, 188
Waikiki, 7, 94–127; beaches & parks, 127; condos, 113–14; dining, 114–20; groceries, 120; lodging, 103–13; map, 97; nightlife, 123–27; shopping, 121–23; sights, 96–103
Waikiki Aquarium, 99
Waikiki Beach, 127
Waikiki Historic Trail, 98
Waikiki Shell, 102
Waimanalo: dining, 180; groceries, 180–81; lodging, 178; shopping, 181; sights, 178
Waimanalo Bay Beach Park, 182–83
Waimanalo Beach Park, 182–83

Waimea Bay, 206
Waimea Bay Beach Park, 215–16
Waimea Falls, 204, 206
Waimea Falls Park, 204, 206
Waioli Tea Room, 162
Waipahu: sights, 220–21
Walking tours, 30, 31, 137
Washington Place, 133
Water safety, 47, 51
Waterskiing, 56
Wawamalu Beach Park, 182
Weather, 8–9
Western Oahu. See Central Oahu and Leeward Coast
Whales, 37
Windsurfing, 52–53, 193
Windward Coast, 7, 184–201; beaches & parks, 197–201; camping, 198, 199, 200–201; dining, 194–96; groceries, 196; lodging, 191–92, 194; map, 187; nightlife, 197; shopping, 196–97; sights, 185–91
Women travelers, 22

Yokohama Bay, 223, 227

Lodging Index

Ala Moana Hotel, 164
Ali'i Bluffs Bed & Breakfast, 192
Ambassador Hotel of Waikiki, 113
Aston at the Waikiki Banyan, 114
Aston Coconut Plaza Hotel, 109
Aston Executive Centre Hotel, 139–40
Aston Honolulu Prince Hotel, 107–108
Aston Pacific Monarch, 113
Aston Waikiki Beach Tower, 113
Aston Waikiki Beachside Hotel, 109–10
Aston Waikiki Circle Hotel, 109
Aston Waikiki Grand Hotel, 108
Atherton YWCA, 164–65

Backpacker's Vacation Inn, 208
Best Western Plaza Hotel, 163
The Breakers, 105

Cabana at Waikiki, 110
Countryside Cabins, 194

Diamond Head Beach Hotel, 110

Estates at Turtle Bay, 208
Ewa Hotel, 107

Fernhurst YWCA, 164

Hale Pua Nui, 105
Halekulani, 107
Hawaii's Hidden Hideaway, 192
Hawaiiana Hotel, 109
Hilton Hawaiian Village, 111
Holiday Inn Waikiki, 108
Hostelling International—Honolulu, 165
Hostelling International—Waikiki, 104–105

Island Hostel/Hotel, 104

JW Marriott Ihilani Resort & Spa, 222

Kahala Mandarin Oriental Resort, 165
Kai Aloha Apartment Hotel, 106
Ke Iki Beach Bungalows, 209
Kom A'ona Inn Bed & Breakfast, 178

Laie Inn, 194
Leisure Resorts Honolulu, 108

Magnolia at Waikiki, 111
Makaha Shores, 223
Makaha Valley Towers, 224
Manoa Valley Inn, 163

Nalo Winds Bed & Breakfast, 178
New Otani Kaimana Beach Hotel, 110
Nuuanu YMCA, 164

OHANA Coral Seas Hotel, 106
OHANA East, 109
OHANA Royal Islander, 106
OHANA Village, 106–107
OHANA Waikiki Tower, 107
Outrigger Waikiki Shore, 114

Pacific Marina Inn, 163–64
Pagoda Hotel, 164
Pat's Kailua Beach Properties, 191
Polynesian Hostel Beach Club, 104

Queen Kapiolani Hotel, 109

Royal Grove Hotel, 105–106
Royal Hawaiian Hotel, 112
Royal Kuhio, 113

Schrader's Windward Country Inn, 192
Sharon's Serenity, 191–92
Sheraton Moana Surfrider Resort, 111–12
Surfhouse, 209

Town Inn, 139
Turtle Bay Condos, 208
Turtle Bay Resort, 208

W Honolulu-Diamond Head, 110
Waikiki Beach Marriott Resort, 112
Waikiki Hana Hotel, 107
Waikiki Prince Hotel, 105
Waikiki Shore, 114
Winston's Waikiki Condos, 113

YMCA Central Branch, 104

LODGING SERVICES
Affordable Accommodations, 18
All-Islands.com, 18
Aston, 15

Bed & Breakfast Hawaii, 17
Bed & Breakfast Honolulu (Statewide), 17
Condo Rentals of Waikiki, 15
CyberRentals, 15
Gold Coast Real Estate, Inc., 15
Hawaiian Condo Resorts, 15
Hawaiian Islands Bed & Breakfast, 15, 17–18

Hawaii's Best Bed & Breakfasts, 18
Luxury Vacation Homes, 15
Marc Resorts, 15
Marina Hawaii Vacations, 15
Naish Hawaii, 191
Pacific Realty, 15
Tropical Villa Vacations, 15
VacationHosts.com, 15
Waikiki Vacation Rentals, 15

Dining Index

Ahi's Restaurant, 195
Alan Wong's Restaurant, 166
Anna Bannana's, 168
Arancino's, 119
Assaggio Hawaii Kai, 178, 180
Assaggio Ristorante Italiano, 194
Auntie Pasto's, 142–43
Azteca Mexican Restaurant, 169
Azul, 224

Baci Bistro, 195
Ba-Le Sandwich Shop, 142
Bali by the Sea, 119
Bautista's Filipino Kitchen, 116
Beachwalk Cafe, 116
Bueno Nalo, 195
Buzz's Original Steak House, 194

Café Haleiwa, 210
Cathay Inn Chop Suey, 224
Cha Cha Cha Restaurant, 118
Chai's Island Bistro, 143
Cheeseburger in Paradise, 117
Chef Mavro's, 167
Choi's Kitchen, 116
Cholos Homestyle Mexican Restaurant, 211
Ciao Mein, 116–17
Cinnamon's Restaurant, 195
Cisco's Cantina, 195
Coconut Willy's Bar & Grill, 116
Coffee Gallery, 211–12
Compadres, 140
Country Kitchen, 209
The Cove, 209–10
Crouching Lion Inn, 196

Daiei Food Court, 168
Dave's Ice Cream, 180
Davey Jones Ribs, 118
Diamond Head Grill, 117
Double Eight Restaurant, 144
Duc's Bistro, 145

Ezogiku, 114–15

Fatty's Chinese Kitchen, 118
Fisherman's Wharf, 142
Flavor Mania, 211

Genki Sushi, 169
Giovanni's Aloha Shrimp Truck, 209
Grace's Inn, 141

Hale Vietnam, 170
Haleiwa Beach Grill, 210–11
Haleiwa Joe's Seafood Grill (Haleiwa), 210
Haleiwa Joe's Seafood Grill (Kaneohe), 196
Hannara Restaurant, 224
Hard Rock Cafe (Waikiki), 120
Harpos, 168
Hau Tree Lanai, 115–16
Helena's Hawaiian Foods, 166

Indigo, 145
International Food Court, 115–16
Irifune, 165
Itochan Sushi, 144

Jameson's By the Sea, 210
Jimbo's Restaurant, 166–67
John Dominis, 142
J.R. Chinese Buffet Garden, 116
JW Marriott Ihilani Resort & Spa, 224

Kau Kau Corner Food Lanai, 143
Keneke's, 180
Keo's in Waikiki, 117
King Tsin Restaurant, 168–69
Koa Omelette House, 195
Kua Aina Sandwich, 211

L & L Drive-Inn (Honolulu), 141
La Mer, 119–20
LaMariana Sailing Club, 143–44
Legend Seafood Restaurant, 145–46
Legend's Buddhist Vegetarian Restaurant, 146
Lewers Street Fish Company, 117–18
Like Like Drive Inn, 141
Liliha Seafood Restaurant, 165
A Little Bit of Saigon, 144

Mabuhay Cafe, 144
Magoo's, 168
Makai Market, 167

Manapua, 168
Maunakea Marketplace, 144
McCully Chop Suey, 167
Meg's Drive-In, 166

Naupaka, 224
Nick's Fishmarket, 114
19th Hole, 224

Ocean Terrace, 115
Odoriko Japanese Restaurant, 114
Old Spaghetti Factory, 140
Olive Tree Cafe, 170
Ono Hawaiian Foods, 169
Orchid Snackshop, 210
Orchids, 120

Pae Thai, 143
Pagoda Floating Restaurant, 166
Palm Terrace, 209–10
Paradise Found Café, 212
Patti's Chinese Kitchen, 167
Peking Garden, 116
People's Café, 143
Perry's Smorgy, 119
Pizza Bob's, 211
Poi Bowl, 167
Prince Court, 168

Rainbow Drive-In, 169
Restaurant Suntory, 115
Rosie's Cantina, 211

Roy's Restaurant, 180
Ryan's Grill, 140

Saeng's Thai Cuisine, 194
Sam Choy, 169
Sam Choy's Breakfast, Lunch & Crab, 146
Sari Sari, 166
Scoozee's, 140
Seaside Bar & Grill, 118
Shirokiya, 167
Shore Bird Beach Broiler, 119
Sugar Bar & Grill, 212
Sunset Grill, 142
Sunset Pizza, 210
Sushi Robot, 168
Swiss Haus, 178

Thai Valley Cuisine, 180
3660 On the Rise, 169–70
Times Coffee Shop, 194
Tsuruya Noodle Shop, 167
Turtle Bay Resort, 209–10

Ushiotei, 224

Waikiki Broiler, 119
Waikiki Shopping Plaza, 115
Wisteria Restaurant, 143

Yong Sing Restaurant, 144

Zaffron Restaurant, 145

HIDDEN GUIDES

Adventure travel or a relaxing vacation?—"Hidden" guidebooks are the only travel books in the business to provide detailed information on both. Aimed at environmentally aware travelers, our motto is "Where Vacations Meet Adventures." These books combine details on unique hotels, restaurants and sightseeing with information on camping, sports and hiking for the outdoor enthusiast.

THE NEW KEY GUIDES

Based on the concept of ecotourism, The New Key Guides are dedicated to the preservation of Central America's rare and endangered species, architecture and archaeology. Filled with helpful tips, they give travelers everything they need to know about these exotic destinations.

PARADISE FAMILY GUIDES

Ideal for families traveling with kids of any age—toddlers to teenagers—Paradise Family Guides offer a blend of travel information unlike any other guides to the Hawaiian islands. With vacation ideas and tropical adventures that are sure to satisfy both action-hungry youngsters and relaxation-seeking parents, these guides meet the specific needs of each and every family member.

Ulysses Press books are available at bookstores everywhere. If any of the following titles are unavailable at your local bookstore, ask the bookseller to order them.

You can also order books directly from Ulysses Press
P.O. Box 3440, Berkeley, CA 94703
800-377-2542 or 510-601-8301
fax: 510-601-8307
www.ulyssespress.com
e-mail: ulysses@ulyssespress.com

HIDDEN GUIDEBOOKS

____ Hidden Arizona, $16.95
____ Hidden Bahamas, $14.95
____ Hidden Baja, $14.95
____ Hidden Belize, $15.95
____ Hidden Big Island of Hawaii, $13.95
____ Hidden Boston & Cape Cod, $14.95
____ Hidden British Columbia, $18.95
____ Hidden Cancún & the Yucatán, $16.95
____ Hidden Carolinas, $17.95
____ Hidden Coast of California, $18.95
____ Hidden Colorado, $15.95
____ Hidden Disneyland, $13.95
____ Hidden Florida, $18.95
____ Hidden Florida Keys & Everglades, $12.95
____ Hidden Georgia, $16.95
____ Hidden Guatemala, $16.95
____ Hidden Hawaii, $18.95
____ Hidden Idaho, $14.95

____ Hidden Kauai, $13.95
____ Hidden Maui, $13.95
____ Hidden Montana, $15.95
____ Hidden New England, $18.95
____ Hidden New Mexico, $15.95
____ Hidden Oahu, $13.95
____ Hidden Oregon, $15.95
____ Hidden Pacific Northwest, $18.95
____ Hidden Salt Lake City, $14.95
____ Hidden San Francisco & Northern California, $18.95
____ Hidden Southern California, $18.95
____ Hidden Southwest, $19.95
____ Hidden Tahiti, $17.95
____ Hidden Tennessee, $16.95
____ Hidden Utah, $16.95
____ Hidden Walt Disney World, $13.95
____ Hidden Washington, $15.95
____ Hidden Wine Country, $13.95
____ Hidden Wyoming, $15.95

THE NEW KEY GUIDEBOOKS

____ The New Key to Costa Rica, $18.95

____ The New Key to Ecuador and the Galápagos, $17.95

PARADISE FAMILY GUIDES

____ Paradise Family Guides: Kaua'i, $16.95
____ Paradise Family Guides: Maui, $16.95

____ Paradise Family Guides: Big Island of Hawai'i, $16.95

Mark the book(s) you're ordering and enter the total cost here ☞ ▭

California residents add 8.25% sales tax here ☞ ▭

Shipping, check box for your preferred method and enter cost here ☞ ▭

❑ BOOK RATE   **FREE! FREE! FREE!**

❑ PRIORITY MAIL/UPS GROUND   cost of postage

❑ UPS OVERNIGHT OR 2-DAY AIR   cost of postage   ▭

Billing, enter total amount due here and check method of payment ☞

❑ CHECK   ❑ MONEY ORDER

❑ VISA/MASTERCARD _____ EXP. DATE _____

NAME _____ PHONE _____

ADDRESS _____

CITY _____ STATE _____ ZIP _____

MONEY-BACK GUARANTEE ON DIRECT ORDERS PLACED THROUGH ULYSSES PRESS.

ABOUT THE AUTHOR

RAY RIEGERT is the author of eight travel books, including *Hidden San Francisco & Northern California*. His most popular work, *Hidden Hawaii*, won the coveted Lowell Thomas Travel Journalism Award for Best Guidebook as well as a similar award from the Hawaii Visitors Bureau. In addition to his role as publisher of Ulysses Press, he has written for the *Chicago Tribune*, *Saturday Evening Post*, *San Francisco Examiner & Chronicle* and *Travel & Leisure*. A member of the Society of American Travel Writers, he lives in the San Francisco Bay area with his wife, co-publisher Leslie Henriques, and their son Keith and daughter Alice.

ABOUT THE UPDATE AUTHOR

JOAN CONROW is a freelance journalist who writes frequently about Hawaii and its natural world. Her work appears regularly in national and regional magazines, and on Reuters news service, and she has contributed to several Hawaii guide books. She has lived on Kauai since 1987.